Construction, Production and Material Management

Construction, Production and Material Management

Sudhindra Nath Bose

RANDOM

RANDOM PUBLICATIONS

NEW DELHI - 110 002 (INDIA)

Construction, Production and Material Management

ISBN 978-93-5111-312-6

Published in 2014 in India by
RANDOM PUBLICATIONS
4376-A/4B, Gali Murari Lal, Ansari Road
New Delhi-110 002
Phone: +9111-43580356, 23289044
E-mail: randomexports@gmail.com; sales@randompublications.com; info@randompublications.com

Reprinted 2026

Type Setting by: Friends Media, Delhi-110089

Preface

Materials management plans and designs for the delivery, distribution, storage, collection, and removal of occupant-generated streams of materials and services. It is usually an additional service that is offered as part of a campus planning process or a building design project. It is most beneficial for university, health care, and corporate environments. Materials management looks at the planning and design considerations needed to support the efficient delivery and removal of goods and services that support occupant activity. The streams of occupant-generated materials and activity include mail, office supplies, lab supplies, food, special deliveries, custodial services, building supplies, waste and recycling, and service calls. A materials management plan may include planning guidelines or full design for the following:

- Truck delivery and service vehicle routes, to reduce vehicle / pedestrian conflict
- Loading docks and delivery points, to increase accommodation and reduce queuing and vehicle idling
- Recycling, trash, and hazardous waste collection and removal, to increase waste diversion and reduce costs
- Service equipment and utility infrastructure relocation or concealment, to improve aesthetics and realize landscaping goals

The effective materials management plan builds from and enhances an institutional master plan by filling in the gaps and producing an environmentally responsible and efficient outcome. An institutional campus, office, or housing complex can expect a myriad of benefits from an effective materials management plan. For starters, there are long-term cost savings, as consolidating, reconfiguring, and better managing a campus' core infrastructure reduces annual operating costs. An institutional campus, office, or housing complex will also get the highest and best use out of campus real estate. An effective materials management plan also means a more holistic approach to managing vehicle use and emissions, solid waste, hazardous waste, recycling, and utility services. As a result, this means a "greener," more sustainable environment and a manifestation of the many demands today for institutions to become more environmentally friendly. In fact, thanks to such environmental advantages, creative materials management plans may qualify for LEAD Innovation in Design credits. And finally, an effective materials management plan can improve aesthetics. Removing unsafe and unsightly conditions, placing core services out of sight, and creating a more pedestrian-friendly environment will improve the visual and physical sense of place for those who live and work there.

This book titled, "Construction, Production and Material Management", provides readers with an introductory overview of construction, production and material management. An introduction to materials management is given. The elements and dimensions of supply chain management are discussed in detail. An overview of construction and production management is provided herein. Efforts have been made to create an understanding of the relationships among logistics, operations and supply chain management. In addition, this book also is helpful in understanding the theory of constraints and role of customer relationship management. Focus lies on purchasing-oriented aspects, other issues and challenges. Focus is also there on select construction production directives. A detailed bibliography and elaborate index makes this publication user-friendly.

—Editor

Contents

1

Construction, Production and Material Management: An Introductory Overview

> The whole difference between construction and creation is exactly this: that a thing constructed can only be loved after it is constructed; but a thing created is loved before it exists.
>
> —*Charles Dickens*

CONSTRUCTION MANAGEMENT: AN INTRODUCTION

Construction management or construction project management (CPM) is the overall planning, coordination, and control of a project from beginning to completion. CPM is aimed at meeting a client's requirement in order to produce a functionally and financially viable project.

Construction as an Industry

The construction industry is composed of five sectors: residential, commercial, heavy civil, industrial, and environmental. A construction manager holds the same responsibilities and completes the same processes in each sector. All that separates a construction manager in one sector from one in another is the knowledge of the construction site. This may include different types of equipment, materials, subcontractors, and possibly locations.

The Role of a Contractor

An contractor is assigned to a construction project once the design has been completed by the architect or is still in progress. This is done by going through a bidding process with different contractors. The contractor is selected by using one of three common selection methods: low-bid selection, best-value selection, or qualifications-based selection. this is the main role of a contractor.

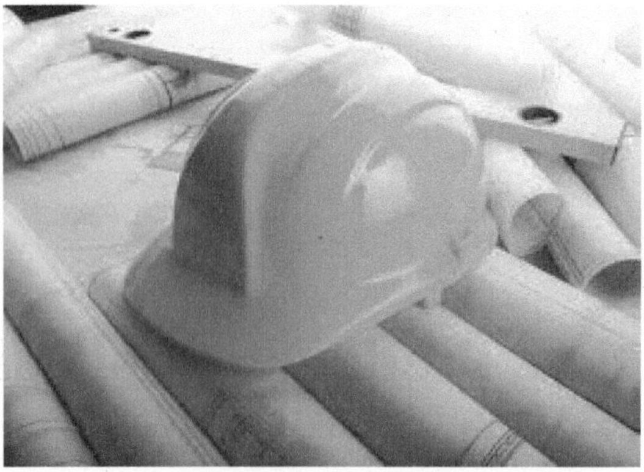

Skills Needed for Construction Management

A construction manager should have the ability to handle public safety, time management, cost management, quality management,decision making, mathematics, working drawings,and human resources.

Functions

The functions of Construction management typically include the following:

1. Specifying project objectives and plans including delineation of scope, budgeting, scheduling, setting performance requirements, and selecting project participants.
2. Maximizing the resource efficiency through procurement of labor, materials and equipment.
3. Implementing various operations through proper coordination and control of planning, design, estimating, contracting and construction in the entire process.
4. Developing effective communications and mechanisms for resolving conflicts.:

The Construction Management Association of America (a US construction management certification and advocacy body) says the 120 most common responsibilities of a Construction Manager fall into the following 7 categories: Project Management Planning, Cost Management, Time Management, Quality Management, Contract Administration, Safety Management, and CM Professional Practice. CM professional practice includes specific activities, such as defining the responsibilities and management structure of the project management team, organizing and leading by implementing project controls, defining roles and responsibilities, developing communication protocols, and identifying elements of project design and construction likely to give rise to disputes and claims.

- The Five Types of Construction
- Residential: Residential construction includes individual homes, apartments, condominiums, townhouses, and other housing types.
- Commercial: This refers to construction dealing with the needs of commerce, trade, and government. Examples include shopping centers, schools, banks, hospitals, theaters, and government buildings.
- Heavy Civil: The construction of transportation infrastructure such as roads, bridges, railroads, tunnels, and airports. Dams are also included here, but other water-related infrastructure is considered environmental.
- Industrial: Buildings and other constructed items used for product production, including chemical plants, steel mills, oil refineries, manufacturing plants, and pipelines.
- Environmental: Environmental construction used to be part of heavy civil, but is now its own section, dealing with projects that improve the environment. Some examples are sanitary sewers, waste management, and clean water.
- Construction Management Jobs
- Planning Engineer
- Project coordinator
- Field Engineer
- Office Engineer
- Quantity Surveyor
- Project Engineer
- Area Superintendent
- Project Superintendent
- Project Manager
- Estimator
- Lead Estimator
- Senior Estimator
- Chief Estimator
- Project Executive
- Obtaining the Project

Bids

A bid is given to the owner by construction managers that are willing to complete their construction project. A bid tells the owner how much money they should expect to pay the construction management company in order for them to complete the project.

- Open Bid: An open bid is used for public projects. Any and all contractors are allowed to submit their bid due to public advertising.
- Closed Bid: A closed bid is used for private projects. A selection of contractors are sent an invitation for bid so only they can submit a bid for the specified project.

Selection Methods

- Low-bid selection: This selection focuses on the price of a project. Multiple construction management companies submit a bid to the owner that is the lowest amount they are willing to do the job for. Then the owner usually chooses the company with the lowest bid to complete the job for them.
- Best-value selection: This selection focuses on both the price and qualifications of the contractors submitting bids. This means that the owner chooses the contractor with the best price and the best qualifications. The owner decides by using a request for proposal (RFP), which provides the owner with the contractor's exact form of scheduling and budgeting that the contractor expects to use for the project.
- Qualifications-based selection: This selection is used when the owner decides to choose the contractor only on the basis of their qualifications. The owner then uses a request for qualifications (RFQ), which provides the owner with the contractor's experience, management plans, project organization, and budget and schedule performance. The owner may also ask for safety records and individual credentials of their members.

Payment Contracts

- Lump-sum: This is the most common type of contract. The construction manager and the owner agree on the overall cost of the construction project and the owner is responsible for paying that amount whether the construction project exceeds or falls below the agreed price of payment.
- Cost-Plus-Fee: This contract provides payment for the contractor including the total cost of the project as well as a fixed fee or percentage of the total cost. This contract is beneficial to the contractor since any additional costs will be paid for even though they were unexpected for the owner.

- Guaranteed Maximum Price: This contract is the same as the cost-plus-fee contract although there is a set price that the overall cost and fee do not go above.
- Unit-Price: This contract is used when the cost cannot be determined ahead of time. The owner provides materials with a specific unit price to limit spending.
- Project Stages

Design

The design stage contains a lot of steps: programming and feasibility, schematic design, design development, and contract documents. It is the responsibility of the design team to ensure that the design meets all building codes and regulations. It is during the design stage that the bidding process takes place.

- Programming and feasibility: The needs, goals, and objectives must be determined for the building. Decisions must be made on the building size, number of rooms, how the space will be used, and who will be using the space. This must all be considered to begin the actual designing of the building.
- Schematic design: Schematic designs are sketches used to identify spaces, shapes, and patterns. Materials, sizes, colors, and textures must be considered in the sketches.
- Design development (DD): This step requires research and investigation into what materials and equipment will be used as well as their cost.
- Contract documents (CDs): Contract documents are the final drawings and specifications of the construction project. They are used by contractors to determine their bid while builders use them for the construction process. Contract documents can also be called working drawings.

Pre-Construction

The pre-construction stage begins when the owner gives a notice to proceed to the contractor that they have chosen through the bidding process. A notice to proceed is when the owner gives permission to the contractor to begin their work on the project. The first step is to assign the project team which includes the project manager (PM), contract administrator, superintendent, and field engineer.

- Project manager: The project manager is in charge of the project team.

- Contract administrator: The contract administrator assists the project manager as well as the superintendent with the details of the construction contract.
- Superintendent: It is the superintendent's job to make sure everything is on schedule including flow of materials, deliveries, and equipment. They are also in charge of coordinating on-site construction activities.
- Field Engineer: A field engineer is considered an entry-level position and is responsible for paperwork.

During the pre-construction stage, a site investigation must take place. A site investigation takes place to discover if any steps need to be implemented on the job site. This is in order to get the site ready before the actual construction begins. This also includes any unforeseen conditions such as historical artifacts or environment problems. A soil test must be done to determine if the soil is in good condition to be built upon.

Procurement

The procurement stage is when labor, materials and equipment needed to complete the project are purchased. This can be done by the general contractor if the company does all their own construction work. If the contractor does not do their own work, they obtain it through subcontractors. Subcontractors are contractors who specialize in one particular aspect of the construction work such as concrete, melding, glass, or carpentry. Subcontractors are hired the same way a general contractor would be, which is through the bidding process. Purchase orders are also part of the procurement stage.

- Purchase orders: A purchase order is used in various types of businesses. In this case, a purchase order is an agreement between a buyer and seller that the products purchased meet the required specifications for the agreed price.

Construction

The construction stage begins with a pre-construction meeting brought together by the superintendent. The pre-construction meeting is meant to make decisions dealing with work hours, material storage, quality control, and site access. The next step is to move everything onto the construction site and set it all up.

At this stage, construction monitoring and supervision is of great importance to ensure that a project is completed on time and on budget, while meeting all relevant regulations and quality standards.

Contractor Progress Payment Schedule

A Contractor progress payment schedule is a schedule of when (according to project milestones or specified dates) contractors and suppliers will be paid for the current progress of installed work.

Progress payments are partial payments for work completed during a portion, usually a month, during a construction period. Progress payments are made to general contractors, subcontractors, and suppliers as construction projects progress. Payments are typically made on a monthly basis but could be modified to meet certain milestones. Progress payments are an important part of contract administration for the contractor. Proper preparation of the information necessary for payment processing can help the contractor financially complete the project.

Post-Construction

Once the construction has been completed there are specific steps that must be taken to prepare the building for occupancy.

- Project punchout: A project punchout means that the project must be looked at for any issues before it is considered completely finished. Issues may include replacing a cracked tile on the floor or changing the color of paint. A list is created containing these issues and it is known as a punch list or a snag list.
- Substantial completion: The architect for the project determines if the building meets every requirement and issues a certificate of substantial completion. This certificate announces the official completion of the project.
- Final inspection: A final inspection is done by the building official once the certificate of substantial completion has been issued.
- Certificate of Occupancy: A certificate of occupancy is issued by the building official which informs the owner that it is now safe to occupy. This is issued by the building official after the final inspection.
- Commissioning: This is the process of testing systems and equipment to ensure that they are working correctly. Then the owner must be trained to properly operate the systems and equipment in the building.
- Final documentation: This provides information on the building to the owner for future references. This includes warranties, operation manuals, inspection and testing reports, and record drawings.
- Final completion: Final completion occurs when all required

paperwork and documentation is completed, including payments to the contractor.

Owner Occupancy

Once the owner moves into the building, a warranty period begins. This is to ensure that all materials, equipment, and quality meet the expectations of the owner that are included within the contract.

- Issues Resulting from Construction

Environmental Protections

- Storm water pollution: As a result of construction, the soil is displaced from its original location which can possibly cause environmental problems in the future. Runoff can occur during storms which can possibly transfer harmful pollutants through the soil to rivers, lakes, wetlands, and coastal waters.
- Endangered species: If endangered species have been found on the construction site, the site must be shut down for some time. The construction site must be shut down for as long as it takes for authorities to make a decision on the situation. Once the situation has been assessed, the contractor makes the appropriate accommodations to not disturb the species.
- Vegetation: There may often be particular trees or other vegetation that must be protected on the job site. This may require fences or security tape to warn builders that they must not be harmed.
- Wetlands: The contractor must make accommodations so that erosion and water flow are not affected by construction. Any liquid spills must be maintained due to contaminants that may enter the wetland.
- Historical or Cultural artifacts: Artifacts may include arrowheads, pottery shards, and bones. All work comes to a halt if any artifacts are found and will not resume until they can be properly examined and removed from the area.
- Construction Activity Documentation

Project Meetings

Project meetings take place at scheduled intervals to discuss the progress on the construction site and any concerns or issues. The discussion and any decisions made at the meeting must be documented.

Diaries, Logs, and Daily Field Reports

Diaries, logs, and daily field reports keep track of the daily activities on a job site each day.

- Diaries: Each member of the project team is expected to keep a project diary. The diary contains summaries of the day's events in the member's own words. They are used to keep track of any daily work activity, conversations, observations, or any other relevant information regarding the construction activities. Diaries can be referred to when disputes arise and a diary happens to contain information connected with the disagreement. Diaries that are handwritten can be used as evidence in court.
- Logs: Logs keep track of the regular activities on the job site such as phone logs, transmittal logs, delivery logs, and RFI (Request for Information) logs.
- Daily Field Reports: Daily field reports are a more formal way of recording information on the job site. They contain information that includes the day's activities, temperature and weather conditions, delivered equipment or materials, visitors on the site, and equipment used that day.
- Resolving Disputes
- Mediation: Mediation uses a third party mediator to resolve any disputes. The mediator helps both disputing parties to come to a mutual agreement. This process ensures that no attorneys become involved in the dispute and is less time-consuming.
- Minitrial: A minitrial takes more time and money than a mediation. The minitrial takes place in an informal setting and involves some type of advisor or attorney that must be paid. The disputing parties may come to an agreement or the third party advisor may offer their advice. The agreement is nonbinding and can be broken.
- Arbitration: Arbitration is the most costly and time-consuming way to resolve a dispute. Each party is represented by an attorney while witnesses and evidence are presented. Once all information is provided on the issue, the arbitrator makes a ruling which provides the final decision. The arbitrator provides the final decision on what must be done and it is a binding agreement between each of the disputing parties.
- Terminology

The following terms are commonly used in the industry:

- Construction management (CM) refers to form of delivery and (in the UK) management of the site.
- Real estate management (REM) is professional property advice (a continuous process, as opposed to a process).

  - Corporate real estate management (CREM) is a company-focused variant.
- Management contracting (MC):
  - UK: form of delivery
  - US: CM at risk
- Programme management (ProgM) is concerned with management of a client's portfolio (the programme, in this sense, is equivalent to a client's brief) or (in the UK) managing time in a project.
- Project control (PC) is the tracking and reporting of the progress, time, cost and quality of a project. This function can be characterized as passive, whereas construction project management (CPM) is active.
- Project leader (PL): The person responsible for achieving the project's objectives; acts as a manager "in-line".
- Project director (PD): The leader of a large project that can be broken down into sub-projects (e.g. the Channel tunnel) or the head of a PM organization
- Owner representative (OR): The representative of the owner; may be internal or external to the company
- Document Control (DC): Key function of a project manager
- Build operate transfer (BOT)
  - Finance build operate transfer (FBOT)
  - Design build operate transfer (DBOT)
- Build own operate (BOO)
- Engineering procurement construction (EPC)
- Private finance initiative (PFI)
- General contract (GC)
- Joint Venture (JV): A collaboration between two or more companies from the same or different backgrounds and/or fields to complete a common project. Joint Ventures typically have a lead contractor that deals with most of the business aspects. The lead will usually have a bigger stake in the partnership (ie. the lead will have a 65% stake while the second contractor might have 30% and a third might have 5%).
- Guaranteed maximum price (GMP): A contract-specified upper limit to the project's final price
- Multiple prime contracts (MPC)
  - UK: One contractor takes responsibility for the development (package deal).

   - o US: A client may have five or six prime contractors.
- Study and Practice

Construction Management education comes in a variety of formats: formal degree programs (Two-year associate degree; four-year baccalaureate degree, masters degree, project management, operations management engineer degree, doctor of philosophy degree, postdoctoral researcher); on-the-job-training; and continuing education and professional development. Information on degree programs is available from the American Council for Construction Education (ACCE) or the Associated Schools of Construction (ASC).

According to the American Council for Construction Education (the academic accrediting body of construction management educational programs in the U.S.), the academic field of construction management encompasses a wide range of topics. These range from general management skills, through management skills specifically related to construction, to technical knowledge of construction methods and practices. There are many schools offering Construction Management programs, including some offering a Masters degree.

- Required Knowledge
- Construction and Building
- Technology
- Public Safety
- Customer Service
- Human Resources
- Mathematics
- Skills and Abilities
- Time Management
- Negotiation
- Decision Making
- Problem Solving
- Business Model

The construction industry typically includes three parties: an owner, a designer (architect or engineer) and a builder (usually known as a general contractor). There are traditionally two contracts between these parties as they work together to plan, design and construct the project. The first contract is the owner-designer contract, which involves planning, design and construction administration. The second contract is the owner-contractor contract, which involves construction. An indirect third-party relationship exists between the designer and the contractor, due to these two contracts. An owner may also contract with a construction project management company as an advisor, creating a third contract relationship in the project. The construction manager's role is to provide construction advice to the designer, design advice to the constructor on the owner's behalf and other advice as necessary.

Design, bid, Build Contracts

The phrase "design, bid, build" describes the prevailing model of construction management, in which the general contractor is engaged through a tender process after designs have been completed by the architect or engineer.

Design-Build Contracts

Many owners – particularly government agencies – let out contracts known as *design-build contracts*. In this type of contract, the construction team (known as the design-builder) is responsible for taking the owner's concept and completing a detailed design before (following the owner's approval of the design) proceeding with construction. Virtual design and construction technology may be used by contractors to maintain a tight construction time. There are three main advantages to a design-build contract. First, the construction team is motivated to work with the design team to develop a practical design. The team can find creative ways to reduce construction costs without reducing the function of the final product. The second major advantage involves the schedule. Many projects are commissioned within a tight time frame. Under a traditional contract, construction cannot begin until after the design is finished and the project has been awarded to a bidder.

In a design-build contract the contractor is established at the outset, and construction activities can proceed concurrently with the design. The third major advantage is that the design-build contractor has an incentive to keep the combined design and construction costs within the owner's budget. The major problem with design-build contracts is an inherent conflict of interest. In a standard contract the designer is responsible to the owner to review the builder's work, ensuring that the products and methods meet specifications and codes. An independent builder may pick up design flaws which might go unnoticed (or unmentioned) if the builder is also the designer.

The owner may get a building that is over-designed to increase profits for the design-builder, or a building built with lesser-grade products to maximize profits. If speed is important, design and construction contracts can be awarded separately; bidding takes place on preliminary plans in a not-to-exceed contract instead of a single, firm design-build contract.

Planning and Scheduling

Project-management methodology is as follows:

- Work breakdown structure
- Project network of activities
  - Critical path method (CPM)
  - Resource management
  - Resource leveling
  - Risk assessment

Architecture–Engineer

- Work inspection
- Change orders
- Review payments
- Materials and samples
- Shop drawings
- Three-dimensional image

Agency CM

Construction cost management is a fee-based service in which the construction manager (CM) is responsible exclusively to the owner, acting in the owner's interests at every stage of the project. The construction manager offers impartial advice on matters such as:

- Optimum use of available funds
- Control of the scope of the work
- Project scheduling
- Optimum use of design and construction firms' skills and talents
- Avoidance of delays, changes and disputes
- Enhancing project design and construction quality
- Optimum flexibility in contracting and procurement
- Cash-flow management

Comprehensive management of every stage of the project, beginning with the original concept and project definition, yields the greatest benefit to owners. As time progresses beyond the pre-design phase, the CM's ability to effect cost savings diminishes. The agency CM can represent the owner by helping select the design and construction teams and managing the design (preventing scope creep), helping the owner stay within a predetermined budget with value engineering, cost-benefit analysis and best-value comparisons. The software-application field of construction collaboration technology has been developed to apply information technology to construction management.

CM at-risk

CM at-risk is a delivery method which entails a commitment by the construction manager to deliver the project within a Guaranteed Maximum Price (GMP). The construction manager acts as a consultant to the owner in the development and design phases (preconstruction services), and as a general contractor during construction. When a construction manager is bound to a GMP, the fundamental character of the relationship is changed. In addition to acting in the owner's interest, the construction manager must control construction costs to stay within the GMP.

CM at-risk is a global term referring to the business relationship of a construction contractor, owner and architect (or designer). Typically, a CM at-risk arrangement eliminates a "low-bid" construction project. A GMP agreement is a typical part of the CM-and-owner agreement (comparable to a "low-bid" contract), but with adjustments in responsibility for the CM. The advantage of a CM at-risk arrangement is budget management. Before a project's design is completed (six to eighteen months of coordination between designer and owner), the CM is involved with estimating the cost of constructing a project based on the goals of the designer and owner (design concept) and the project's scope. In balancing the costs, schedule, quality and scope of the project, the design may be modified instead of redesigned; if the owner decides to expand the project, adjustments can be made before pricing. To manage the budget before design is complete and construction crews mobilized, the CM conducts site management and purchases major items to efficiently manage time and cost.

CONSTRUCTION ENGINEERING

Construction engineering is a professional discipline that deals with the designing, planning, construction, and management of infrastructures such as highways, bridges, airports, railroads, buildings, dams, and utilities. Construction Engineers are unique such that they are a cross between civil engineers and construction managers. Construction engineers learn the designing aspect much like civil engineers and construction site management functions much like construction managers. The primary difference between a construction engineer and a construction manager is that the construction engineer has the ability to sit for the Professional Engineer license (PE) whereas a construction manager cannot. At the educational level, construction managers are not as focused on design work as they are on construction procedures, methods, and people management. Their primary concern is to deliver a project on time, within budget, and of the desired quality.

The difference between a construction engineer and civil engineer is only at the educational level as both disciplines are able to sit for the PE exam giving them the same title of engineer. Civil engineering students concentrate more on the design work, gearing them toward a career as a design professional. This essentially requires them to take a multitude of design courses. Construction engineering students take design courses as well as construction management courses. This allows them to understand both the design functions as well as the building requirements needed to design and build today's infrastructures.

Work Activities

Depending on which career the construction engineer has chosen to follow, an entry-level design engineer normally provides support to project managers and assist with creating conceptual designs, scopes, and cost estimates for the planning and construction of approved projects. It should be noted that a career in design work does require a professional engineer license (PE). Individuals who pursue this career path are strongly advised to sit for the Engineer In Training exam (EIT) while in college as it takes five years (4 years in USA) post graduate to obtain the PE license. Entry-level construction manager positions are typically called project engineers or assistant project engineers.

They are responsible for preparing purchasing requisitions, processing change orders, preparing monthly budgeting reports, and handling meeting minutes. The construction management position does not necessarily require a PE license; however possessing one does make the individual more marketable, as the PE license allows the individual to sign off on temporary structure designs.

Abilities

Construction engineers are problem solvers, they help create infrastructure that best meets the unique demands of its environment. They must be able to understand infrastructure life cycles and have the perspective to solve technical challenges with clarity and imagination. Therefore individuals should have a strong understanding of maths and science, but many other skills are required, including critical and analytical thinking, time management, people management and good communication skills.

Educational Requirements

Individuals looking to obtain a construction engineering degree must first ensure that the program is accredited by EAC or Technology Accreditation Commission (TAC) of the Accreditation Board for Engineering and Technology (ABET). ABET accreditation is assurance that a college or university program meets the quality standards established by the profession for which it prepares its students. In the US there are currently twenty-five programs that exist in the entire country so careful college consideration is advised. A typical construction engineering curriculum is a mixture of engineering mechanics, engineering design, construction management and general science and mathematics. This usually leads to a Bachelor of Science degree. The B.S. degree along with some design or construction experience is sufficient for most entry level positions. Graduate schools may be an option for those who want to go further in depth of the construction and engineering subjects taught at the undergraduate level. In most cases construction engineering graduates look to either civil engineering, engineering management, or business administration as a possible graduate degree. For authority to approve any final designs of public projects (and most any project), a construction engineer must have a professional engineers (P.E.) license.

Job Prospects

Job prospects for construction engineers generally have a strong cyclical variation. For example, starting in 2008 - continuing until at least 2011 - job prospects have been poor due to the collapse of housing bubbles in many parts of the world. This sharply reduced demand for construction, forced construction professionals towards infrastructure construction and therefore increased the competition faced by established and new construction engineers. This increased competition, and a core reduction in quantity demand is in parallel with a possible shift in the demand for construction engineers due to the automation of many engineering tasks, overall resulting in reduced prospects for construction engineers. In early 2010 the United States construction industry had a 27%

unemployment rate, this is nearly three times higher than the 9.7% national average unemployment rate. The construction unemployment rate (including tradesmen) is comparable to the United States 1933 unemployment rate - the lowest point of the Great Depression - of 25%.

Remuneration

The average salary for a civil engineer in the UK depends on the sector, and more specifically the level of experience of the individual. A 2010 survey of the remuneration and benefits of those occupying jobs in construction and the built environment industry showed that the average salary of a civil engineer in the UK is £29,582. The average salary varies depending on experience, for example the average annual salary for a civil engineer with between 3 and 6 years experience is £23,813. For those with between 14 and 20 years experience the average is £38,214.

INVENTORY

The word inventory doesn't have the same meaning in the USA and in the UK:

- In American English and in a business accounting context, the word inventory is commonly used to describe the goods and materials that a business holds for the ultimate purpose of resale (or repair). In American English, the word stock is commonly used to describe the capital invested in a business, while in British English, the sentence stock shared is used in the same context.
- In the rest of the English-speaking world, stock is more commonly used, although the word inventory is recognised as a synonym. In British English, the word inventory is more commonly thought of as a list compiled for some formal purpose, such as the details of an estate going to probate, or the contents of a house let furnished.

In both British and American English, stock is the collective noun for one hundred shares as shares were usually traded in stocks on Stock Exchanges. For this reason the word stock is used by both American and British English in the term Stock Exchange. Inventory management is a science primarily about specifying the shape and percentage of stocked goods. It is required at different locations within a facility or within many locations of a supply network to precede the regular and planned course of production and stock of materials. The scope of inventory management concerns the fine lines between replenishment lead time, carrying costs of inventory, asset management, inventory forecasting, inventory valuation, inventory visibility, future inventory price forecasting, physical inventory, available physical space for inventory, quality management, replenishment, returns and defective goods, and demand forecasting. Balancing these competing requirements leads to optimal inventory levels, which is an on-going process as the business needs shift and react to the wider environment.

Inventory management involves a retailer seeking to acquire and maintain a proper merchandise assortment while ordering, shipping, handling, and related costs are kept in check. It also involves systems and processes that identify inventory requirements, set targets, provide replenishment techniques, report actual and projected inventory status and handle all functions related to the tracking and management of material. This would include the monitoring of material moved into and out of stockroom locations and the reconciling of the inventory balances. It also may include ABC analysis, lot tracking, cycle counting support, etc. Management of the inventories, with the primary objective of determining/controlling stock levels within the physical distribution system, functions to balance the need for product availability against the need for minimizing stock holding and handling costs.

Definition

Inventory management is primarily about specifying the size and placement of stocked goods. Inventory management is required at different locations within a facility or within multiple locations of a supply network to protect the regular and planned course of production against the random disturbance of running out of materials or goods. The scope of inventory management also concerns the fine lines between replenishment lead time, carrying costs of inventory, asset management, inventory forecasting, inventory valuation, inventory visibility, future inventory price forecasting, physical inventory, available physical space for inventory, quality management, replenishment, returns and defective goods and demand forecasting and also by replenishment Or can be defined as the left out stock of any item used in an organization.

- Business Inventory

Reasons for Keeping Stock

There are four basic reasons for keeping an inventory

1. Time - The time lags present in the supply chain, from supplier to user at every stage, requires that you maintain certain amounts of inventory to use in this lead time. However, in practice, inventory is to be maintained for consumption during

'variations in lead time'. Lead time itself can be addressed by ordering that many days in advance.

2. Uncertainty - Inventories are maintained as buffers to meet uncertainties in demand, supply and movements of goods.
3. Economies of scale - Ideal condition of "one unit at a time at a place where a user needs it, when he needs it" principle tends to incur lots of costs in terms of logistics. So bulk buying, movement and storing brings in economies of scale, thus inventory.
4. Appreciation in Value - In some situations, some stock gains the required value when it is kept for some time to allow it reach the desired standard for consumption, or for production. For example; beer in the brewing industry

All these stock reasons can apply to any owner or product

Special Terms used in Dealing with Inventory

- *Stock Keeping Unit* (SKU) is a unique combination of all the components that are assembled into the purchasable item. Therefore, any change in the packaging or product is a new SKU. This level of detailed specification assists in managing inventory.
- *Stockout* means running out of the inventory of an SKU.
- "New old stock" (sometimes abbreviated NOS) is a term used in business to refer to merchandise being offered for sale that was manufactured long ago but that has never been used. Such merchandise may not be produced anymore, and the new old stock may represent the only market source of a particular item at the present time.

Typology

1. Buffer/safety stock
2. Reorder level
3. Cycle stock (Used in batch processes, it is the available inventory, excluding buffer stock)
4. De-coupling (Buffer stock held between the machines in a single process which serves as a buffer for the next one allowing smooth flow of work instead of waiting the previous or next machine in the same process)
5. Anticipation stock (Building up extra stock for periods of increased demand - e.g. ice cream for summer)

6. Pipeline stock (Goods still in transit or in the process of distribution - have left the factory but not arrived at the customer yet)

Inventory Examples

While accountants often discuss inventory in terms of goods for sale, organizations - manufacturers, service-providers and not-for-profits - also have inventories (fixtures, furniture, supplies, etc.) that they do not intend to sell. Manufacturers', distributors', and wholesalers' inventory tends to cluster in warehouses. Retailers' inventory may exist in a warehouse or in a shop or store accessible to customers. Inventories not intended for sale to customers or to clients may be held in any premises an organization uses. Stock ties up cash and, if uncontrolled, it will be impossible to know the actual level of stocks and therefore impossible to control them.

While the reasons for holding stock were covered earlier, most manufacturing organizations usually divide their "goods for sale" inventory into:

- Raw materials - materials and components scheduled for use in making a product.
- Work in process, WIP - materials and components that have begun their transformation to finished goods.
- Finished goods - goods ready for sale to customers.
- Goods for resale - returned goods that are salable.
- Stocks in Transit.
- Consignment Stocks.

For example:

Manufacturing

A canned food manufacturer's materials inventory includes the ingredients to form the foods to be canned, empty cans and their lids (or coils of steel or aluminum for constructing those components), labels, and anything else (solder, glue, etc.) that will form part of a finished can. The firm's work in process includes those materials from the time of release to the work floor until they become complete and ready for sale to wholesale or retail customers. This may be vats of prepared food, filled cans not yet labeled or sub-assemblies of food components. It may also include finished cans that are not yet packaged into cartons or pallets. Its finished good inventory consists of all the filled and labeled cans of food in its warehouse that it has manufactured and wishes to sell to food distributors (wholesalers), to grocery stores (retailers), and even perhaps to consumers through arrangements like factory stores and outlet centers.

Principle of Inventory Proportionality

Purpose

Inventory proportionality is the goal of demand-driven inventory management. The primary optimal outcome is to have the same number of days' (or hours', etc.) worth of inventory on hand across all products so that the time of runout of all products would be simultaneous. In such a case, there is no "excess inventory," that is, inventory that would be left over of another product when the first product runs out. Excess inventory is sub-optimal because the money spent to obtain it could have been utilized better elsewhere, i.e. to the product that just ran out.

The secondary goal of inventory proportionality is inventory minimization. By integrating accurate demand forecasting with inventory management, rather than to past averages, a much more accurate and optimal outcome.

Integrating demand forecasting into inventory management in this way also allows for the prediction of the "can fit" point when inventory storage is limited on a per-product basis.

Applications

The technique of inventory proportionality is most appropriate for inventories that remain unseen by the consumer, as opposed to "keep full" systems where a retail consumer would like to see full shelves of the product they are buying so as not to think they are buying something old, unwanted or stale; and differentiated from the "trigger point" systems where product is reordered when it hits a certain level; inventory proportionality is used effectively by just-in-time manufacturing processes and retail applications where the product is hidden from view.

One early example of inventory proportionality used in a retail application in the United States was for motor fuel. Motor fuel (e.g. gasoline) is generally stored in underground storage tanks. The motorists do not know whether they are buying gasoline off the top or bottom of the tank, nor need they care. Additionally, these storage tanks have a maximum capacity and cannot be overfilled. Finally, the product is expensive. Inventory proportionality is used to balance the inventories of the different grades of motor fuel, each stored in dedicated tanks, in proportion to the sales of each grade. Excess inventory is not seen or valued by the consumer, so it is simply cash sunk (literally) into the ground. Inventory proportionality minimizes the amount of excess inventory carried in underground storage tanks. This application for motor fuel was first developed and implemented by Petrolsoft Corporation in 1990 for Chevron Products Company. Most major oil companies use such systems today.

Roots

The use of inventory proportionality in the United States is thought to have been inspired by Japanese just-in-time parts inventory management made famous by Toyota Motors in the 1980s.[3] the shieft of the stock in the common in the used in the college.

High-Level Inventory Management

It seems that around 1880 there was a change in manufacturing practice from companies with relatively homogeneous lines of products to horizontally integrated companies with unprecedented diversity in processes and products. Those companies (especially in metalworking) attempted to achieve success through economies of scope - the gains of jointly producing two or more products in one facility. The managers now needed information on the effect of product-mix decisions on overall profits and therefore needed accurate product-cost information. A variety of attempts to achieve this were unsuccessful due to the huge overhead of the information processing of the time.

However, the burgeoning need for financial reporting after 1900 created unavoidable pressure for financial accounting of stock and the management need to cost manage products became overshadowed. In particular, it was the need for audited accounts that sealed the fate of managerial cost accounting. The dominance of financial reporting accounting over management accounting remains to this day with few exceptions, and the financial reporting definitions of 'cost' have distorted effective management 'cost' accounting since that time. This is particularly true of inventory.

Hence, high-level financial inventory has these two basic formulas, which relate to the accounting period:

1. Cost of Beginning Inventory at the start of the period + inventory purchases within the period + cost of production within the period = cost of goods available
2. Cost of goods available " cost of ending inventory at the end of the period = cost of goods sold

The benefit of these formulas is that the first absorbs all overheads of production and raw material costs into a value of inventory for reporting. The second formula then creates the new start point for the next period and gives a figure to be subtracted from the sales price to determine some form of sales-margin figure. Manufacturing management is more interested in *inventory turnover ratio* or *average days to sell inventory* since it tells them something about relative inventory levels.

Inventory turnover ratio (also known as inventory turns) = cost of goods sold / Average Inventory = Cost of Goods Sold / ((Beginning Inventory + Ending Inventory) / 2) and its inverse

Average Days to Sell Inventory = Number of Days a Year / Inventory Turnover Ratio = 365 days a year / Inventory Turnover Ratio

This ratio estimates how many times the inventory turns over a year. This number tells how much cash/goods are tied up waiting for the process and is a critical measure of process reliability and effectiveness. So a factory with two inventory turns has six months stock on hand, which is generally not a good figure (depending upon the industry), whereas a factory that moves from six turns to twelve turns has probably improved effectiveness by 100%. This improvement will have some negative results in the financial reporting, since the 'value' now stored in the factory as inventory is reduced.

While these accounting measures of inventory are very useful because of their simplicity, they are also fraught with the danger of their own assumptions. There are, in fact, so many things that can vary hidden under this appearance of simplicity that a variety of 'adjusting' assumptions may be used. These include:

- Specific Identification
- Weighted Average Cost
- Moving-Average Cost
- FIFO and LIFO.

Inventory Turn is a financial accounting tool for evaluating inventory and it is not necessarily a management tool. Inventory management should be forward looking. The methodology applied is based on historical cost of goods sold. The ratio may not be able to reflect the usability of future production demand, as well as customer demand.

Business models, including Just in Time (JIT) Inventory, Vendor Managed Inventory (VMI) and Customer Managed Inventory (CMI), attempt to minimize on-hand inventory and increase inventory turns. VMI and CMI have gained considerable attention due to the success of third-party vendors who offer added expertise and knowledge that organizations may not possess.

Accounting for Inventory

Each country has its own rules about accounting for inventory that fit with their financial-reporting rules.

For example, organizations in the U.S. define inventory to suit their needs within US Generally Accepted Accounting Practices (GAAP), the rules defined by the Financial Accounting Standards Board (FASB) (and others) and enforced by the U.S. Securities and Exchange Commission (SEC) and other federal and state agencies. Other countries often have similar arrangements but with their own accounting standards and national agencies instead.

It is intentional that financial accounting uses standards that allow the public to compare firms' performance, cost accounting functions internally to an organization and potentially with much greater flexibility. A discussion of inventory from standard and Theory of Constraints-based (throughput) cost accounting perspective follows some examples and a discussion of inventory from a financial accounting perspective.

The internal costing/valuation of inventory can be complex. Whereas in the past most enterprises ran simple, one-process factories, such enterprises are quite probably in the minority in the 21st century. Where 'one process' factories exist, there is a market for the goods created, which establishes an independent market value for the good. Today, with multistage-process companies, there is much inventory that would once have been finished goods which is now held as 'work in process' (WIP). This needs to be valued in the accounts, but the valuation is a management decision since there is no market for the partially finished product. This somewhat arbitrary 'valuation' of WIP combined with the allocation of overheads to it has led to some unintended and undesirable results.

Financial Accounting

An organization's inventory can appear a mixed blessing, since it counts as an asset on the balance sheet, but it also ties up money that could serve for other purposes and requires additional expense for its protection. Inventory may also cause significant tax expenses, depending on particular countries' laws regarding depreciation of inventory, as in Thor Power Tool Company v. Commissioner.

Inventory appears as a current asset on an organization's balance sheet because the organization can, in principle, turn it into cash by selling it. Some organizations hold larger inventories than their operations require in order to inflate their apparent asset value and their perceived profitability. In addition to the money tied up by acquiring inventory, inventory also brings associated costs for warehouse space, for utilities, and for insurance to cover staff to handle and protect it from fire and other disasters, obsolescence, shrinkage (theft and errors), and others. Such holding costs can mount up: between a third and a half of its acquisition value per year. Businesses that stock too little inventory cannot take advantage of large orders from customers if they cannot deliver. The conflicting objectives of cost control and customer service often pit an organization's financial and operating managers against its sales and marketing departments. Salespeople, in particular, often receive sales-commission payments, so unavailable goods may reduce their potential personal income. This conflict can be minimised by reducing production time to being near or less than customers' expected delivery time. This effort, known as "Lean production" will significantly reduce working capital tied up in inventory and reduce manufacturing costs.

Role of Inventory Accounting

By helping the organization to make better decisions, the accountants can help the public sector to change in a very positive way that delivers increased value for the taxpayer's investment. It can also help to incentivise progress and to ensure that reforms are sustainable and effective in the long term, by ensuring that success is appropriately recognized in both the formal and informal reward systems of the organization. To say that they have a key role to play is an understatement. Finance is connected to most, if not all, of the key business processes within the organization. It should be steering the stewardship and accountability systems that ensure that the organization is conducting its business in an appropriate, ethical manner. It is critical that these foundations are firmly laid. So often they are the litmus test by which public confidence in the institution is either won or lost.

Finance should also be providing the information, analysis and advice to enable the organizations' service managers to operate effectively. This goes beyond the traditional preoccupation with budgets – how much have we spent so far, how much do we have left to spend? It is about helping the organization to better understand its own performance. That means making the connections and understanding the relationships between given inputs – the resources brought to bear – and the outputs and outcomes that they achieve. It is also about understanding and actively managing risks within the organization and its activities.

FIFO vs. LIFO Accounting

When a merchant buys goods from inventory, the value of the inventory account is reduced by the cost of goods sold (COGS). This is simple where the CoG has not varied across those held in stock; but where it has, then an agreed method must be derived to evaluate it. For commodity items that one cannot track individually, accountants must choose a method that fits the nature of the sale. Two popular methods that normally exist are: FIFO and LIFO accounting (first in - first out, last in - first out).

FIFO regards the first unit that arrived in inventory as the first one sold. LIFO considers the last unit arriving in inventory as the first one sold. Which method an accountant selects can have a significant effect on net income and book value and, in turn, on taxation. Using LIFO accounting for inventory, a company generally reports lower net income and lower book value, due to the effects of inflation. This generally results in lower taxation. Due to LIFO's potential to skew inventory value, UK GAAP and IAS have effectively banned LIFO inventory accounting.

Standard Cost Accounting

Standard cost accounting uses ratios called efficiencies that compare the labour and materials actually used to produce a good with those that the same goods would have required under "standard" conditions. As long as actual and standard conditions are similar, few problems arise. Unfortunately, standard cost accounting methods developed about 100 years ago, when labor comprised the most important cost in manufactured goods. Standard methods continue to emphasize labor efficiency even though that resource now constitutes a (very) small part of cost in most cases. Standard cost accounting can hurt managers, workers, and firms in several ways. For example, a policy decision to increase inventory can harm a manufacturing manager's performance evaluation. Increasing inventory requires increased production, which means that processes must operate at higher rates. When (not if) something goes wrong, the process takes longer and uses more than the standard labor time. The manager appears responsible for the excess, even though s/he has no control over the production requirement or the problem.

In adverse economic times, firms use the same efficiencies to downsize, rightsize, or otherwise reduce their labor force. Workers laid off under those circumstances have even less control over excess inventory and cost efficiencies than their managers. Many financial and cost accountants have agreed for many years on the desirability of replacing standard cost accounting. They have not, however, found a successor.

Theory of Constraints Cost Accounting

Eliyahu M. Goldratt developed the Theory of Constraints in part to address the cost-accounting problems in what he calls the "cost world." He offers a substitute, called throughput accounting, that uses throughput (money for goods sold to customers) in place of output (goods produced that may sell or may boost inventory) and considers labor as a fixed rather than as a variable cost. He defines inventory simply as everything the organization owns that it plans to sell, including buildings, machinery, and many other things in addition to the categories listed here. Throughput accounting recognizes only one class of variable costs: the truly variable costs, like materials and components, which vary directly with the quantity produced

Finished goods inventories remain balance-sheet assets, but labor-efficiency ratios no longer evaluate managers and workers. Instead of an incentive to reduce labor cost, throughput accounting focuses attention on the relationships between throughput (revenue or income) on one hand and controllable operating expenses and changes in inventory on the other.

National Accounts

Inventories also play an important role in national accounts and the analysis of the business cycle. Some short-term macroeconomic fluctuations are attributed to the inventory cycle.

Distressed Inventory

Also known as distressed or expired stock, distressed inventory is inventory whose potential to be sold at a normal cost has passed or will soon pass. In certain industries it could also mean that the stock is or will soon be impossible to sell. Examples of distressed inventory include products that have reached their expiry date, or have reached a date in advance of expiry at which the planned market will no longer purchase them (e.g. 3 months left to expiry), clothing that is defective or out of fashion, music that is no longer popular and old newspapers or magazines. It also includes computer or consumer-electronic equipment that is obsolete or discontinued and whose manufacturer is unable to support it. One current example of distressed inventory is the VHS format. In 2001, Cisco wrote off inventory worth US $2.25 billion due to duplicate orders. This is one of the biggest inventory write-offs in business history.

Stock Rotation

Stock Rotation is the practice of changing the way inventory is displayed on a regular basis. This is most commonly used in hospitably and retail - particularity where food products are sold. For example, in the case of supermarkets that a customer frequents on a regular basis, the customer may know exactly where they want and where it is. This results in many customers going straight to the product they seek and do not look at other items on sale. To discourage this practice, stores will rotate the location of stock to encourage customers to look through the entire store. This is in hopes the customer will pick up items they would not normally see.

Inventory Credit

Inventory credit refers to the use of stock, or inventory, as collateral to raise finance. Where banks may be reluctant to accept traditional collateral, for example in developing countries where land title may be lacking, inventory credit is a potentially important way of overcoming financing constraints. This is not a new concept; archaeological evidence suggests that it was practiced in Ancient Rome. Obtaining finance against stocks of a wide range of products held in a bonded warehouse is common in much of the world. It is, for example, used with Parmesan cheese in Italy. Inventory credit on the basis of stored agricultural produce is widely used in Latin American countries and in some Asian countries. A precondition for such credit is that banks must be confident that the stored product will be available if they need to call on the collateral; this implies the existence of a reliable network of certified warehouses. Banks also face problems in valuing the inventory. The possibility of sudden falls in commodity prices means that they are usually reluctant to lend more than about 60% of the value of the inventory at the time of the loan.

INVENTORY MANAGEMENT SOFTWARE

Inventory management software is a computer-based system for tracking inventory levels, orders, sales and deliveries. It can also be used in the manufacturing industry to create a work order, bill of materials and other production-related documents. Companies use inventory management software to avoid product overstock and outages. It is a tool for organizing inventory data that before was generally stored in hard-copy form or in spreadsheets. It is often associated with and is similar to distribution software.

Inventory management software is made up of several key components, all working together to create a cohesive inventory for many organizations' systems. These features include:

Order Management

Should inventory reach a certain threshold, a company's inventory management system can be programmed to tell managers to reorder that product. This helps companies avoid running out of products or tying up too much capital in inventory.

Asset Tracking

When a product is in a warehouse or store, it can be tracked via its barcode and/or other tracking criteria, such as serial number, lot number or revision number. Nowadays, inventory management software often utilizes barcode, radio-frequency identification (RFID), and/or wireless tracking technology.

Service Management

Companies that are primarily service-oriented rather than product-oriented can use inventory management software to track the cost of the materials they use to provide services, such as cleaning supplies. This way, they can attach prices to their services that reflect the total cost of performing them.

Product Identification

Barcodes are often the means whereby data on products and orders is inputted into inventory management software. A barcode reader is used to read barcodes and look up information on the products they represent. Radio-frequency identification (RFID) tags and wireless methods of product identification are also growing in popularity.

History

The Universal Product Code (UPC) was adopted by the grocery industry in April 1973 as the standard barcode for all grocers, though it was not introduced at retailing locations until 1974. This helped drive down costs for inventory management because retailers in the United States and Canada didn't have to purchase multiple barcode readers to scan competing barcodes. There was now one primary barcode for grocers and other retailers to buy one type of reader for. In the early 1980s, personal computers debuted and started becoming popular. This further pushed down the cost of barcodes and readers. It also allowed the first versions of inventory management software to be put into place. One of the biggest hurdles in selling readers and barcodes to retailers was the fact that they didn't have a place to store the information they scanned. As computers became more common and affordable, this hurdle was overcome. Once barcodes and inventory management programs started spreading through grocery stores, inventory management by hand became less practical. Writing inventory data by hand on paper was replaced by scanning products and inputting information into a computer by hand.

Starting in the early 2000s, inventory management software progressed to the point where businesspeople no longer needed to input data by hand but could instantly update their database with barcode readers.

Purpose

Companies often use inventory management software to reduce their carrying costs. The software is used to track products and parts as they are transported from a vendor to a warehouse, between warehouses, and finally to a retail location or directly to a customer.

Inventory management software is used for a variety of purposes, including:

- Maintaining a balance between too much and too little inventory.
- Tracking inventory as it is transported between locations.
- Receiving items into a warehouse or other location.
- Picking, packing and shipping items from a warehouse.
- Keeping track of product sales and inventory levels.
- Cutting down on product obsolescence and spoilage.
- Manufacturing Uses

Manufacturers primarily use inventory management software to create work orders and bills of materials. This facilitates the manufacturing process by helping manufacturers efficiently assemble the tools and parts they need to perform specific tasks. For more complex manufacturing jobs, manufacturers can create multilevel work orders and bills of materials, which have a timeline of processes that need to happen in the proper order to build a final product. Other work orders that can be created using inventory management software include reverse work orders and auto work orders. Manufacturers also use inventory management software for tracking assets, receiving new inventory and additional tasks businesses in other industries use it for.

Advantages

There are several advantages to using inventory management software in a business setting.

Cost Savings

In many cases, a company's inventory represents one of its largest investments, along with its workforce and locations. Inventory management software helps companies cut expenses by minimizing the amount of unnecessary parts and products in storage. It also helps companies keep lost sales to a minimum by having enough stock on hand to meet demand.

Increased Efficiency

Inventory management software often allows for automation of many inventory-related tasks. For example, software can automatically collect data, conduct calculations, and create records. This not only results in time savings, cost savings, but also increases business efficiency.

Warehouse Organization

Inventory management software can help distributors, wholesalers, manufacturers and retailers optimize their warehouses. If certain products are often sold together or are more popular than others, those products can be grouped together or placed near the delivery area to speed up the process of picking,

Updated Data

Up-to-date, real-time data on inventory conditions and levels is another advantage inventory management software gives companies. Company executives can usually access the software through a mobile device, laptop or PC to check current inventory numbers. This automatic updating of inventory records allows businesses to make informed decisions.

Data Security

With the aid of restricted user rights, company managers can allow many employees to assist in inventory management. They can grant employees enough information access to receive products, make orders, transfer products and do other tasks without compromising company security. This can speed up the inventory management process and save managers' time.

Insight into Trends

Tracking where products are stocked, which suppliers they come from, and the length of time they are stored is made possible with inventory management software. By analysing such data, companies can control inventory levels and maximize the use of warehouse space. Furthermore, firms are more prepared for the demands and supplies of the market, especially during special circumstances such as a peak season on a particular month. Through the reports generated by the inventory management software, firms are also able to gather important data that may be put in a model for it to be analyzed.

Disadvantages

The main disadvantages of inventory management software are its cost and complexity.

Expense

Cost can be a major disadvantage of inventory management software. Many large companies use inventory management software, but small businesses can find it difficult to afford it. Barcode readers and other hardware can compound this problem by adding even more cost to companies. The advantage of allowing multiple employees to perform inventory-management tasks is tempered by the cost of additional barcode readers.

Complexity

Inventory management software is not necessarily simple or easy to learn. A company's management team must dedicate a certain amount of time to learning a new system, including both software and hardware, in order to put it to use. Most inventory management software includes training manuals and other information available to users. Despite its apparent complexity, inventory management software offers a degree of stability to companies. For example, if an IT employee in charge of the system leaves the company, a replacement can be comparatively inexpensive to train compared to if the company used multiple programs to store inventory data.

PROCUREMENT

Procurement is the acquisition of goods, services or works from an outside external source. It is favourable that the goods, services or works are appropriate and that they are procured at the best possible cost to meet the needs of the purchaser in terms of quality and quantity, time, and location. Corporations and public bodies often define processes intended to promote fair and open competition for their business while minimizing exposure to fraud and collusion.

Overview

Almost all purchasing decisions include factors such as delivery and handling, marginal benefit, and price fluctuations. Procurement generally involves making buying decisions under conditions of scarcity. If good data is available, it is good practice to make use of economic analysis methods such as cost-benefit analysis or cost-utility analysis.

An important distinction s hould be made between analyses without risk and those with risk. Where risk is involved, either in the costs or the benefits, the concept of expected value may be employed. Direct procurement occurs in manufacturing settings only. It encompasses all items that are part of finished products, such as raw material, components and parts. Direct procurement, which is the focus in supply chain management, directly affects the production process of manufacturing firms. In contrast, Indirect procurement activities concern "operating resources" that a company purchases to enable its operations. It comprises a wide variety of goods and services, from standardized low value items like office supplies and machine lubricants to complex and costly products and services; like heavy equipment and consulting services.

History

Prior to 1900, purchasing was recognized as an independent function by many railroad organizations, but not in most other industries. Prior to World War I, purchasing was regarded as primarily clerical.

During World War I & II - The function increased due to the importance of obtaining raw materials, supplies, and services needed to keep the factories and mines operating.

1950s & 1960s - Purchasing continued to gain stature as the techniques for performing the function became more refined and as the number of trained professionals increased. The emphasis became more managerial. With introduction of major public bodies and intergovernmental organizations, such as United Nations, procurement becomes a well-recognized science.

1970s & 1980s - More emphasis was placed on purchasing strategy as the ability to obtain needed items from suppliers at realistic prices increased.

1983 - In September 1983, Harvard Business Review published a ground-breaking article by Peter Kraljic on purchasing strategy that is widely cited today as the beginning of the transformation of the function from "purchasing", to something that is viewed as highly tactical to procurement or supply management, something that is viewed as very strategic to the business.

1990s - Procurement starts to become more integrated into the overall corporate strategy and a broad-based transformation of the business function is ignited, fueled strongly by the development of supply management software solutions which help automate the source-to-settle process.

2000s - The leader of the procurement function within many enterprises is established with a C-Level title - the Chief Procurement Officer (sometimes called the Head of Procurement). Websites, publications, and events, and that are dedicated solely to the advancement of Chief Procurement Officers and the procurement function arise. The global recession of 2008-2009 places procurement at the crux of business strategy.

2010s - The elevation of the function continues as Chief Procurement Officers are recognized as important business leaders and begin to take on broader operation responsibility.

Topics

Procurement vs Acquisition

The US Defense Acquisition University (DAU) defines procurement as the act of buying goods and services for the government.

DAU defines acquisition as the conceptualization, initiation, design, development, test, contracting, production, deployment, Logistics Support (LS), modification, and disposal of weapons and other systems, supplies, or services (including construction) to satisfy Department of Defense needs, intended for use in or in support of military missions.

Acquisition is therefore a much wider concept than procurement, covering the whole life cycle of acquired systems. Multiple acquisition models exist, one of which is provided in the following section.

Acquisition Process

The revised acquisition process for major systems in industry and defense. The process is defined by a series of phases during which technology is defined and matured into viable concepts, which are subsequently developed and readied for production, after which the systems produced are supported in the field. The process allows for a given system to enter the process at any of the development phases. For example, a system using unproven technology would enter at the beginning stages of the process and would proceed through a lengthy period of technology maturation, while a system based on mature and proven technologies might enter directly into engineering development or, conceivably, even production. The process itself includes four phases of development:

- Concept and Technology Development: is intended to explore alternative concepts based on assessments of operational needs, technology readiness, risk, and affordability.
- Concept and Technology Development phase begins with concept exploration. During this stage, concept studies are undertaken to define alternative concepts and to provide information about capability and risk that would permit an objective comparison of competing concepts.
- System Development and Demonstration phase. This phase could be entered directly as a result of a technological opportunity and urgent user need, as well as having come through concept and technology development.
- The last, and longest phase is the Sustainable and Disposal phase of the program. During this phase all necessary activities are accomplished to maintain and sustain the system in the field in the most cost-effective manner possible.

Procurement Systems

Another common procurement issue is the timing of purchases.

Procurement Process

Procurement may involve bidding process known as *tendering*. A company or organisation may require some product or service. If the price exceeds a threshold that has been set (e.g.: government department procurement policy: "any product or service desired whose price is over X must be put to tender"), depending on policy or legal requirements, the purchaser is required to state what is required and make the contract open to the bidding process. The concept of total cost also comes into play. At times, not just price, but other factors such as reliability, quality, flexibility and timing, are considered in the tendering process. A number of potential suppliers then submit proposals of what they will provide and at what price. Then the purchaser will usually select the lowest bidder; however if the lowest bidder is deemed incompetent to provide what is required despite quoting the lowest price, the purchaser will select the lowest bidder deemed competent. In the European Union, strict rules on procurement must be followed by public bodies, with contract value thresholds determining the processes required (relating to advertising the contract, the actual process etc.).

Procurement Steps

Procurement life cycle in modern businesses usually consists of seven steps:

- Identification of need: This is an internal step for a company that involves understanding of the company needs by establishing a short term strategy (three to five years) followed by defining the technical direction and requirements.
- Supplier Identification: Once the company has answered important questions like: Make-buy, multiple vs. single suppliers, then it needs to identify who can provide the required product/ service. There are many sources to search for supplier; more popular ones being Ariba, Alibaba, other suppliers and trade shows.
- Supplier Communication: When one or more suitable suppliers have been identified, requests for quotation, requests for proposals, requests for information or requests for tender may be advertised, or direct contact may be made with the suppliers. References for product/service quality are consulted, and any requirements for follow-up services including installation, maintenance, and warranty are investigated. Samples of the P/S being considered may be examined, or trials undertaken.
- Negotiation: Negotiations are undertaken, and price, availability,

and customization possibilities are established. Delivery schedules are negotiated, and a contract to acquire the P/S is completed.

- Supplier Liaison: During this phase, the company evaluates the performance of the P/S and any accompanying service support, as they are consumed.Supplier scorecard is a popular tool for this purpose.When the P/S has been consumed or disposed of, the contract expires, or the product or service is to be re-ordered, company experience with the P/S is reviewed. If the P/S is to be re-ordered, the company determines whether to consider other suppliers or to continue with the same supplier.
- Logistics Management: Supplier preparation, expediting, shipment, delivery, and payment for the P/S are completed, based on contract terms. Installation and training may also be included.
- Additional Step - Tender Notification: Some institutions choose to use a notification service in order to raise the competition for the chosen opportunity. These systems can either be direct from their e-tendering software, or as a re-packaged notification from an external notification company.

Procurement Performance

In July 2011, Ardent Partners, published a research report that presented a comprehensive, industry-wide view into what is happening in the world of procurement today by drawing on the experience, performance, and perspective of nearly 250 Chief Procurement Officers and other procurement executives. The report includes the main procurement performance and operational benchmarks that procurement leaders use to gauge the success of their organizations. This report found that the average procurement department manages 60.6% of total enterprise spend. This measure commonly called “spend under management” refers to the percentage of total enterprise spend (which includes all direct, indirect, and services spend) that a procurement organization manages or influences. The average procurement department also achieved an annual savings of 6.7% in the last reporting cycle, sourced 52.6% of its addressable spend, and has a contract compliance rate of 62.6%.

Public Procurement

Public procurement generally is an important sector of the economy. In Europe, public procurement accounts for 16.3% of the Community GDP.

Green Public Procurement

In Green public procurement (GPP), contracting authorities and entities take environmental issues into account when tendering for goods or services. The goal is to reduce the impact of the procurement on human health and the environment. In the European Union, the Commission has adopted its Communication on public procurement for a better environment, where proposes a political target of 50% Green public procurement to be reached by the Member States by the year 2010.

Alternative Procurement Procedures

There are several alternatives to tendering which are available in formal procurement. One system which has gained increasing momentum in the construction industry and among developing economies is the Selection in planning process which enables project developers and equipment purchasers to make significant changes to their requirements with relative ease. The SIP process also enables vendors and contractors to respond with greater accuracy and competitiveness as a result of the generally longer lead times they are afforded.

Procurement Frauds

Procurement fraud can be defined as dishonestly obtaining an advantage, avoiding an obligation or causing a loss to public property or various means during procurement process by public servants, contractors or any other person involved in the procurement. An example is the kickback, whereby a dishonest agent of the supplier pays a dishonest agent of the purchaser to select the supplier's bid, often at an inflated price.

WAREHOUSE MANAGEMENT SYSTEM

A warehouse management system (WMS) is a key part of the supply chain and primarily aims to control the movement and storage of materials within a warehouse and process the associated transactions, including shipping, receiving, putaway and picking. The systems also direct and optimize stock putaway based on real-time information about the status of bin utilization. A WMS monitors the progress of products through the warehouse. It involves the physical warehouse infrastructure, tracking systems, and communication between product stations.

More precisely, warehouse management involves the receipt, storage and movement of goods, (normally finished goods), to intermediate storage locations or to a final customer. In the multi-echelon model for distribution, there may be multiple levels of warehouses. This includes a central warehouse, a regional warehouses (serviced by the central warehouse) and potentially retail warehouses (serviced by the regional warehouses). Warehouse management systems often utilize automatic identification and data capture technology, such as barcode scanners, mobile computers, wireless LANs and potentially radio-frequency identification (RFID) to efficiently monitor the flow of products. Once data has been collected, there is either a batch synchronization with, or a real-time wireless transmission to a central database. The database can then provide useful reports about the status of goods in the warehouse. Warehouse design and process design within the warehouse (e.g. wave picking) is also part of warehouse management. Warehouse management is an aspect of logistics and supply chain management.

Objective

The objective of a warehouse management system is to provide a set of computerized procedures for management of warehouse inventory with the goal of minimizing cost and fulfillment times.

This includes:

- A standard receiving process to properly handle a shipment when it arrives. This process can be individualized to each warehouse or product type.
- The receipt of stock and returns into a warehouse facility. An efficient warehouse management system helps companies cut expenses by minimizing the amount of unnecessary parts and products in storage. It also helps companies keep lost sales to a minimum by having enough stock on hand to meet demand.
- Modeling and managing the logical representation of the physical storage facilities (e.g. racking, etc.). For example, if certain products are often sold together or are more popular than others, those products can be grouped together or placed near the delivery area to speed up the process of picking, packing and shipping to customers.
- Enabling a seamless link to order processing and logistics management in order to pick, pack, and ship product out of the facility.
- Tracking where products are stocked, which suppliers they come from, and the length of time they are stored. By analysing such data, companies can control inventory levels and maximize the use of warehouse space. Furthermore, firms are more prepared for the demands and supplies of the market, especially during special circumstances such as a peak season on a particular month. Through the reports generated by the inventory

management software, firms are also able to gather important data that may be put in a model for it to be analyzed.

Alone warehouse management cannot automate the process. It also involves the combination of business process to be followed along with system to achieve 100% productivity and accuracy .

Types

Warehouse management systems can be standalone systems, or modules of an ERP system or supply chain execution suite. Depending on the size and sophistication of the organization, the system can be as simple as a handwritten list that are updated when required, spreadsheets using software such as Microsoft Excel or Access or purpose-built software programs. In its simplest form, the WMS can data track products during the production process and act as an interpreter and message buffer between existing ERP and WMS systems.

MATERIALS SCIENCE

Materials science, also commonly known as materials engineering, is an interdisciplinary field applying the properties of matter to various areas of science and engineering. This relatively new scientific field investigates the relationship between the structure of materials at atomic or molecular scales and their macroscopic properties. It incorporates elements of applied physics and chemistry. With significant media attention focused on Nano science and nanotechnology in recent years, materials science is becoming more widely known as a specific field of science and engineering. It is an important part of forensic engineering (Forensic engineering is the investigation of materials, products, structures or components that fail or do not operate or function as intended, causing personal injury or damage to property.) and failure analysis, the latter being the key to understanding, for example, the cause of various aviation accidents. Many of the most pressing scientific problems that are currently faced today are due to the limitations of the materials that are currently available and, as a result, breakthroughs in this field are likely to have a significant impact on the future of technology.

History

The material of choice of a given era is often a defining point. Phrases such as Stone Age, Bronze Age, Iron Age, and Steel Age are good examples. Originally deriving from the manufacture of ceramics and its putative derivative metallurgy, materials science is one of the oldest forms of engineering and applied science. Modern materials science evolved directly from metallurgy, which itself evolved from mining and (likely) ceramics and the use of fire. A major breakthrough in the understanding of materials occurred in the late 19th century, when the American scientist Josiah Willard Gibbs demonstrated that the thermodynamic properties related to atomic structure in various phases are related to the physical properties of a material. Important elements of modern materials science are a product of the space race: the understanding and engineering of the metallic alloys, and silica and carbon materials, used in the construction of space vehicles enabling the exploration of space. Materials science has driven, and been driven by, the development of revolutionary technologies such as plastics, semiconductors, and biomaterials.

Before the 1960s (and in some cases decades after), many *materials science* departments were named *metallurgy* departments, from a 19th and early 20th century emphasis on metals. The field has since broadened to include every class of materials, including ceramics, polymers, semiconductors, magnetic materials, medical implant materials, biological materials and nanomaterials (materiomics).

Fundamentals

The basis of materials science involves relating the desired properties and relative performance of a material in a certain application to the structure of the atoms and phases in that material through characterization. The major determinants of the structure of a material and thus of its properties are its constituent chemical elements and the way in which it has been processed into its final form. These characteristics, taken together and related through the laws of thermodynamics, govern a material's microstructure, and thus its properties. The manufacture of a perfect crystal of a material is currently physically impossible. Instead materials scientists manipulate the defects in crystalline materials such as precipitates, grain boundaries (Hall–Petch relationship), interstitial atoms, vacancies or substitutional atoms, to create materials with the desired properties.

Not all materials have a regular crystal structure. Polymers display varying degrees of crystallinity, and many are completely non-crystalline. Glass as, some ceramics, and many natural materials are amorphous, not possessing any long-range order in their atomic arrangements. The study of polymers combines elements of chemical and statistical thermodynamics to give thermodynamic, as well as mechanical, descriptions of physical properties. In addition to industrial interest, materials science has gradually developed into a field which provides tests for condensed matter or solid state theories. New physics emerge because of the diverse new material properties that need to be explained.

Classes of Materials

Materials science encompasses various classes of materials, each of which may constitute a separate field. There are several ways to classify materials. For instance by the type of bonding between the atoms. The traditional groups are ceramics, metals and polymers based on atomic structure and chemical composition. New materials have resulted in more classes. One way of classifying materials is:

- Biomaterials
- Carbon
- Ceramics
- Composite materials
- Glass
- Metals
- Nanomaterials
- Polymers
- Refractory
- Semiconductors
- Thin Films
- Functionally Graded Materials
- Materials in Industry

Radical materials advances can drive the creation of new products or even new industries, but stable industries also employ materials scientists to make incremental improvements and troubleshoot issues with currently used materials. Industrial applications of materials science include materials design, cost-benefit tradeoffs in industrial production of materials, processing techniques (casting, rolling, welding, ion implantation, crystal growth, thin-film deposition, sintering, glassblowing, etc.), and analytical techniques (characterization techniques such as electron microscopy, x-ray diffraction, calorimetry, nuclear microscopy (HEFIB), Rutherford backscattering, neutron diffraction, small-angle X-ray scattering (SAXS), etc.).

Besides material characterization, the material scientist/engineer also deals with the extraction of materials and their conversion into useful forms. Thus ingot casting, foundry techniques, blast furnace extraction, and electrolytic extraction are all part of the required knowledge of a metallurgist/engineer. Often the presence, absence or variation of minute quantities of secondary elements and compounds in a bulk material will have a great impact on the final properties of the materials produced, for instance, steels are classified based on 1/10 and 1/100 weight percentages of the carbon and other alloying elements they contain. Thus, the extraction and purification techniques employed in the extraction of iron in the blast furnace will have an impact of the quality of steel that may be produced. The overlap between physics and materials science has led to the offshoot field of *materials physics*, which is concerned with the physical properties of materials. The approach is generally more macroscopic and applied than in condensed matter physics. See important publications in materials physics for more details on this field of study.

Ceramics and Glasses

Another application of the material sciences is the structures of glass and ceramics, typically associated with the most brittle materials. Bonding in ceramics and glasses use covalent and ionic-covalent types with SiO2 (silica or sand) as a fundamental building block. Ceramics are as soft as clay and as hard as stone and concrete. Usually, they are crystalline in form. Most glasses contain a metal oxide fused with silica. At high temperatures used to prepare glass, the material is a viscous liquid. The structure of glass forms into an amorphous state upon cooling. Windowpanes and eyeglasses are important examples. Fibers of glass are also available. Scratch resistant Corning Gorilla Glass is a well-known example of the application of materials science to drastically improve the properties of common components. Diamond and carbon in its graphite form are considered to be ceramics.

Engineering ceramics are known for their stiffness and stability under high temperatures, compression and electrical stress. Alumina, silicon carbide, and tungsten carbide are made from a fine powder of their constituents in a process of sintering with a binder. Hot pressing provides higher density material. Chemical vapor deposition can place a film of a ceramic on another material. Cermets are ceramic particles containing some metals. The wear resistance of tools is derived from cemented carbides with the metal phase of cobalt and nickel typically added to modify properties.

Composite Materials

Filaments are commonly used for reinforcement in composite materials.

Another application of material science in industry is the making of composite materials. Composite materials are structured materials composed of two or more macroscopic phases. Applications range from structural elements such as steel-reinforced concrete, to the thermally insulative tiles which play a key and integral role in NASA's Space Shuttle thermal protection system which is used to protect the surface of the shuttle from the heat of re-entry into the Earth's atmosphere. One example is reinforced Carbon-Carbon (RCC), the light gray material which withstands re-entry temperatures up to 1510 °C (2750 °F) and protects the Space Shuttle's wing leading edges and nose cap. RCC is a laminated composite material made from graphite rayon cloth and impregnated with a phenolic resin. After curing at high temperature in an autoclave, the laminate is pyrolized to convert the resin to carbon, impregnated with furfural alcohol in a vacuum chamber, and cured/pyrolized to convert the furfural alcohol to carbon. In order to provide oxidation resistance for reuse capability, the outer layers of the RCC are converted to silicon carbide.

Other examples can be seen in the "plastic" casings of television sets, cell-phones and so on. These plastic casings are usually a composite material made up of a thermoplastic matrix such as acrylonitrile-butadiene-styrene (ABS) in which calcium carbonate chalk, talc, glass fibers or carbon fibers have been added for added strength, bulk, or electrostatic dispersion. These additions may be referred to as reinforcing fibers, or dispersants, depending on their purpose.

Polymers

Polymers are also an important part of materials science. Polymers are the raw materials (the resins) used to make what we commonly call plastics. Plastics are really the final product, created after one or more polymers or additives have been added to a resin during processing, which is then shaped into a final form. Polymers which have been around, and which are in current widespread use, include polyethylene, polypropylene, PVC, polystyrene, nylons, polyesters, acrylics, polyurethanes, and polycarbonates. Plastics are generally classified as "commodity", "specialty" and "engineering" plastics.

PVC (polyvinyl-chloride) is widely used, inexpensive, and annual production quantities are large. It lends itself to an incredible array of applications, from artificial leather to electrical insulation and cabling, packaging and containers. Its fabrication and processing are simple and well-established. The versatility of PVC is due to the wide range of plasticisers and other additives that it accepts. The term "additives" in polymer science refers to the chemicals and compounds added to the polymer base to modify its material properties. Polycarbonate would be normally considered an engineering plastic (other examples include PEEK, ABS). Engineering plastics are valued for their superior strengths and other special material properties. They are usually not used for disposable applications, unlike commodity plastics. Specialty plastics are materials with unique characteristics, such as ultra-high strength, electrical conductivity, electro-fluorescence, high thermal stability, etc.

The dividing lines between the various types of plastics is not based on material but rather on their properties and applications. For instance, polyethylene (PE) is a cheap, low friction polymer commonly used to make disposable shopping bags and trash bags, and is considered a commodity plastic, whereas medium-density polyethylene (MDPE) is used for underground gas and water pipes, and another variety called Ultra-high Molecular Weight Polyethylene UHMWPE is an engineering plastic which is used extensively as the glide rails for industrial equipment and the low-friction socket in implanted hip joints.

Metal Alloys

The study of metal alloys is a significant part of materials science. Of all the metallic alloys in use today, the alloys of iron (steel, stainless steel, cast iron, tool steel, alloy steels) make up the largest proportion both by quantity and commercial value. Iron alloyed with various proportions of carbon gives low, mid and high carbon steels. An iron carbon alloy is only considered steel if the carbon level is between 0.01% and 2.00%. For the steels, the hardness and tensile strength of the steel is related to the amount of carbon present, with increasing carbon levels also leading to lower ductility and toughness. Heat treatment processes such as quenching and tempering can significantly change these properties however. Cast Iron is defined as an iron–carbon alloy with more than 2.00% but less than 6.67% carbon. Stainless steel is defined as a regular steel alloy with greater than 10% by weight alloying content of Chromium. Nickel and Molybdenum are typically also found in stainless steels.

Other significant metallic alloys are those of aluminium, titanium, copper and magnesium. Copper alloys have been known for a long time (since the Bronze Age), while the alloys of the other three metals have been relatively recently developed. Due to the chemical reactivity of these metals, the electrolytic extraction processes required were only developed relatively recently. The alloys of aluminium, titanium and magnesium are also known and valued for their high strength-to-weight ratios and, in the case of magnesium, their ability to provide electromagnetic shielding. These materials are ideal for situations where high strength-to-weight ratios are more important than bulk cost, such as in the aerospace industry and certain automotive engineering applications.

Sub-Disciplines of Materials Science

Below is a list of disciplines within or related to the materials science field. These range from biomaterials, to ceramics, to metals, to textile reinforced materials. Also note that these are linked to the respective main article.

- Biomaterials – materials that are derived from and/or used with life forms.
- Ceramography – the study of the microstructures of high-temperature materials and refractories, including structural ceramics such as RCC, polycrystalline silicon carbide and transformation toughened ceramics
- Crystallography – the study of regular arrangement of atoms and ions in a solid, the defects associated with crystal structures such as grain boundaries and dislocations, and the characterization of these structures and their relation to physical properties.
- Electronic and magnetic materials – materials such as semiconductors used to create integrated circuits, storage media, sensors, and other devices.
- Forensic engineering – the study of how products fail, and the vital role of the materials of construction
- Forensic materials engineering – the study of material failure, and the light it sheds on how engineers specify materials in their product
- Glass science – any non-crystalline material including inorganic glasses, vitreous metals and non-oxide glasses.
- Materials characterization – such as diffraction with x-rays, electrons, or neutrons, and various forms of spectroscopy and chemical analysis such as Raman spectroscopy, energy-dispersive spectroscopy (EDS), chromatography, thermal analysis, electron microscope analysis, etc., in order to understand and define the properties of materials.
- Metallography - Metallography is the study of the physical structure and components of metals, typically using microscopy.
- Metallurgy – the study of metals and their alloys, including their extraction, microstructure and processing.
- Microtechnology – study of materials and processes and their interaction, allowing microfabrication of structures of micrometric dimensions, such as Microelectromechanical systems (MEMS).
- Nanotechnology – rigorously, the study of materials where the effects of quantum confinement, the Gibbs–Thomson effect, or any other effect only present at the nanoscale is the defining property of the material; but more commonly, it is the creation and study of materials whose defining structural properties

are anywhere from less than a nanometer to one hundred nanometers in scale, such as molecularly engineered materials.

- Rheology – Some practitioners consider rheology a sub-field of materials science, because it can cover any material that flows. However, modern rheology typically deals with non-Newtonian fluid dynamics, so it is often considered a sub-field of continuum mechanics.
- Surface science/catalysis – interactions and structures between solid-gas solid-liquid or solid-solid interfaces.
- Textile reinforced materials – materials in the form of ceramic or concrete are reinforced with a primarily woven or non-woven textile structure to impose high strength with comparatively more flexibility to withstand vibrations and sudden jerks.
- Tribology – the study of the wear of materials due to friction and other factors.

Methods, Processes, and Related Topics

Below are links to topics that explain methods, processes and related topics in order to enhance understanding of materials science.

- Alloying, corrosion, and thermal or mechanical processing, for a specialized treatment of metallurgical materials—with applications ranging from aerospace and industrial equipment to the civil industries
- Biomaterials, physiology, biomechanics, biochemistry, for a specialized understanding of how materials integrate into biological systems, e.g., through materiomics
- Crystallography, quantum chemistry or quantum physics, for the structure (symmetry and defects) and bonding in materials (e.g., ionic, metallic, covalent, and van der Waals bonding)
- Diffraction and wave mechanics, for the science behind characterization systems, e.g., X-ray diffraction (XRD) transmission electron microscopy (TEM)
- Electronic properties of materials, and solid-state physics, for the understanding of the electronic, thermal, magnetic, and optical properties of materials
- Mechanical behavior of materials, to understand the mechanical properties of materials, defects and their propagation, and their behavior under static, dynamic, and cyclic loads
- Phase transformation kinetics, for the kinetics of phase

transformations (with particular emphasis on solid-solid phase transitions)

- Polymer properties, synthesis, and characterization, for a specialized understanding of how polymers behave, how they are made, and how they are characterized; exciting applications of polymers include liquid crystal displays (LCDs, the displays found in most cell phones, cameras, and iPods), novel photovoltaic devices based on semiconductor polymers (which, unlike the traditional silicon solar panels, are flexible and cheap to manufacture, albeit with lower efficiency), and membranes for room-temperature fuel cells (as proton exchange membranes) and filtration systems in the environmental and biomedical fields
- Semiconductor materials and semiconductor devices, for a specialized understanding of the advanced processes used in industry (e.g. crystal growth techniques, thin-film deposition, ion implantation, photolithography), their properties, and their integration in electronic devices
- Solid-state physics is the study of rigid matter, or solids, through methods such as quantum mechanics, crystallography, electromagnetism, and metallurgy. It is the largest branch of condensed matter physics. Solid-state physics studies how the large-scale properties of solid materials result from their atomic-scale properties. Thus, solid-state physics forms the theoretical basis of materials science. It also has direct applications, for example in the technology of transistors and semiconductors.
- Thermodynamics, statistical mechanics, and physical chemistry, for phase equilibrium conditions, phase diagrams of materials systems (multi-phase, multi-component, reacting and non-reacting systems)

SERVICE MANAGEMENT

Service management is integrated into supply chain management as the intersection between the actual sales and the customer. The aim of high performance service management is to optimize the service-intensive supply chains, which are usually more complex than the typical finished-goods supply chain. Most service-intensive supply chains require larger inventories and tighter integration with field service and third parties. They also must accommodate inconsistent and uncertain demand by establishing more advanced information and product flows. Moreover, all processes must be coordinated across numerous service locations with large numbers of parts and multiple levels in the supply chain.

Among typical manufacturers, post-sale services (maintenance, repair and parts) comprise less than 20 percent of revenue. But among the most innovative companies in Service, those same activities often generate more than 50 percent of the profits.

- Benefits

The main drivers for a company to establish or optimize its service management practices are varied:

- High service costs can be reduced, i.e. by integrating the service and products supply chain.
- Inventory levels of service parts can be reduced and therefore reduce total inventory costs.
- Customer service or parts/service quality can be optimized.
- Increasing service revenue.
- Reduce obsolescence costs of service parts through improved forecasting.
- Improve customer satisfaction levels.
- Reduce expediting costs - with optimized service parts inventory, there is no need to rush orders to customers.
- Minimize technician visits - if they have the right part in hand, they can fix the problem on the first visit.
- Components

Generally, service management comprises six different capabilities that companies should consider for optimization:

- Service strategy and service offerings
  - o Service strategy definition
  - o Service offerings definition & positioning
  - o Go-to-market strategy
  - o Service portfolio management
- Spare parts management
  - o Parts supply management
  - o Inventory management
  - o Parts demand management
  - o Fulfillment operations & logistics
  - o Service parts management
- Returns, repairs, and warranties
  - o Warranty & claims management

  - Reverse logistics
  - Returns processing
  - Remanufacturing
- Field service management or field force effectiveness
  - Technician enablement
  - Mobility
  - E-learning
  - Activity scheduling
  - Service billing
- Customer management
  - Order management & availability
  - Channel & partner management
  - Customer insight
  - Technical documentation
- Assets, maintenance, task scheduling, event management
  - Remote monitoring
  - Diagnostics & testing
  - Asset management/optimization
  - Configuration management

ORDER FULFILLMENT

Order fulfillment (in British English order fulfilment) is in the most general sense the complete process from point of sales inquiry to delivery of a product to the customer. Sometimes *Order fulfillment* is used to describe the more narrow act of distribution or the logistics function, however, in the broader sense it refers to the way firms respond to customer orders.

Options

The first research towards defining order fulfillment strategies was published by Mather (1988) and his discussion of the P:D ratio, whereby P is defined as the production lead-time, i.e. how long it takes to manufacture a product, and D is the demand lead-time, i.e. how long customers are willing to wait for the order to be completed. Based on comparing P and D, a firm has several basic strategic order fulfillment options:

- Engineer-to-Order (ETO) - (D>>P) Here, the product is designed and built to customer specifications; this approach is most common for large construction projects and one-off products, such as Formula 1 cars

- Build-to-Order (BTO); syn: Make-to-Order (MTO) - (D>P) Here, the product is based on a standard design, but component production and manufacture of the final product is linked to the order placed by the final customer's specifications; this strategy is typical for high-end motor vehicles and aircraft
- Assemble-to-Order (ATO) - (D<P) Here, the product is built to customer specifications from a stock of existing components. This assumes a modular product architecture that allows for the final product to be configured in this way; a typical example for this approach is Dell's approach to customizing its computers.
- Make-to-Stock (MTS); syn: Build-to-Forecast (BTF) - (D=0) Here, the product is built against a sales forecast, and sold to the customer from finished goods stock; this approach is common in the grocery and retail sectors.
- Digital Copy (DC) - (D=0, P=0) Where products are digital assets and inventory is maintained with a single digital master. Copies are created on-demand, downloaded and saved on customers' storage devices.
- Process

In its broadest definition, the possible steps in the process are

- Product Inquiry - Initial inquiry about offerings, visit to the web-site, catalog request
- Sales Quote - Budgetary or availability quote
- Order Configuration - Where ordered items need selection of options or order lines need to be compatible with each other
- Order Booking - The formal order placement or closing of the deal (issuing by the customer of a Purchase Order)
- Order Acknowledgment / Confirmation - Confirmation that the order is booked and/or received
- Invoicing / Billing - The presentment of the commercial invoice / bill to the customer
- Order Sourcing / Planning - Determining the source / location of item(s) to be shipped
- Order Changes - Changes to orders, if needed
- Order Processing - Process step where the distribution center or warehouse is responsible to fill order (receive and stock inventory, pick, pack and ship orders).

- Shipment - The shipment and transportation of the goods
- Delivery - The delivery of the goods to the consignee / customer
- Settlement - The payment of the charges for goods / services / delivery
- Returns - In case the goods are unacceptable / not required
- Advantages

The order fulfillment strategy also determines the de-coupling point in the supply chain, which describes the point in the system where the "push" (or forecast-driven) and "pull" (or demand-driven see Demand chain management) elements of the supply chain meet. The decoupling point always is an inventory buffer that is needed to cater for the discrepancy between the sales forecast and the actual demand (i.e. the forecast error). It has become increasing necessary to move the de-coupling point in the supply chain to minimize the dependence on forecast and to maximize the reactionary or demand-driven supply chain elements. This initiative in the distribution elements of the supply chain corresponds to the Just-in-time initiatives pioneered by automobile manufacturers in the 1970s.

The order fulfillment strategy has also strong implications on how firms customize their products and deal with product variety. Strategies that can be used to mitigate the impact of product variety include modularity, option bundling, late configuration, and build to order (BTO) strategies—all of which are generally referred as mass customization strategies.

OPERATIONS MANAGEMENT

Operations management is an area of management concerned with overseeing, designing, and controlling the process of production and redesigning business operations in the production of goods or services. It involves the responsibility of ensuring that business operations are efficient in terms of using as few resources as needed, and effective in terms of meeting customer requirements. It is concerned with managing the process that converts inputs (in the forms of materials, labor, and energy) into outputs (in the form of goods and/or services). The relationship of operations management to senior management in commercial contexts can be compared to the relationship of line officers to highest-level senior officers in military science. The highest-level officers shape the strategy and revise it over time, while the line officers make tactical decisions in support of carrying out the strategy. In business as in military affairs, the boundaries between levels are not always distinct; tactical information dynamically informs strategy, and individual people often move between roles over time.

According to the U.S. Department of Education, operations management is the field concerned with managing and directing the physical and/or technical functions of a firm or organization, particularly those relating to development, production, and manufacturing. Operations management programs typically include instruction in principles of general management, manufacturing and production systems, factory management, equipment maintenance management, production control, industrial labor relations and skilled trades supervision, strategic manufacturing policy, systems analysis, productivity analysis and cost control, and materials planning. Management, including operations management, is like engineering in that it blends art with applied science. People skills, creativity, rational analysis, and knowledge of technology are all required for success.

History

Industrial Revolution

Before the First industrial revolution work was mainly done through two systems: domestic system and craft guilds. In the domestic system merchants took materials to homes where artisans performed the necessary work, craft guilds on the other hand were associations of artisans which passed work from one shop to another, for example: leather was tanned by a tanner, passed to curriers, and finally arrived at shoemakers and saddlers. The beginning of the industrial revolution is usually associated with 18th century English textile industry, with the invention of flying shuttle by John Kay in 1733, the spinning jenny by James Hargreaves in 1765, the water frame by Richard Arkwright in 1769 and the steam engine by James Watt in 1765. In 1851 at the Crystal Palace Exhibition the term American system of manufacturing was used to describe the new approach that was evolving in the United States of America which centered on two central features: interchangeable parts and extensive use of mechanization to produce them.

In 1913 Henry Ford first used the concept of the assembly line in Highland Park, he characterized it as follows:

> "The thing is to keep everything in motion and take the work to the man and not the man to the work. That is the real principle of our production, and conveyors are only one of many means to an end"

This became one the central ideas that led to mass production, one of the main elements of the Second Industrial Revolution, along with emergence of the electrical industry and petroleum industry.

Operations Management

In 1911 Frederick Taylor published his "The Principles of Scientific Management", in which he characterized scientific management as:

1. The development of a true science
2. The scientific selection of the worker
3. Their scientific education and development
4. Intimate friendly cooperation between management and the workers

Taylor is also credited for developing stopwatch time study, this combined with Frank and Lillian Gilbreth motion study gave way to time and motion study which is centered on the concepts of standard method and standard time. Other contemporaries of Taylor worth remembering are Morris Cooke (rural electrification in 1920s) and Henry Gantt (Gantt chart). Also in 1910 Hugo Diemer published the first industrial engineering book: Factory Organization and Administration.

In 1913 Ford W. Harris published his "How Many parts to make at once" in which he presented the idea of the economic order quantity model. He described the problem as follows:

> "Interest on capital tied up in wages, material and overhead sets a maximum limit to the quantity of parts which can be profitably manufactured at one time; "set-up" costs on the job fix the minimum. Experience has shown one manager a way to determine the economical size of lots"

In 1931 Walter Shewhart published his Economic Control of Quality of Manufactured Product, the first systematic treatment of the subject of Statistical Process Control.

In 1943, in Japan, Taiichi Ohno arrived at Toyota Motor company. Toyota evolved a unique manufacturing system centered on two complementary notions: just in time (produce only what is needed) and autonomation (automation with a human touch). Regarding JIT, Ohno was inspired by American supermarkets: workstations functioned like a supermarket shelf where the customer can get products they need, at the time they need and in the amount needed, the workstation (shelf) is then restocked. Autonomation was developed by Toyoda Sakichi in Toyoda Spinning and Weaving: an automatically activated loom that was also foolproof, that is automatically detected problems. In 1983 J.N Edwards published his "MRP and Kanban-American style" in which he described JIT goals in terms of seven zeros: zero defects, zero (excess) lot size, zero setups, zero breakdowns, zero handling, zero lead time and zero surging. This periods also marks the spread of Total Quality Management in Japan, ideas initially developed by American authors such as Deming, Juran and Armand V. Feigenbaum. Schnonberger identified seven fundamentals principles essential to the Japanese approach:

1. Process control: SPC and worker responsibility over quality
2. Easy-to-see quality: boards, gauges, meters, etc. and poka-yoke
3. Insistence on compliance: "quality first"
4. Line stop: stop the line to correct quality problems
5. Correcting one's own errors: worker fixed a defective part if he produced it
6. The 100% check: automated inspection techniques and foolproof machines
7. Continual improvement: ideally zero defects

In 1987 the International Organization for Standardization (ISO), recognizing the growing importance of quality, issued the ISO 9000, a family of standards related to quality management systems. There has been some controversy thought regarding the proper procedures to follow and the amount of paperwork involved.

Meanwhile in 1964, a different approach was developed by Joseph Orlicky as a response to the TOYOTA Manufacturing Program: Material Requirements Planning (MRP) at IBM, latter gaining momentum in 1972 when the American Production and Inventory Control Society launched the "MRP Crusade". One of the key insights of this management system was the distinction between dependent demand and independent demand.

Recent trends in the field revolve around concepts such as Business Process Re-engineering (launched by Michael Hammer in 1993), Lean Manufacturing, Six Sigma (an approach to quality developed at Motorola between 1985-1987) and Reconfigurable Manufacturing Systems.

The term lean manufacturing was coined in the book The Machine that Changed the World. Six Sigma refers to a control limits placed at 6 [standard deviations]] of the mean of a normal distribution, this became very famous after Jack Welch of General Electric launched a company-wide initiative in 1995 to adopt this set of methods. More recently Six Sigma developed in DMAIC (for improving processes) and DFSS (for designing new products and new processes)

Topics

Production Systems

A first possible distinction in production systems (technological classification) is between process production and part production.

- Process production means that the product undergoes physical -chemical

- transformations and lacks assembly operations, therefore raw materials cant easily be obtained from the final product, examples include: paper, cement and nylon.
- Part production (ex:cars and ovens) comprises both manufacturing systems and assembly systems. In the first category we find job shops, manufacturing cells, flexible manufacturing systems and transfer lines, in the assembly category we have fixed position systems, assembly lines and assembly shops (both manual and/or automated operations).

Another possible classification is one based on Lead Time (manufacturing lead time vs delivery lead time): Engineer to Order, Purchase to Order, Make to Order, Assemble to Order and Make to Stock. According to this classification different kinds of systems will have different customer order decoupling points (CODP), meaning that Work in Progress cycle stock levels are practically nonexistent regarding operations located after the CODP (except for WIP due to queues).

The concept of production systems can be expanded to the service sector world keeping in mind that services have some fundamental differences in respect to material goods: intangibility, client always present during transformation processes, no stocks for "finished goods". Services can be classified according to a service process matrix: degree of labor intensity (volume) vs degree of customization (variety). For high degree of labor intensity we have Mass Services (ex: commercial banking bill payments and state schools) and Professional Services (ex:personal physicians and lawyers), while for low degree of labor intensity we have Service Factories (ex:airlines and hotels) and Service Shops (ex:hospitals and auto mechanics).

The systems described above are ideal types, real systems may present themselves as hybrids of those categories.

Metrics: Efficiency and Effectiveness

Operations strategy concerns policies and plans of use of the firm productive resources with the aim of supporting long term competitive strategy. Metrics in operations management can be broadly classified into efficiency metrics and effectiveness metrics. Effectiveness metrics involve:

1. Price (actually fixed by marketing, but lower bounded by production cost): purchase price, use costs, maintenance costs, upgrade costs, disposal costs
2. Quality: specification and compliance

3. Time: productive lead time, information lead time, punctuality
4. Flexibility: mix, volume, gamma
5. Stock availability

A more recent approach, introduced by Terry Hill, involves distinguishing competitive variables in order winner and order qualifiers when defining operations strategy. Order winners are variables which permit differentiating the company from competitors, while order qualifiers are prerequisites for engaging in a transaction. This view can be seen as a unifying approach between operations management and marketing.

Productivity is a standard efficiency metric for evaluation of production systems, broadly speaking a ratio between outputs and inputs, and can assume many specific forms, for example: machine productivity, workforce productivity, raw material productivity, warehouse productivity (=inventory turnover). It is also useful to break up productivity in use U (productive percentage of total time) and yield ç (ratio between produced volume and productive time) to better evaluate production systems performances. Cycle times can be modeled through manufacturing engineering if the individual operations are heavily automated, if the manual component is the prevalent one, methods used include: time and motion study, predetermined motion time systems and work sampling.

ABC analysis is a method for analyzing inventory based on Pareto distribution, it posits that since revenue from items on inventory will be power law distributed then it makes sense to manage items differently based on their position on a revenue-inventory level matrix, 3 classes are constructed (A,B and C) from cumulative item revenues, so in a matrix each item will have a letter (A,B or C) assigned for revenue and inventory. This method posits that items away from the diagonal should be managed differently: items in the upper part are subject to risk of obsolescence, items in the lower part are subject to risk of stockout.

Throughput is a variable which quantifies the number of parts produced in the unit of time. Although estimating throughput for a single process maybe fairly simple, doing so for an entire production system involves an additional difficulty due to the presence of queues which can come from: machine breakdowns, processing time variability, scraps, setups, maintenance time, lack of orders, lack of materials, strikes, bad coordination between resources, mix variability, plus all these inefficiencies tend to compound depending on the nature of the production system. One important example of how system throughput is tied to system design are bottlenecks: in job shops bottlenecks are typically dynamic and dependent on scheduling while on transfer lines it makes sense to speak of "the bottleneck" since it can be univocally associated with a specific station on the line. This leads to the problem of how to define capacity measures, that is an estimation of the maximum output of a given production system, and capacity utilization.

Overall Equipment Effectiveness (OEE) is defined as the product between system availability, cycle time efficiency and quality rate. OEE is typically used as key performance indicator (KPI) in conjunction with the lean manufacturing approach.

Configuration and Management

Designing the configuration of production systems involves both technological and organizational variables. Choices in production technology involve: dimensioning capacity, fractioning capacity, capacity location, outsourcing processes, process technology, automation of operations, tradeoff between volume and variety. Choices in the organizational area involve: defining worker skills and responsibilities, team coordination, worker incentives and information flow.

Regarding the planning of production there is a basic distinction between the push approach and the pull approach, with the later including the singular approach of Just in Time. Regarding the traditional pull approach a number of techniques have been developed based on the work of Ford W. Harris (1913) which came to be know as the Economic Order Quantity Model (EOQ), which formed the basis of subsequent techniques as the Wagner-Within Procedure, the News Vendor Model, Base Stock Model and the Fixed Time Period Model. These models usually involve the calculation of cycle stocks and buffer stocks, the latter usually modeled as a function of demand variability. The Economic Production Quantity (EPQ) differs from the EOQ model only in that it assumes a constant fill rate for the part being produced, instead of the instantaneous refilling of the EOQ model.

Joseph Orlickly and others developed Material Requirement Planning (MRP) at IBM, essentially a push approach to inventory control and production planning, which takes as input both the Master Production Schedule (MPS) and the Bill of Materials (BOM) and gives as output a schedule for the materials needed in the production process. The MPS can be seen as a kind of aggregate planning for production coming in two fundamentally opposing varieties: plans which try to chase demand and level plans which try to keep uniform capacity utilization. Many models have been proposed to solve MPS problems:

- Analytical models (e.g. Magee Boodman model)
- Exact optimization algorithmic models (e.g. LP and ILP)
- Heuristic models (e.g. Aucamp model).

MRP can be briefly described as a 3s procedure: sum (different orders), split (in lots), shift (in time according to item lead time) To avoid an "explosion" of data processing in MRP (number of BOMs required in input) planning bills (such as family bills or super bills) can be useful since they allow a rationalization of input data into common codes. MRP had some notorious problems such as infinite capacity and fixed lead times, giving way later on to modifications of original software implementation in the form of MRP II and ERP. In this context problems of scheduling (sequencing of production), loading (tools to use), part type selection (parts to work on) and applications of operations research have a significant role to play.

Lean Manufacturing is an approach to production which arose in Toyota between the end of World War II and the seventies. It comes mainly from the ideas of Taiichi Ohno and Toyoda Sakichi which are centered on the complementary notions of Just in Time and Autonomation (jidoka), all aimed at reducing waste (usually applied in PDCA style). Some additional elements are also fundamental: production smoothing (Heijunka), capacity buffers, setup reduction, cross-training and plant layout.

- Heijunka: production smoothing presupposes a level strategy for the MPS and a final assembly schedule developed from the MPS by smoothing aggregate production requirements in smaller time buckets and sequencing final assembly to achieve repetitive manufacturing. In this case throughput can be equaled to takt time. Besides volume, heijunka also means attaining mixed model production, which however may only be feasible trough set-up reduction. A standard tool for achieving this is the Heijunka box
- Capacity buffers: ideally a JIT system would work with zero breakdowns, this however is very hard to achieve in practice, nonetheless Toyota favors acquiring extra capacity over extra WIP to deal with starvation.
- Set-up reduction: typically necessary to achieve mixed model production, a key distinction can be made between internal and external setup. Internal setups (ex:removing a die) refers to tasks when the machine is not working, while external setups can be completed while the machine is running (ex:transporting dies).
- Cross training: important as an element of Autonomation, Toyota cross trained their employees through rotation, this served as an element of production flexibility, reducing boredom and holistic thinking.

- Layout: U-shaped lines or cells are common in the lean approach since they allow for minimum walking, greater worker efficiency and flexible capacity.

A series of tools have been developed mainly with the objective of replicating Toyota success: a very common implementation involves small cards known as kanbans, these also come in some varieties: reorder kanbans, allarm kanbans, triangle kanbans, etc. In the classic kanban procedure with one card:

- Parts are kept in containers with their respective kanbans
- The downstream station moves the kanban to the upstream station and starts producing the part at the downstream station
- The upstream operator takes the most urgent kanban from his list (compare to queue discipline from queue theory) and produces it and attach its respective kanban

The two-card kanban procedure differs a bit:

- The downstream operator takes the production kanban from his list
- If required parts are available he removes the move kanban and places them in another box, otherwise he chooses another production card
- He produces the part and attach its respective production kanban
- Periodically a mover picks up the move kanbans in upstream stations and search for the respective parts, when found he exchanges production kanbans for move kanbans and move the parts to downstream stations

Since the number of kanbans in the production system is set by managers as a constant number, the kanban procedure works as WIP controlling device, which for a given arrival rate, per Little's Law, works as lead time controlling device.

In Toyota the TPS represented more of a philosophy of production than a set of specific tools, the latter would include: SMED, Value Stream Mapping, 5S, poka-yoke, elimination of time batching, lot-size reduction, Rank Order Clustering, single point scheduling, multi-process handling and backflush accounting. Seen more broadly JIT can include methods such as: product standardization and modularity, group technology, total productive maintenance, job enlargement, job enrichment, flat organization and vendor rating (JIT production is very sensitive to replenishment conditions).

Modeling

There are also fields of mathematical theory which have found applications in the field of operations management such as operations research, mainly mathematical optimization problems and queue theory. Queue theory is employed in modeling queue and processing times in production systems while mathematical optimization draws heavily from multivariate calculus and linear algebra. Queue theory is based on markov chains and stochastic processes. It also worth noticing that computations of safety stocks are usually based on modeling demand as a normal distribution.

When analytical models are not enough, managers may resort to using simulation. Simulation has been traditionally done thought the Discrete event simulation paradigm, where the simulation model posses a state which can only change when a discrete event happens, which consists of a clock and list of events. The more recent Transaction-level modeling paradigm consists of a set of resources and a set of transactions: transactions move thought a network of resources (nodes) according to a code, called process. Since real production processes are always affected by disturbances in both inputs and outputs, many companies implement some form of Quality management or quality control. Quality control tools include check sheets, pareto charts, Ishikawa diagrams, control charts, which are used in approaches like Total quality management and Six Sigma. Keeping quality under control is relevant to both increasing customer satisfaction and reducing processing waste.

Operations management textbooks usually cover

demand forecasting, even though it is not strictly speaking an operations problem, because demand is related to some production systems variables. For example, a classic approach in dimensioning safety stocks requires calculating standard deviation of forecast errors. Demand forecasting is also a critical part of push systems, since order releases have to be planned ahead of actual clients orders. Also any serious discussion of capacity planning involves adjusting company outputs with market demands.

Safety, Risk and Maintenance

Other important management problems involve maintenance policies, safety management systems, facility management and supply chain integration.

Organizations

The following organizations support and promote operations management:

- Association for Operations Management (APICS) which supports the *Production and Inventory Management Journal*
- European Operations Management Association (EurOMA) which supports the International Journal of Operations & Production Management
- Production and Operations Management Society (POMS) which supports the journal: *Production and Operations Management*
- Institute for Operations Research and the Management Sciences (INFORMS)
- The Manufacturing and Service Operations Management Society (MSOM) which supports the journal: Manufacturing & Service Operations Management
- Institute of Operations Management (UK)
- Association of Technology, Management, and Applied Engineering (ATMAE)
- Journals

The following high-ranked academic journals are concerned with Operations Management issues:

- *Management Science*
- *Manufacturing & Service Operations Management*
- *Operations Research*
- *Journal of Operations Management*
- *International Journal of Operations & Production Management*
- *Production and Operations Management*

INFORMATION TECHNOLOGY MANAGEMENT

IT management is the discipline whereby all of the information technology resources of a firm are managed in accordance with its needs and priorities. These resources may include tangible investments like computer hardware, software, data, networks and data centre facilities, as well as the staff who are hired to maintain them. Managing this responsibility within a company entails many of the basic management functions, like budgeting, staffing, change management, and organizing and controlling, along with other aspects that are unique to technology, like software design, network planning, tech support etc.

Overview

The central aim of IT management is to generate value through the use of technology. To achieve this, business strategies and technology must be aligned. IT Management is different from management information systems. The latter refers to management methods tied to the automation or support of human decision making. IT Management refers to IT related management activities in organizations. MIS is focused mainly on the business aspect, with strong input into the technology phase of the business/organization.

A primary focus of IT management is the value creation made possible by technology. This requires the alignment of technology and business strategies. While the value creation for an organization involves a network of relationships between internal and external environments, technology plays an important role in improving the overall value chain of an organization. However, this increase requires business and technology management to work as a creative, synergistic, and collaborative team instead of a purely mechanistic span of control. Historically, one set of resources was dedicated to one particular computing technology, business application or line of business, and managed in a silo-like fashion. These resources supported a single set of requirements and processes, and couldn't easily be optimized or reconfigured to support actual demand. This led technology providers to build out and complement their product-centric infrastructure and management offerings with Converged Infrastructure environments that converge servers, storage, networking, security, management and facilities. The efficiencies of having this type of integrated and automated management environment allows enterprises to get their applications up and running faster, with simpler manageability and maintenance, and enables IT to adjust IT resources (such as servers, storage and networking) quicker to meet unpredictable business demand.

IT Infrastructure

The term *IT infrastructure* is defined in a standard called Information Technology Infrastructure Library (ITIL) v3 as a combined set of hardware, software, networks, facilities, etc. (including all of the information technology), in order to develop, test, deliver, monitor, control or support IT services. Associated people, processes and documentation are not part of IT Infrastructure. ITIL documents define best practices and accepted techniques in the information technology community. This set of guidelines is widely used in both the public and private sector, essentially providing companies with a blueprint on how to organize and manage information technology operations at the company. The library is constantly updated to ensure accuracy and to include emerging technological advances. ITIL provides a systematic and professional approach to the management of IT service provision, and offers the following benefits:

1. Reduced IT costs

2. Improved IT services through the use of proven best practice processes
3. Improved customer satisfaction through a more professional approach to service delivery
4. Standards and guidance
5. Improved productivity
6. Improved use of skills and experience
7. Improved delivery of third-party services through the specification of ITIL or BS15000 as the standard for service delivery in services procurements.

IT Management Disciplines

The below concepts are commonly listed or investigated under the broad term IT Management:

- Business/IT alignment
- IT governance
- IT financial management
- IT service management
- Sourcing
- IT configuration management
- IT Managers

IT managers have a lot in common with project managers but their main difference is one of focus: an IT manager is responsible and accountable for an ongoing program of IT services while the project manager's responsibility and accountability are both limited to a project with a clear start and end date.

Most IT management programs are designed to educate and develop managers who can effectively manage the planning, design, selection, implementation, use, and administration of emerging and converging information and communications technologies. The program curriculum provides students with the technical knowledge and management knowledge and skills needed to effectively integrate people, information and communication technologies, and business processes in support of organizational strategic goals.

Graduates should be able

1. to explain the important terminology, facts, concepts, principles, analytic techniques, and theories used in IT management.
2. to apply important terminology, facts, concepts, principles,

analytic techniques, and theories in IT management when analyzing complex factual situations.

3. to integrate (or synthesize) important facts, concepts, principles, and theories in IT management when developing solutions to IT management multifaceted problems in complex situations.

The importance of IT management is to understand the managing data. There are also difficulties IT managers overcome. The amount of data is increasing, most of the data in is separated between the organizations and collected by different departments. They may not be using the same method or procedure. Data security, quality and integrity is most informant in receiving information. The sources have an impact also on the sources obtained; they may be internal or external. When the information structures do not transfer properly with each other, that can result in unreliable data. An important part to understand in an IT management is Data Governance.

It is an approach to managing information across the entire organization or company. Many will also need to know master data management, which is a process that spans all of the companies processes and business. Without a structure your company will not be able to function properly. Applying these processes in Data bases, it your job to be able to communicate with other departments systems and develop precise communication and holding your organization accountable of certain data issues. Your design and programs helps increase design and technical knowledge throughout the business.

ROLE OF SUPPLY CHAIN MANAGEMENT

Supply chain management (SCM) is the management of the flow of goods. It includes the movement and storage of raw materials, work-in-process inventory, and finished goods from point of origin to point of consumption. Interconnected or interlinked networks, channels and node businesses are involved in the provision of products and services required by end customers in a supply chain. Supply chain management has been defined as the "design, planning, execution, control, and monitoring of supply chain activities with the objective of creating net value, building a competitive infrastructure, leveraging worldwide logistics, synchronizing supply with demand and measuring performance globally."

SCM draws heavily from the areas of operations management, logistics, procurement, and information technology, and strives for an integrated approach.

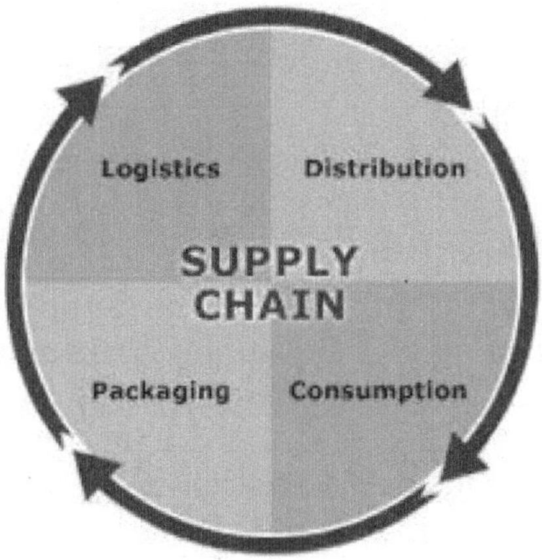

Origin of the Term and Definitions

The term "supply chain management" entered the public domain when Keith Oliver, a consultant at Booz Allen Hamilton (now Booz & Company), used it in an interview for the Financial Times in 1982. The term was slow to take hold. It gained currency in the mid-1990s, when a flurry of articles and books came out on the subject. In the late 1990s it rose to prominence as a management buzzword, and operations managers began to use it in their titles with increasing regularity.

Commonly accepted definitions of supply chain management include:

- The management of upstream and downstream value-added flows of materials, final goods, and related information among suppliers, company, resellers, and final consumers
- The systematic, strategic coordination of traditional business functions and tactics across all business functions within a particular company and across businesses within the supply chain, for the purposes of improving the long-term performance of the individual companies and the supply chain as a whole
- A customer-focused definition is given by Hines (2004:p76): "Supply chain strategies require a total systems view of the links in the chain that work together efficiently to create customer satisfaction at the end point of delivery to the consumer. As a consequence, costs must be lowered throughout the chain by driving out unnecessary expenses, movements, and handling. The main focus is turned to efficiency and added value, or the end-user's perception of value. Efficiency must be increased, and bottlenecks removed. The measurement of performance focuses on total system efficiency and the equitable monetary

reward distribution to those within the supply chain. The supply chain system must be responsive to customer requirements."

- The integration of key business processes across the supply chain for the purpose of creating value for customers and stakeholders (Lambert, 2008)
- According to the Council of Supply Chain Management Professionals (CSCMP), supply chain management encompasses the planning and management of all activities involved in sourcing, procurement, conversion, and logistics management. It also includes coordination and collaboration with channel partners, which may be suppliers, intermediaries, third-party service providers, or customers. Supply chain management integrates supply and demand management within and across companies. More recently, the loosely coupled, self-organizing network of businesses that cooperate to provide product and service offerings has been called the *Extended Enterprise*.

A supply chain, as opposed to supply chain management, is a set of organizations directly linked by one or more upstream and downstream flows of products, services, finances, or information from a source to a customer. Supply chain management is the management of such a chain.

Supply chain management software includes tools or modules used to execute supply chain transactions, manage supplier relationships, and control associated business processes.

Supply chain event management (SCEM) considers all possible events and factors that can disrupt a supply chain. With SCEM, possible scenarios can be created and solutions devised.

In many cases the supply chain includes the collection of goods after consumer use for recycling. Including third-party logistics or other gathering agencies as part of the RM re-patriation process is a way of illustrating the new endgame strategy...

Problems Addressed

Supply chain management addresses the following problems:

- Distribution network configuration: the number, location, and network missions of suppliers, production facilities, distribution centers, warehouses, cross-docks, and customers.
- Distribution strategy: questions of operating control (e.g., centralized, decentralized, or shared); delivery scheme (e.g., direct shipment, pool point shipping, cross docking, direct store

delivery, or closed loop shipping); mode of transportation (e.g., motor carrier, including truckload, less than truckload (LTL), parcel, railroad, intermodal transport, including trailer on flatcar (TOFC) and container on flatcar (COFC), ocean freight, airfreight); replenishment strategy (e.g., pull, push, or hybrid); and transportation control (e.g., owner operated, private carrier, common carrier, contract carrier, or third-party logistics (3PL)).

- Trade-offs in logistical activities: The above activities must be coordinated in order to achieve the lowest total logistics cost. Trade-offs may increase the total cost if only one of the activities is optimized. For example, full truckload (FTL) rates are more economical on a cost-per-pallet basis than are LTL shipments. If, however, a full truckload of a product is ordered to reduce transportation costs, there will be an increase in inventory holding costs, which may increase total logistics costs. The planning of logistical activities therefore takes a systems approach. These trade-offs are key to developing the most efficient and effective logistics and SCM strategy.
- Information: The integration of processes through the supply chain in order to share valuable information, including demand signals, forecasts, inventory, transportation, and potential collaboration.
- Inventory management: Management of the quantity and location of inventory, including raw materials, work in process (WIP), and finished goods.
- Cash flow: Arranging the payment terms and methodologies for exchanging funds across entities within the supply chain.

Supply chain execution means managing and coordinating the movement of materials, information and funds across the supply chain. The flow is bi-directional. SCM applications provide real-time analytical systems that manage the flow of products and information throughout the supply chain network.

Functions

Supply chain management is a cross-functional approach that includes managing the movement of raw materials into an organization, certain aspects of the internal processing of materials into finished goods, and the movement of finished goods out of the organization and toward the end consumer. As organizations strive to focus on core competencies and becoming more flexible, they reduce their ownership of raw materials sources and distribution channels. These functions are increasingly being outsourced to other firms that can perform the activities better or more cost effectively. The effect is to increase the number of organizations involved in satisfying customer demand, while reducing managerial control of daily logistics operations. Less control and more supply chain partners led to the creation of the concept of supply chain management. The purpose of supply chain management is to improve trust and collaboration among supply chain partners, thus improving inventory visibility and the velocity of inventory movement.

Importance

Organizations increasingly find that they must rely on effective supply chains, or networks, to compete in the global market and networked economy. In Peter Drucker's (1998) new management paradigms, this concept of business relationships extends beyond traditional enterprise boundaries and seeks to organize entire business processes throughout a value chain of multiple companies. In recent decades, globalization, outsourcing, and information technology have enabled many organizations, such as Dell and Hewlett Packard, to successfully operate collaborative supply networks in which each specialized business partner focuses on only a few key strategic activities (Scott, 1993). This inter-organisational supply network can be acknowledged as a new form of organisation. However, with the complicated interactions among the players, the network structure fits neither "market" nor "hierarchy" categories (Powell, 1990). It is not clear what kind of performance impacts different supply network structures could have on firms, and little is known about the coordination conditions and trade-offs that may exist among the players. From a systems perspective, a complex network structure can be decomposed into individual component firms (Zhang and Dilts, 2004). Traditionally, companies in a supply network concentrate on the inputs and outputs of the processes, with little concern for the internal management working of other individual players. Therefore, the choice of an internal management control structure is known to impact local firm performance (Mintzberg, 1979).

In the 21st century, changes in the business environment have contributed to the development of supply chain networks. First, as an outcome of globalization and the proliferation of multinational companies, joint ventures, strategic alliances, and business partnerships, significant success factors were identified, complementing the earlier "just-in-time", lean manufacturing, and agile manufacturing practices. Second, technological changes, particularly the dramatic fall in communication costs (a significant component of transaction costs), have led to changes in coordination among the members of the supply chain network (Coase, 1998). Many researchers have recognized supply network structures as a new organisational form, using terms such as "Keiretsu", "Extended

Enterprise", "Virtual Corporation", "Global Production Network", and "Next Generation Manufacturing System". In general, such a structure can be defined as "a group of semi-independent organisations, each with their capabilities, which collaborate in ever-changing constellations to serve one or more markets in order to achieve some business goal specific to that collaboration" (Akkermans, 2001).

The security management system for supply chains is described in ISO/IEC 28000 and ISO/IEC 28001 and related standards published jointly by the ISO and the IEC.Supply Chain Management draws heavily from the areas of operations management, logistics, procurement, and information technology, and strives for an integrated approach.

Historical Developments

Six major movements can be observed in the evolution of supply chain management studies: creation, integration, and globalization (Movahedi et al., 2009), specialization phases one and two, and SCM 2.0.

Creation Era

The term "supply chain management" was first coined by Keith Oliver in 1982. However, the concept of a supply chain in management was of great importance long before, in the early 20th century, especially with the creation of the assembly line. The characteristics of this era of supply chain management include the need for large-scale changes, re-engineering, downsizing driven by cost reduction programs, and widespread attention to Japanese management practices.

Integration Era

This era of supply chain management studies was highlighted with the development of electronic data interchange (EDI) systems in the 1960s, and developed through the 1990s by the introduction of enterprise resource planning (ERP) systems. This era has continued to develop into the 21st century with the expansion of Internet-based collaborative systems. This era of supply chain evolution is characterized by both increasing value added and cost reductions through integration.

A supply chain can be classified as a stage 1, 2 or 3 network. In a stage 1–type supply chain, systems such as production, storage, distribution, and material control are not linked and are independent of each other. In a stage 2 supply chain, these are integrated under one plan and is ERP enabled. A stage 3 supply chain is one that achieves vertical integration with upstream suppliers and downstream customers. An example of this kind of supply chain is Tesco.

Globalization Era

The third movement of supply chain management development, the globalization era, can be characterized by the attention given to global systems of supplier relationships and the expansion of supply chains over national boundaries and into other continents. Although the use of global sources in organizations' supply chains can be traced back several decades (e.g., in the oil industry), it was not until the late 1980s that a considerable number of organizations started to integrate global sources into their core business. This era is characterized by the globalization of supply chain management in organizations with the goal of increasing their competitive advantage, adding value, and reducing costs through global sourcing.

Specialization Era (phase I): Outsourced Manufacturing and Distribution

In the 1990s, companies began to focus on "core competencies" and specialization. They abandoned vertical integration, sold off non-core operations, and outsourced those functions to other companies. This changed management requirements, by extending the supply chain beyond the company walls and distributing management across specialized supply chain partnerships. This transition also refocused the fundamental perspectives of each organization. Original equipment manufacturers (OEMs) became brand owners that required visibility deep into their supply base. They had to control the entire supply chain from above, instead of from within. Contract manufacturers had to manage bills of material with different part-numbering schemes from multiple OEMs and support customer requests for work-in-process visibility and vendor-managed inventory (VMI).

The specialization model creates manufacturing and distribution networks composed of several individual supply chains specific to producers, suppliers, and customers that work together to design, manufacture, distribute, market, sell, and service a product. This set of partners may change according to a given market, region, or channel, resulting in a proliferation of trading partner environments, each with its own unique characteristics and demands.

Specialization Era (phase II): Supply Chain Management as a Service

Specialization within the supply chain began in the 1980s with the inception of transportation brokerages, warehouse management, and non-asset-based carriers, and has matured beyond transportation and logistics into aspects of supply planning, collaboration, execution, and performance management. Market forces sometimes demand rapid changes from suppliers, logistics providers, locations, or customers in their role as components of supply chain networks. This variability has significant effects on supply chain infrastructure, from the foundation layers of establishing and managing electronic communication between trading partners, to more complex requirements such as the configuration of processes and work flows that are essential to the management of the network itself.

Supply chain specialization enables companies to improve their overall competencies in the same way that outsourced manufacturing and distribution has done; it allows them to focus on their core competencies and assemble networks of specific, best-in-class partners to contribute to the overall value chain itself, thereby increasing overall performance and efficiency. The ability to quickly obtain and deploy this domain-specific supply chain expertise without developing and maintaining an entirely unique and complex competency in house is a leading reason why supply chain specialization is gaining popularity. Outsourced technology hosting for supply chain solutions debuted in the late 1990s and has taken root primarily in transportation and collaboration categories. This has progressed from the application service provider (ASP) model from roughly 1998 through 2003, to the on-demand model from approximately 2003 through 2006, to the software as a service (SaaS) model currently in focus today.

Supply Chain Management 2.0 (SCM 2.0)

Building on globalization and specialization, the term "SCM 2.0" has been coined to describe both changes within supply chains themselves as well as the evolution of processes, methods, and tools to manage them in this new "era". The growing popularity of collaborative platforms is highlighted by the rise of TradeCard's supply chain collaboration platform, which connects multiple buyers and suppliers with financial institutions, enabling them to conduct automated supply-chain finance transactions. Web 2.0 is a trend in the use of the World Wide Web that is meant to increase creativity, information sharing, and collaboration among users. At its core, the common attribute of Web 2.0 is to help navigate the vast information available on the Web in order to find what is being bought. It is the notion of a usable pathway. SCM 2.0 replicates this notion in supply chain operations. It is the pathway to SCM results, a combination of processes, methodologies, tools, and delivery options to guide companies to their results quickly as the complexity and speed of the supply chain increase due to global competition; rapid price fluctuations; surging oil prices; short product life cycles; expanded specialization; near-, far-, and off-shoring; and talent scarcity.

SCM 2.0 leverages solutions designed to rapidly deliver results with the agility to quickly manage future change for continuous flexibility, value, and success. This is delivered through competency networks composed of best-of-breed supply chain expertise to understand which elements, both operationally and organizationally, deliver results, as well as through intimate understanding of how to manage these elements to achieve the desired results. The solutions are delivered in a variety of options, such as no-touch via business process outsourcing, mid-touch via managed services and software as a service (SaaS), or high-touch in the traditional software deployment model.

Business Process Integration

Successful SCM requires a change from managing individual functions to integrating activities into key supply chain processes. In an example scenario, a purchasing department places orders as its requirements become known. The marketing department, responding to customer demand, communicates with several distributors and retailers as it attempts to determine ways to satisfy this demand. Information shared between supply chain partners can only be fully leveraged through process integration.

Supply chain business process integration involves collaborative work between buyers and suppliers, joint product development, common systems, and shared information. According to Lambert and Cooper (2000), operating an integrated supply chain requires a continuous information flow. However, in many companies, management has concluded that optimizing product flows cannot be accomplished without implementing a process approach. The key supply chain processes stated by Lambert (2004) are:

- Customer relationship management
- Customer service management
- Demand management style
- Order fulfillment
- Manufacturing flow management
- Supplier relationship management
- Product development and commercialization
- Returns management

Much has been written about demand management. Best-in-class companies have similar characteristics, which include the following:

- Internal and external collaboration
- Initiatives to reduce lead time

- Tighter feedback from customer and market demand
- Customer-level forecasting

One could suggest other critical supply business processes that combine these processes stated by Lambert, such as:

a. Customer service management
b. Procurement
c. Product development and commercialization
d. Manufacturing flow management/support
e. Physical distribution
f. Outsourcing/partnerships
g. Performance measurement
h. Warehousing management

a) Customer Service Management Process

Customer relationship management concerns the relationship between an organization and its customers. Customer service is the source of customer information. It also provides the customer with real-time information on scheduling and product availability through interfaces with the company's production and distribution operations. Successful organizations use the following steps to build customer relationships:

- determine mutually satisfying goals for organization and customers
- establish and maintain customer rapport
- induce positive feelings in the organization and the customers

b) Procurement Process

Strategic plans are drawn up with suppliers to support the manufacturing flow management process and the development of new products. In firms whose operations extend globally, sourcing may be managed on a global basis. The desired outcome is a relationship where both parties benefit and a reduction in the time required for the product's design and development. The purchasing function may also develop rapid communication systems, such as electronic data interchange (EDI) and Internet linkage, to convey possible requirements more rapidly. Activities related to obtaining products and materials from outside suppliers involve resource planning, supply sourcing, negotiation, order placement, inbound transportation, storage, handling, and quality assurance, many of which include the responsibility to coordinate with suppliers on matters of scheduling, supply continuity, hedging, and research into new sources or programs.

c) Product Development and Commercialization

Here, customers and suppliers must be integrated into the product development process in order to reduce the time to market. As product life cycles shorten, the appropriate products must be developed and successfully launched with ever-shorter time schedules in order for firms to remain competitive. According to Lambert and Cooper (2000), managers of the product development and commercialization process must:

1. coordinate with customer relationship management to identify customer-articulated needs;
2. select materials and suppliers in conjunction with procurement; and
3. develop production technology in manufacturing flow to manufacture and integrate into the best supply chain flow for the given combination of product and markets.

d) Manufacturing Flow Management Process

The manufacturing process produces and supplies products to the distribution channels based on past forecasts. Manufacturing processes must be flexible in order to respond to market changes and must accommodate mass customization. Orders are processes operating on a just-in-time (JIT) basis in minimum lot sizes. Changes in the manufacturing flow process lead to shorter cycle times, meaning improved responsiveness and efficiency in meeting customer demand. This process manages activities related to planning, scheduling, and supporting manufacturing operations, such as work-in-process storage, handling, transportation, and time phasing of components, inventory at manufacturing sites, and maximum flexibility in the coordination of geographical and final assemblies postponement of physical distribution operations.

e) Physical Distribution

This concerns the movement of a finished product or service to customers. In physical distribution, the customer is the final destination of a marketing channel, and the availability of the product or service is a vital part of each channel participant's marketing effort. It is also through the physical distribution process that the time and space of customer service become an integral part of marketing. Thus it links a marketing channel with its customers (i.e., it links manufacturers, wholesalers, and retailers).

f) Outsourcing/Partnerships

This includes not just the outsourcing of the procurement of materials and components, but also the outsourcing of services that traditionally have been provided in house. The logic of this trend is that the company will increasingly focus on those activities in the value chain in which it has a distinctive advantage and outsource everything else. This movement has been particularly evident in logistics, where the provision of transport, warehousing, and inventory control is increasingly subcontracted to specialists or logistics partners. Also, managing and controlling this network of partners and suppliers requires a blend of central and local involvement: strategic decisions are taken centrally, while the monitoring and control of supplier performance and day-to-day liaison with logistics partners are best managed locally.

g) Performance Measurement

Experts found a strong relationship from the largest arcs of supplier and customer integration to market share and profitability. Taking advantage of supplier capabilities and emphasizing a long-term supply chain perspective in customer relationships can both be correlated with a firm's performance. As logistics competency becomes a critical factor in creating and maintaining competitive advantage, measuring logistics performance becomes increasingly important, because the difference between profitable and unprofitable operations becomes narrower. A.T. Kearney Consultants (1985) noted that firms engaging in comprehensive performance measurement realized improvements in overall productivity. According to experts, internal measures are generally collected and analyzed by the firm, including cost, customer service, productivity, asset measurement, and quality. External performance is measured through customer perception measures and "best practice" benchmarking.

h) Warehousing Management

To reduce a company's cost and expenses, warehousing management is carrying the valuable role against operations. In the case of perfect storage and office with all convenient facilities in company level, reducing manpower cost, dispatching authority with on time delivery, loading & unloading facilities with proper area, area for service station, stock management system etc.

Theories

Currently there's a gap in the literature on supply chain management studies present: there is no theoretical support for explaining the existence or the boundaries of supply chain management. A few authors, such as Halldorsson et al. (2003), Ketchen and Hult (2006), and Lavassani et al. (2009), have tried to provide theoretical foundations for different areas related to supply chain by employing organizational theories. These theories include:

- Resource-based view (RBV)
- Transaction cost analysis (TCA)
- Knowledge-based view (KBV)
- Strategic choice theory (SCT)
- Agency theory (AT)
- Channel coordination
- Institutional theory (InT)
- Systems theory (ST)
- Network perspective (NP)
- Materials logistics management (MLM)
- Just-in-time (JIT)
- Material requirements planning (MRP)
- Theory of constraints (TOC)
- Total quality management (TQM)
- Agile manufacturing
- Time-based competition (TBC)
- Quick response manufacturing (QRM)
- Customer relationship management (CRM)
- Requirements chain management (RCM)
- Available-to-promise (ATP)

However, the unit of analysis of most of these theories is not the supply chain but rather another system, such as the firm or the supplier-buyer relationship. Among the few exceptions is the relational view, which outlines a theory for considering dyads and networks of firms as a key unit of analysis for explaining superior individual firm performance (Dyer and Singh, 1998).

Supply Chain Centroids

In the study of supply chain management, the concept of centroids has become an important economic consideration. A centroid is a location that has a high proportion of a country's population and a high proportion of its manufacturing, generally within 500 mi (805 km). In the US, two major supply chain centroids have been defined, one near Dayton, Ohio, and a second near Riverside, California. The centroid near Dayton is particularly important because it is closest to the population center of the US and Canada. Dayton is within 500 miles of 60% of the US population and manufacturing capacity, as well as 60% of Canada's population. The region includes the interchange between I-70 and I-75, one of the busiest in the nation, with 154,000 vehicles passing through per day, 30–35% of which are trucks hauling goods. In addition, the I-75 corridor is home to the busiest north-south rail route east of the Mississippi River.

Tax Efficient Supply Chain Management

Tax efficient supply chain management is a business model that considers the effect of tax in the design and implementation of supply chain management. As the consequence of globalization, cross-national businesses pay different tax rates in different countries. Due to these differences, they may legally optimize their supply chain and increase profits based on tax efficiency.

Sustainability and Social Responsibility in Supply Chains

Supply chain sustainability is a business issue affecting an organization's supply chain or logistics network, and is frequently quantified by comparison with SECH ratings, which uses a triple bottom line incorporating economic, social, and environmental aspects. SECH ratings are defined as social, ethical, cultural, and health' footprints. Consumers have become more aware of the environmental impact of their purchases and companies' SECH ratings and, along with non-governmental organizations (NGOs), are setting the agenda for transitions to organically grown foods, anti-sweatshop labor codes, and locally produced goods that support independent and small businesses. Because supply chains may account for over 75% of a company's carbon footprint, many organizations are exploring ways to reduce this and thus improve their SECH rating.

For example, in July 2009, Wal-Mart announced its intentions to create a global sustainability index that would rate products according to the environmental and social impacts of their manufacturing and distribution. The index is intended to create environmental accountability in Wal-Mart's supply chain and to provide motivation and infrastructure for other retail companies to do the same. More recently, the US Dodd–Frank Wall Street Reform and Consumer Protection Act, signed into law by President Obama in July 2010, contained a supply chain sustainability provision in the form of the Conflict Minerals law. This law requires SEC-regulated companies to conduct third party audits of their supply chains in order to determine whether any tin, tantalum, tungsten, or gold (together referred to as *conflict minerals*) is mined or sourced from the Democratic Republic of the Congo, and create a report (available to the general public and SEC) detailing the due diligence efforts taken and the results of the audit. The chain of suppliers and vendors to these reporting companies will be expected to provide appropriate supporting information.

Incidents like the 2013 Savar building collapse with more than 1,100 victims have led to widespread discussions about corporate social responsibility across global supply chains. Wieland and Handfield (2013) suggest that companies need to audit products and suppliers and that supplier auditing needs to go beyond direct relationships with first-tier suppliers. They also demonstrate that visibility needs to be improved if supply cannot be directly controlled and that smart and electronic technologies play a key role to improve visibility. Finally, they highlight that collaboration with local partners, across the industry and with universities is crucial to successfully managing social responsibility in supply chains.

Components

Management Components

SCM components are the third element of the four-square circulation framework. The level of integration and management of a business process link is a function of the number and level of components added to the link (Ellram and Cooper, 1990; Houlihan, 1985). Consequently, adding more management components or increasing the level of each component can increase the level of integration of the business process link.

Literature on business process re-engineering buyer-supplier relationships, and SCM suggests various possible components that should receive managerial attention when managing supply relationships. Lambert and Cooper (2000) identified the following components:

- Planning and control
- Work structure
- Organization structure
- Product flow facility structure
- Information flow facility structure
- Management methods
- Power and leadership structure
- Risk and reward structure
- Culture and attitude

However, a more careful examination of the existing literature leads to a more comprehensive understanding of what should be the key critical supply chain components, or "branches" of the previously identified supply chain business processes—that is, what kind of relationship the components may have that are related to suppliers and customers. Bowersox and Closs (1996) state that the emphasis on cooperation represents the synergism leading to the highest level of joint achievement. A primary-level channel participant is a business that is willing to participate in responsibility for inventory ownership or assume other financial risks, thus including primary level components (Bowersox and Closs, 1996). A secondary-level participant (specialized) is a business that participates in channel relationships by performing essential services for primary participants, including secondary level components, which support primary participants. Third-level channel participants and components that support primary-level channel participants and are the fundamental branches of secondary-level components may also be included.

Consequently, Lambert and Cooper's framework of supply chain components does not lead to any conclusion about what are the primary- or secondary-level (specialized) supply chain components—that is, which supply chain components should be viewed as primary or secondary, how these components should be structured in order to achieve a more comprehensive supply chain structure, and how to examine the supply chain as an integrative one.

Reverse Supply Chain

Reverse logistics is the process of managing the return of goods. It is also referred to as "aftermarket customer services". Any time money is taken from a company's warranty reserve or service logistics budget, one can speak of a reverse logistics operation.

Systems and Value

Supply chain systems configure value for those that organize the networks. Value is the additional revenue over and above the costs of building the network. Co-creating value and sharing the benefits appropriately to encourage effective participation is a key challenge for any supply system. Tony Hines defines value as follows: "Ultimately it is the customer who pays the price for service delivered that confirms value and not the producer who simply adds cost until that point".

Global Applications

Global supply chains pose challenges regarding both quantity and value. Supply and value chain trends include:

- Globalization
- Increased cross-border sourcing
- Collaboration for parts of value chain with low-cost providers
- Shared service centers for logistical and administrative functions
- Increasingly global operations, which require increasingly global coordination and planning to achieve global optimums

- Complex problems involve also midsized companies to an increasing degree

These trends have many benefits for manufacturers because they make possible larger lot sizes, lower taxes, and better environments (e.g., culture, infrastructure, special tax zones, or sophisticated OEM) for their products. There are many additional challenges when the scope of supply chains is global. This is because with a supply chain of a larger scope, the lead time is much longer, and because there are more issues involved, such as multiple currencies, policies, and laws. The consequent problems include different currencies and valuations in different countries, different tax laws, different trading protocols, and lack of transparency of cost and profit.

Certification

There are several certification programs for SCM staff development, including the Association for Operations Management (APICS), the International Supply Chain Education Alliance (ISCEA), and the Institute of Supply Chain Management (IOSCM). The APICS certification is called the Certified Supply Chain Professional (CSCP); the ISCEA certification is called the Certified Supply Chain Manager (CSCM). Additionally, the Institute for Supply Management is developing a certification called the Certified Professional in Supply Management (CPSM), focused on procurement and sourcing, also called supply management. The Purchasing Management Association of Canada is the main Canadian certifying body; its designations have global recipricocity. The main designation is the Supply Chain Management Professional (SCMP), with several others progressing toward it.

Supply Chain Management College Level Education

Many of the top universities offer supply chain management programs at the undergraduate and graduate levels. Some of them are:

United States

- Michigan State University
- Massachusetts Institute of Technology
- Arizona State University
- Pennsylvania State University
- Ohio State University
- Carnegie Mellon University
- University of Tennessee
- Purdue University

- University of Maryland
- University of Michigan
- University of Texas at Dallas
- Western Michigan University
- Texas State University

United Kingdom

- Cranfield University
- Huddersfield University
- Northumbria University
- University of Sunderland
- University of Liverpool
- University of Lincoln
- University of Birmingham
- University of Hull
- University of Central Lancashire
- Brunel University
- University of Westminster

HOW TO MANAGE CONSTRUCTION WASTE ?

Construction waste consists of unwanted material produced directly or incidentally by the construction or industries. This includes building materials such as insulation, nails, electrical wiring, and rebar, as well as waste originating from site preparation such as dredging materials, tree stumps, and rubble. Construction waste may contain lead, asbestos, or other hazardous substances. Much building waste is made up of materials such as bricks, concrete and wood damaged or unused for various reasons during construction. Observational research has shown that this can be as high as 10 to 15% of the materials that go into a building, a much higher percentage than the 2.5-5% usually assumed by quantity surveyors and the construction industry. Since considerable variability exists between construction sites, there is much opportunity for reducing this waste. Certain components of construction waste such as plasterboard are hazardous once landfilled. Plasterboard is broken down in landfill conditions releasing hydrogen sulfide, a toxic gas.

There is the potential to recycle many elements of construction waste. Often roll-off containers are used to transport the waste. Rubble can be crushed and reused in construction projects. Waste wood can also be recovered and recycled. Government or local authorities often make rules about how much waste should be sorted before it is hauled away to landfills or other waste treatment facilities. Some hazardous materials may not be moved, before the authorities have ascertained that safety guidelines and restrictions have been followed. Among their concerns would be the proper handling and disposal of such toxic elements as lead, asbestos or radioactive materials. In Kuwait, The Ministry of Finance granted a BOT (Build Operate and Transfer) contract to the Environmental Preservation Industries Company to build the first construction waste recycle plant in the middle east with a daily production of 2,500 tonnes. The government pays tipping fee to the company for waste removal as an incentive to relieve the stress on the environment. The construction waste is recycled to several sizes of gravels that can be reused in construction beside the screened sand can be used in ancillary construction uses.

REFERENCES

A. Portioli, A.Pozzetti, Progettazione dei sistemi produttivi, Hoepli 2003 *Note: this classification is very old but it has been subject to update as production systems have evolved over the 20th century, for a complete picture consult recent texts*

ABET. (2010, April 8). Accrediting College Programs in Applied Science, Computing,

Andrew Feller, Dan Shunk, & Tom Callarman (2006). BPTrends, March 2006 - Value Chains Vs. Supply Chains

Armony, Mor. "The Impact of Duplicate Orders on Demand Estimation and Capacity Investment".

Ashby, Michael; Hugh Shercliff and David Cebon (2007). *Materials: engineering, science, processing and design* (1st ed.). Butterworth-Heinemann.

Askeland, Donald R.; Pradeep P. Phulé (2005). *The Science & Engineering of Materials* (5th ed.). Thomson-Engineering.

Barbara J. Jackson (2010). *Construction Management Jumpstart* (2nd ed.). Indianapolis, Indiana: Wiley.

Bartsch, Frank. "Supply Chain Management (SCM)". BB Handel. Retrieved 19 June 2013.

Bird, M. (2010). Modern Management Guide to Information Technology. Create Space.

Brooame, Jr., J. Tol (June 1999). "The Benefits of Smart Inventory Management Software". CBS Interactive.

Caldwell, N.D. Roehrich, J.K. and Davies, A.C. (2009). Procuring complex performance in construction: London Heathrow Terminal 5 and a private finance initiative Hospital. Journal of Purchasing and Supply Management15(3):178-186.

Callister, Jr., William D. (2000). *Materials Science and Engineering – An Introduction* (5th ed.). John Wiley and Sons.

Callister, William (2007). *Materials Science and Engineering - An Introduction*. United States of America: John Wiley & Sons, Inc. pp. 5–13.

Chambers Dictionary, 1998, Chambers Harrap, Edinburgh, p. 845

Chris Hendrickson (September 2008). "What Is Construction Project Management?". PM Hut. Retrieved 2010-07-04.

CIO Wisdom: Best Practise from Silicon Valley's Leading IT Experts, Lane, D. (ed), Prentice Hall 2004

David Blanchard (2010), Supply Chain Management Best Practices, 2nd. Edition, John Wiley & Sons.

David Jacoby (2009), Guide to Supply Chain Management: How Getting it Right Boosts Corporate Performance (The Economist Books), Bloomberg Press; 1st edition.

DeBaise, Colleen (August 10, 2010). "Technology Basics for Business". *The Wall Street Journal Complete Small Business Guidebook.*

DesMarais, Christina (24 May 2011). "Choosing the Best Inventory Tracking Software". Inc.com. Retrieved 23 November 2012.

Dolinsky, Anton (Retrieved August 17, 2010). "Inventory Management History Part Four". Almyta Systems.

Eberhart, Mark (2003). *Why Things Break: Understanding the World by the Way It Comes Apart.* Harmony.

Financial dictionary, formerly at http://www.specialinvestor.com/terms/1072.html, Special Investor

Gardner, Dana, "Converged Infrastructure Approach Paves Way for Improved Data Center Productivity, Private Clouds," February 9, 2010, IT Business Edge

Gaskell, David R. (1995). *Introduction to the Thermodynamics of Materials* (4th ed.). Taylor and Francis Publishing.

Golden, Bernard, "Cloud Computing: Two Kinds of Agility," CIO, July 16, 2010.

Gordon, James Edward (1984). *The New Science of Strong Materials or Why You Don't Fall Through the Floor* (eissue ed.). Princeton University Press.

Harland, C.M. (1996) Supply Chain Management, Purchasing and Supply Management, Logistics, Vertical Integration, Materials Management and Supply Chain Dynamics. In: Slack, N (ed.) Blackwell Encyclopedic Dictionary of Operations Management. UK: Blackwell.

Harris, Derrick, "Can Open Converged Infrastructure Compete?" GigaOM, October 10, 2010.

Harris, Ford W. (1990, reprint from 1913). "How Many Parts to Make at Once". *Operations Research* (INFORMS) 38 (6): 947–950. JSTOR 170962. Retrieved Nov 21 2012. edit

Hines, T. 2004. Supply chain strategies: Customer driven and customer focused. Oxford: Elsevier.

Huff, Lisa, "The Battle for the Converged Data Center Network," Data Center Knowledge, August 18, 2011.

Italian Notebook.com "Who moved my parmigiano?" 24 February 2009

J. N. Edwards, MRP and Kanban-American style, APICS 26th Conference Proceedings,pp586-603 1983

J.C. Wortmann, Chapter: "A classification scheme for master production schedule", in Efficiency of Manufacturing Systems, C. Berg, D. French and B. Wilson (eds) New York, Plenum Press 1983

Japanese Manufacturing Techniques:Nine Hidden Lessons in Simplicity, New York 1982

Jonathan Coulter and Andrew W. Shepherd, Inventory Credit – An approach to developing agricultural markets, FAO, Rome, 1995

K, Scholasticus (May 26, 2010). "Inventory Management Techniques". Buzzle.com.

Lee, Perlitz (2012). *Retail Services*. Australia: McGraw HIll. p. 440. ISBN 9781743070741.

Lewis, M.A. and Roehrich, J.K. (2009). Contracts, relationships and integration: Towards a model of the procurement of complex performance. International Journal of Procurement Management, 2(2):125-142.

Lewis, P.R., Reynolds, K. & Gagg, C. (2003). *Forensic Materials Engineering: Case Studies*. Boca Raton: CRC Press.

M.Hammer, J.Champy, Reengineering the Corporation: A Manifesto for Business Revolution, Harper Business 1993

MacDuffie and Helper, 1997; Monden, 1993; Womack and Jones, 1996; Gunasekaran, 1999

Mathews, F.L. & Rawlings, R.D. (1999). *Composite Materials: Engineering and Science*. Boca Raton: CRC Press.

McKeen, James D., and Smith, Heather A., Making IT Happen: Critical Issues in IT Management, Wiley Series in Information Systems, 2003

McNurlin, Barbara, et al. (2009). "Information Systems Management in Practice (8th ed.)". Prentice Hall.

Mentzer, J.T. et al. (2001): Defining Supply Chain Management, in: *Journal of Business Logistics*, Vol. 22, No. 2, 2001, pp. 1–25

Moskowitz, Robert (Retrieved August 17, 2010). "Using Your Computer for Inventory Control". Accvision.

O'Brien, J (1999). *Management Information Systems – Managing Information Technology in the Internetworked Enterprise*. Boston: Irwin McGraw-Hill.

Oestreich, Ken, "Converged Infrastructure," CTO Forum, November 15, 2010.

Piasecki, Dave (Retrieved August 17, 2010). "Optimizing Economic Order Quantity – Carrying Costs". Inventoryops.com.

Polsson, Ken (Retrieved August 17, 2010). "Chronology of Personal Computers – 1981". Polsson's WebWorld.

R. S. SAXENA (1 December 2009). *INVENTORY MANAGEMENT: Controlling in a Fluctuating Demand Environment*. Global India Publications. pp. 24–. ISBN 978-93-8022-821-1. Retrieved 7 April 2012.

Relevance Lost, Johnson and Kaplan, Harvard Business School Press, 1987, p126

Roger W. Schmenner, How Can Service Businesses Survive and Prosper?, Sloan Management Review, vol. 27, no. 3, Spring 1986 http://umairbali.ekalaam.com/Business%20Process%20Workflow%20Analysis/Week6/SMR-ServiceBusiness.pdf

Shewhart, Walter A[ndrew]. (1931). Economic control of quality of manufactured product. New York: D. Van Nostrand Company. pp. 501 p.. ISBN 0-87389-076-0 (edition ??). LCCN 3132090. OCLC 1045408. LCC TS155 .S47.

Skoyles ER. Skoyles JR. (1987) Waste Prevention on Site. Mitchell Publishing, London. ISBN 0-7134-5380-X

Stagner, Steve. "Design-Build and Alternative Project Delivery in Texas" (PDF). Texas Council of Engineering Companies. Retrieved 18 October 2011.

Taft, E. W. "The most economical production lot." Iron Age 101.18 (1918): 1410-1412.

Talbot, Chris, "HP Adds to Converged Infrastructure Lineup," ChannelInsider, June 7, 2011.

Taylor, Frederick Winslow (1911). The Principles of Scientific Management. New York, NY, US and London, UK: Harper & Brothers. LCCN 11010339. OCLC 233134. Also available from Project Gutenberg.

The Book of Knowledge. (1992). Engineering. In The New Book of Knowledge (Vol. 5, pp. 224–225). Danbury, CT: Grolier Incorporated.

Thomas, Rhané (June 15, 2009). "IT Managers and Project Management". PM Hut. Retrieved December 13, 2009.

U.S. Department of Education Institute of Education Sciences: Classification of Instructional Programs (CIP). Retrieved on October 26, 2009 from CIP 2000 - CIP Lookup to Occupational Crosswalks

Veen, Annelies van der; Jan van Bon (2007). *Foundations of ITIL V3*. Van Haren Publishing.

Weele, Arjan J. van (2010). *Purchasing and Supply Chain Management: Analysis, Strategy, Planning and Practice* (5th ed. ed.). Andover: Cengage Learning.

2

Introduction to Materials Management

What conditions of work, what kinds of work, what kinds of management, and what kinds of reward or pay will help human stature to grow healthy, to its fuller and fullest stature ? Classic economic theory, based as it is on an inadequate theory of hum

—*Abraham Maslow*

MATERIALS MANAGEMENT

First, it must be remembered that materials management can deal with campus planning and building design for the movement of materials, or with logistics that deal with the tangible components of a supply chain. Specifically, this covers the acquisition of spare parts and replacements, quality control of purchasing and ordering such parts, and the standards involved in ordering, shipping, and warehousing the said parts.

In fact, the goal of materials management is to provide an unbroken chain of components for production to manufacture goods on time for the customer base. The materials department is charged with releasing materials to a supply base, ensuring that the materials are delivered on time to the company using the correct carrier. Materials is generally measured by accomplishing on time delivery to the customer, on time delivery from the supply base, attaining a freight budget, inventory shrink management, and inventory accuracy.

The materials department is also charged with the responsibility of managing new launches. In some companies materials management is also charged with the procurement of materials by establishing and managing a supply base.

In other companies the procurement and management of the supply base is the responsibility of a separate purchasing department. The purchasing department is then responsible for the purchased price variances from the supply base.

It is significant to note that in large companies with multitudes of customer changes to the final product over the course of a year, there may be a separate logistics department that is responsible for all new acquisition launches and customer changes. This logistics department ensures that the launch materials are procured for production and then transfers the responsibility to the plant materials management

Standards

There are no standards for materials management that are practiced from company to company. Most companies use ERP systems such as SAP, Oracle, BPCS, MAPICS, and other systems to manage materials control. Small concerns that do not have or cannot afford ERP systems use a form of spreadsheet application to manage materials. Materials management is not a science and depending upon the relevance and importance that company officials place upon controlling material flow, the level of expertise changes.

Some companies place materials management on a level whereby there is a logistics director, other companies see the importance level as managing at the plant level by hiring an inventory manager or materials manager, and still other companies employ the concept that the supervisors in the plant are responsible accompanied by a planners. Because there are no standards there is only best practices for any particular business sector that are widely used. For example, the generation of releases to the supply base come in many forms from the lowest level that requires sending facsimilies and PDF files, the EDI information exchange, to the ultimate practice of a supplier web base site.

Management is doing things right; leadership is doing the right things.

—*Peter F Drucker quotes*

Challenges

Remarkably, the major challenge that materials managers face is maintaining a consistent flow of materials for production. There are many factors that inhibit the accuracy of inventory which results in production shortages, premium freight, and often inventory adjustments. The major issues that all materials managers face are incorrect bills of materials, inaccurate cycle counts, un-reported scrap, shipping errors, receiving errors, and production reporting errors. Materials managers have striven to determine how to manage these issues in the business sectors of manufacturing since the beginning of the industrial revolution. Although there are no known methods that eliminate the afore mentioned inventory accuracy inhibitors, there are best methods available to eliminate the impact upon maintaining an interrupted flow of materials for production.

One challenge for materials managers is to provide timely releases to the supply base. On the scale of worst to best practices, sending releases via facsimile or PDF file is the worst practice and transmitting releases to the supplier based web site is the best practice. Why? The flaw in transmitting releases via facsimile or email is that they can get lost or even interpreted incorrectly into the suppliers system resulting in a stock out. The problem with transmitting EDI releases is that not all suppliers have EDI systems capable of receiving the release information. The best practice is to transmit the releases to a common supplier web base site where the suppliers can view (for free) the releases. The other advantage is that the supplier is required to use the carrier listed in the web site, must transmit an ASN (advanced shipping notification), and review the accumulative balances of the order

Improving Circulation Infrastructure

Redundancy can be reduced and effectiveness is increased when service points are clustered to reduce the amount of redundancy. An effective materials management programme can also resolve "island" approaches to shipping, receiving, and vehicle movement. Solutions can include creating a new central loading location, as well consolidating service areas and docks from separate buildings into one. Developing better campus circulation infrastructure also means re-evaluating truck delivery and service vehicle routes. Vehicle type, size, and schedules are studied to make these more onment for other uses.

Each year, an entire week is dedicated to celebrating resource and materials management professionals for their outstanding contributions to healthcare and the overall success of the supply chain. Sponsored by the Association for Healthcare Resource & Materials Management (AHRMM), National Healthcare Resource & Materials Management Week (MM Week) provides an opportunity to recognize the integral role materials management professionals play in delivering high-quality patient care throughout the health care industry. In 2010 Material Management Week is October 4-10.

Materials management plans and designs for the delivery, distribution, storage, collection, and removal of occupant-generated streams of materials and services. It is usually an additional service that is offered as part of a campus planning process or a building design project. It is most beneficial for university, health care, and corporate environments. Materials management looks at the planning and design considerations needed to support the efficient delivery and removal of goods and services that support occupant activity. The streams of occupant-generated materials and activity include mail, office supplies, lab supplies, food, special deliveries, custodial services, building supplies, waste and recycling, and service calls.

A materials management plan may include planning guidelines or full design for the following:

- Truck delivery and service vehicle routes, to reduce vehicle / pedestrian conflict
- Loading docks and delivery points, to increase accommodation and reduce queuing and vehicle idling
- Recycling, trash, and hazardous waste collection and removal, to increase waste diversion and reduce costs
- Service equipment and utility infrastructure relocation or concealment, to improve aesthetics and realize landscaping goals
- Regulatory and operation planning

Benefits

The effective materials management plan builds from and enhances an institutional master plan by filling in the gaps and producing an environmentally responsible and efficient outcome. An institutional campus, office, or housing complex can expect a myriad of benefits from an effective materials management plan. For starters, there are long-term cost savings, as consolidating, reconfiguring, and better managing a campus' core infrastructure reduces annual operating costs. An institutional campus, office, or housing complex will also get the highest and best use out of campus real estate. An effective materials management plan also means a more holistic approach to managing vehicle use and emissions, solid waste, hazardous waste, recycling, and utility services. As a result, this means a "greener," more sustainable environment and a manifestation of the many demands today for institutions to become more environmentally friendly. In fact, thanks to such environmental advantages, creative materials management plans may qualify for LEED Innovation in Design credits.

And finally, an effective materials management plan can improve aesthetics. Removing unsafe and unsightly conditions, placing core services out of sight, and creating a more pedestrian-friendly environment will improve the visual and physical sense of place for those who live and work there.

ROLE OF MATERIAL FLOW ANALYSIS

It is significant to note that material flow analysis (MFA) (also referred to as substance flow analysis; SFA) is an analytical method of quantifying flows and stocks of materials or substances in a well-defined system. MFA is an important tool to assess the physical consequences of human activities and needs in the field of Industrial Ecology, where it is used on different spatial and temporal scales. Examples are accounting of material flows within certain industries and connected ecosystems, determination of indicators of material use by different societies, and development of strategies for improving the material flow systems in form of material flow management. The most prolific writer on the topic is Paul H. Brunner.

Motivation

Human needs such as shelter, food, transport, or communication require materials such as wood, starch, sugar, iron and steel, copper, or semiconductors. As society develops and economic activity grows, production, use, and disposal of the materials employed increases to a scale where unwanted impacts on environment and society cannot be neglected anymore, neither locally nor globally: Material flows represent the core of local environmental problems such as leaching from landfills or oil spills. Rising concern about global climate change put a previously unimportant waste flow, carbon dioxide, on the top of the political and scientific agenda. In addition the gradual shift from traditional to urban mining in developed countries requires a detailed assessment of in-use and obsolete stocks of materials within the human environment. Industries, government bodies, and other organisations therefore need a tool to complement economic accounting with systematic book-keeping of materials entering, staying, and leaving the anthroposphere. Material flow analysis is such a tool.

Basic Principles

MFA is based on two fundamental and well-established scientific principles, system approach and mass balance. While these principles are applied wide across science and technology, it is the way they are applied to the socioeconomic metabolism that makes MFA a special method.

System Definition

An MFA system is a model of a process, industry sector or region of concern. Its level of detail is chosen according to the purpose of the study. An MFA system consists of the system boundary, processes, flows, and stocks. Contrary to e.g. chemical engineering where such a system would represent a specific physical setup, systems and processes in MFA can represent much larger and more abstract things as long as they are well-defined. The concept of the system is central as it allows to allocate quantitative information either as stocks within certain processes or as flows between processes. In other words an MFA system allows to graphically allocate the meaning of measurements or statistical data in form of stocks or flows that are related to certain processes in a given system.

MFA studies can be refined by disaggregating or simplified by aggregating processes.

Next to the system and the arrangement of processes and flows in between, scale and scope of the system need to be specified. The spatial scale is the geographic entity that is covered by the system. A system representing a certain industrial sector can be applied to the US, China, certain world regions, or the world as a whole. The temporal scale is the point in time or time span for which the system shall be considered. A system can represent a snapshot of stocks and flows at a certain point in time or it can contain time series which describe the temporal evolution of the system variables. The material (scope) of the system is the actual physical entity that shall be quantified. This can be a certain chemical element such as cadmium or a substance such as CO2. More general things can be quantified as well as long as some kind of balance can be established. Examples are goods such as passenger cars or other physical quantities such as energy.

Unlike in daily life, MFA requires a more precise use of the terms material, substance, or good due to the way they are affected by the mass balance principle. We refer to chapter 2.1 from Brunner and Rechberger:

- A chemical element is "a pure chemical substance consisting of one type of atom distinguished by its atomic number".
- A substance is "any (chemical) element or compound composed of uniform units. All substances are characterized by a unique and identical constitution and are thus homogeneous." From chapter 2.1.1 in Brunner&Rechberger.
- A good is defined as "economic entity of matter with a positive or negative economic value. Goods are made up of one or several substances". From chapter 2.1.2 in Brunner&Rechberger.
- The term material in MFA "serves as an umbrella term for both substances and goods." From chapter 2.1.3 in Brunner&Rechberger.

Process balance: One of the main purposes of MFA is to obtain a complete picture of the metabolism of certain elements or substances within the scope of the system. Such an analysis must also cover the stocks and flows that are not covered by financial accounting such as some waste flows, exhausts, or stocks of obsolete products. Mass balance or more general process balance is a first order physical principle that turns MFA into a powerful tool. The requirement for a balance to hold for each process facilitates a complete picture of the materials used, produced, and discarded within the various processes. Which balances hold for a given system depends on the specific processes that are considered: While for a process 'oil refinery' one can establish a mass balance for each chemical element, this is not possible for a nuclear power station.

A car factory respects the balance for steel, but a steel mill doesn't. Mass balance is a powerful and surprisingly versatile concept for the quantification of MFA systems. When quantifying MFA systems either by measurements or from statistical data, mass balance and other process balances have to be checked to ensure the correctness of the quantification and to reveal possible data inconsistencies or even misconceptions in the system such as the omission of a flow or a process.

Applications on Different Spatial and Temporal Scales

Material flow analyses are conducted on various spatial and temporal scales, for a variety of elements, substances, and goods, and cover a wide range of process chains and material cycles. Examples are

- *MFA on a national or regional scale* (also referred to as Material Flow Accounting): In this type of studies the material exchanges between an economy and the natural environment are analyzed. Several indicators are calculated in order to assess the level of resource intensity of the system.
- *Corporate material flow analysis*, or MFA along an *industrial supply chain* involving a number of companies: The goal of material flow analysis within a company is to optimize the production processes in such a way that materials and energy are used in the most efficient manner (e.g. by recycling and reduction of waste). Companies that implement material flow analysis can use the results to improve their operations costs and environmental performance.
- In the *life cycle of a product*: The life cycle inventory as part of life cycle assessment can be considered an MFA as it involves system definition and balances.

Historic Development of the Discipline

- Mass balance or the conservation of matter has been postulated already in ancient Greece, and it was introduced into modern chemistry by Lavoisier (cf. chapter 2.1.3 in Brunner&Rechberger.), from where it found its way to chemical engineering and finally to environmental science.
- Dennis Meadows made a wide audience aware of the physical foundation of the economy when he co-authored the bestseller Limits to Growth in 1971. Meadows et al. based their predictions on an analysis of resource stocks; see in the Glossary Glossary of environmental science#R.
- Friedrich Schmidt-Bleek is considered by many to be the father of MFA with his concept of Material Input Per Service unit (MIPS). Dr. Schmidt-Bleek is known for his work which claims that resource efficiency could be increased by a Factor 10. In the 1980s he inspired others to conduct MFA studies with him at the Wuppertal Institute and to establish research groups at other academic institutions. One example is the Sustainable Europe Research Institute (SERI) in Vienna, Austria which has developed a data base called materialflows.net.
- Mathis Wackernagel is known for co-developing the concept of the ecological footprint. Dr. Wackernagel founded the Global Footprint Network.
- The UNEP Resource Panel was set up in 2008 by the United Nations Environment Programme, and is headed by Ernst Ulrich von Weizsaecker. In analogy to the Intergovernmental Panel on Climate Change (IPCC) it brings together experts from many disciplines and institutions to review the current state of research on societal metabolism and to communicate the latest findings to policymakers and stakeholders.

Recent Development

- MFA concepts have been or are being incorporated in national accounts in several countries and regions such as the EU and Japan.
- Several international conferences or other meetings provide a platform for researchers and policymakers to meet and exchange results and ideas. A prominent example is the World Resources Forum, a bi-annual international conference on material flow analysis and sustainable development held in Davos, Switzerland. Friedrich Schmidt-Bleek, Dennis Meadows, and Ernst Ulrich

von Weizsaecker from the UNEP Resource Panel were among the keynote speakers during the 2009 event.

- MFA-IO is an approach to establish an MFA system of the whole economy using monetary and physical Input-Output tables.
- Dynamic MFA aims for long-term quantification of MFA systems and uses historic development patterns of physical stocks and flows to create robust scenarios for the years and decades to come.
- The current centre for MFA research is Japan. The country has scarce mineral resources and is therefore dependent on imports of energy carriers, ores, and other raw materials. The Japanese government fosters research on material cycles and also inaugurated the 3-R concept.

MFA is complementary to Life Cycle Assessment and Input-output models. Some overlaps between the different methods exist as they all share the system approach and to some extent the mass balance principle. The methods mainly differ in purpose, scope, and data requirements. MFA studies often cover the entire cycle (mining, production, manufacturing, use, waste handling) of a certain substance within a given geographical boundary and time frame. The level of detail of the system is adapted to the substance considered. Material stocks are considered explicitly which makes MFA suitable to tackle resource scarcity and recycling from old scrap. The common use of time series and lifetime models makes MFA a suitable forecasting tool for long-term trends in material use.

- Life cycle assessments and inventories focus on the various material demands and subsequent impacts for single products, whereas MFA studies typically focus on a single material in many different products. When scaling up LCA studies to cover a whole market or sector, feedbacks on the industry, such as flows of old scrap or resource constraints should be considered, topics that are traditionally covered by MFA studies.
- Compared to IO analyses the number of processes considered in MFA systems is usually much lower. On the other hand mass balance ensures that flows of by-products or waste are not overlooked in MFA studies, whereas in IO tables these flows are often not listed due to their lack in economic value. In addition, physical IO models are much less common than economic ones. Material stocks are also only indirectly covered by IO analysis in form of capital accumulation. Moreover, IO models do not have an upper limit: Any given final demand can be

satisfied. MFA systems on the other hand usually contain stocks of resources and hence a physical upper boundary of material turnover can be established.

REFERENCES

Brunner, P.H.; Rechberger, H. (2004). *Practical Handbook of Material Flow Analysis.* Lewis Publishers, New York.

Daniel B. Müller, Stock dynamics for forecasting material flows—Case study for housing in The Netherlands, Ecological Economics 59(1), 2006, pp 142-156.

IUPAC, Compendium of Chemical Terminology, 2nd ed. (the "Gold Book") (1997). Online corrected version: (2006–) "chemical element".

Marina Fischer-Kowalski, The Intellectual History of Materials Flow Analysis, Part I, 1860-1970, Journal of Industrial Ecology 2(1), 1998, pp 61-78.

Marina Fischer-Kowalski, The Intellectual History of Materials Flow Analysis, Part II, 1970-1998, Journal of Industrial Ecology 2(4), 1998, pp 107-136.

Nakamura, S.; Kondo, Y. (2009). *Waste Input-Output Analysis. Concepts and Application to Industrial Ecology*. Springer.

3

Elements and Dimensions of Supply Chain Management

> Supply chains cannot tolerate even 24 hours of disruption. So if you lose your place in the supply chain because of wild behavior you could lose a lot. It would be like pouring cement down one of your oil wells.
>
> —*Thomas Friedman quotes*

It is significant to note that supply chain management (SCM) is the management of a network of interconnected businesses involved in the provision of product and service packages required by the end customers in a supply chain. Supply chain management spans all movement and storage of raw materials, work-in-process inventory, and finished goods from point of origin to point of consumption. Another definition is provided by the APICS Dictionary when it defines SCM as the "design, planning, execution, control, and monitoring of supply chain activities with the objective of creating net value, building a competitive infrastructure, leveraging worldwide logistics, synchronizing supply with demand and measuring performance globally."

The term "supply chain management" entered the public domain when Keith Oliver, a consultant at Booz Allen Hamilton, used it in an interview for the Financial Times in 1982. The term was slow to take hold and the lexicon was slow to change. It gained currency in the mid-1990s, when a flurry of articles and books came out on the subject. In the late 1990s it rose to prominence as a management buzzword, and operations managers began to use it in thier titles with increasing regularity.

Common and accepted definitions of supply chain management are:

- Managing upstream and down stream value added flow of materials, final goods and related information among suppliers;

company; resellers; final consumers is supply chain management.

- Supply chain management is the systematic, strategic coordination of the traditional business functions and the tactics across these business functions within a particular company and across businesses within the supply chain, for the purposes of improving the long-term performance of the individual companies and the supply chain as a whole (Mentzer *et al.*, 2001).
- A customer focused definition is given by Hines (2004:p76) "Supply chain strategies require a total systems view of the linkages in the chain that work together efficiently to create customer satisfaction at the end point of delivery to the consumer. As a consequence costs must be lowered throughout the chain by driving out unnecessary costs and focusing attention on adding value. Throughout efficiency must be increased, bottlenecks removed and performance measurement must focus on total systems efficiency and equitable reward distribution to those in the supply chain adding value. The supply chain system must be responsive to customer requirements."
- Global supply chain forum - supply chain management is the integration of key business processes across the supply chain for the purpose of creating value for customers and stakeholders (Lambert, 2008).
- According to the Council of Supply Chain Management Professionals (CSCMP), supply chain management encompasses the planning and management of all activities involved in sourcing, procurement, conversion, and logistics management. It also includes the crucial components of coordination and collaboration with channel partners, which can be suppliers, intermediaries, third-party service providers, and customers. In essence, supply chain management integrates supply and demand management within and across companies. More recently, the loosely coupled, self-organizing network of businesses that cooperate to provide product and service offerings has been called the *Extended Enterprise*.

A supply chain, as opposed to supply chain management, is a set of organizations directly linked by one or more of the upstream and downstream flows of products, services, finances, and information from a source to a customer. Managing a supply chain is 'supply chain management' (Mentzer *et al.*, 2001). Supply chain management software includes tools or modules used to execute supply chain transactions, manage supplier relationships and control associated business processes. Supply chain event management (abbreviated as SCEM) is a consideration of all possible events and factors that can disrupt a supply chain. With SCEM possible scenarios can be created and solutions devised. In many cases the supply chain includes the collection of goods after consumer use for recycling. Including 3PL or other gathering agencies as part of the RM re-patriation process is a way of illustrating the new end-game strategy.

Supply chain management must address the following problems:

- Distribution Network Configuration: number, location and network missions of suppliers, production facilities, distribution centers, warehouses, cross-docks and customers.
- Distribution Strategy: questions of operating control (centralized, decentralized or shared); delivery scheme, e.g., direct shipment, pool point shipping, cross docking, DSD (direct store delivery), closed loop shipping; mode of transportation, e.g., motor carrier, including truckload, LTL, parcel; railroad; intermodal transport, including TOFC (trailer on flatcar) and COFC (container on flatcar); ocean freight; airfreight; replenishment strategy (e.g., pull, push or hybrid); and transportation control (e.g., owner-operated, private carrier, common carrier, contract carrier, or 3PL).
- Trade-Offs in Logistical Activities: The above activities must be well coordinated in order to achieve the lowest total logistics cost. Trade-offs may increase the total cost if only one of the activities is optimized. For example, full truckload (FTL) rates are more economical on a cost per pallet basis than less than truckload (LTL) shipments. If, however, a full truckload of a product is ordered to reduce transportation costs, there will be an increase in inventory holding costs which may increase total logistics costs. It is therefore imperative to take a systems approach when planning logistical activities. These trade-offs are key to developing the most efficient and effective Logistics and SCM strategy.
- Information: Integration of processes through the supply chain to share valuable information, including demand signals, forecasts, inventory, transportation, potential collaboration, etc.
- Inventory Management: Quantity and location of inventory, including raw materials, work-in-process (WIP) and finished goods.
- Cash-Flow: Arranging the payment terms and methodologies for exchanging funds across entities within the supply chain.

Supply chain execution means managing and coordinating the movement of materials, information and funds across the supply chain. The flow is bi-directional.

Understanding Activities/Functions

Supply chain management is a cross-function approach including managing the movement of raw materials into an organization, certain aspects of the internal processing of materials into finished goods, and the movement of finished goods out of the organization and toward the end-consumer. As organizations strive to focus on core competencies and becoming more flexible, they reduce their ownership of raw materials sources and distribution channels. These functions are increasingly being outsourced to other entities that can perform the activities better or more cost effectively. The effect is to increase the number of organizations involved in satisfying customer demand, while reducing management control of daily logistics operations. Less control and more supply chain partners led to the creation of supply chain management concepts. The purpose of supply chain management is to improve trust and collaboration among supply chain partners, thus improving inventory visibility and the velocity of inventory movement.

Several models have been proposed for understanding the activities required to manage material movements across organizational and functional boundaries. SCOR is a supply chain management model promoted by the Supply Chain Council. Another model is the SCM Model proposed by the Global Supply Chain Forum (GSCF). Supply chain activities can be grouped into strategic, tactical, and operational levels. The CSCMP has adopted The American Productivity & Quality Center (APQC) Process Classification Framework a high-level, industry-neutral enterprise process model that allows organizations to see their business processes from a cross-industry viewpoint.

Strategic Level

- Strategic network optimization, including the number, location, and size of warehousing, distribution centers, and facilities.
- Strategic partnerships with suppliers, distributors, and customers, creating communication channels for critical information and operational improvements such as cross docking, direct shipping, and third-party logistics.
- Product life cycle management, so that new and existing products can be optimally integrated into the supply chain and capacity management activities.
- Information technology chain operations.
- Where-to-make and make-buy decisions.

- Aligning overall organizational strategy with supply strategy.
- It is for long term and needs resource commitment.

Tactical Level

- Sourcing contracts and other purchasing decisions.
- Production decisions, including contracting, scheduling, and planning process definition.
- Inventory decisions, including quantity, location, and quality of inventory.
- Transportation strategy, including frequency, routes, and contracting.
- Benchmarking of all operations against competitors and implementation of best practices throughout the enterprise.
- Milestone payments.
- Focus on customer demand and Habits.

Operational Level

- Daily production and distribution planning, including all nodes in the supply chain.
- Production scheduling for each manufacturing facility in the supply chain (minute by minute).
- Demand planning and forecasting, coordinating the demand forecast of all customers and sharing the forecast with all suppliers.
- Sourcing planning, including current inventory and forecast demand, in collaboration with all suppliers.
- Inbound operations, including transportation from suppliers and receiving inventory.
- Production operations, including the consumption of materials and flow of finished goods.
- Outbound operations, including all fulfillment activities, warehousing and transportation to customers.
- Order promising, accounting for all constraints in the supply chain, including all suppliers, manufacturing facilities, distribution centers, and other customers.
- From production level to supply level accounting all transit damage cases & arrange to settlement at customer level by maintaining company loss through insurance company.
- Managing non-moving, short-dated inventory and avoiding more products to go short-dated.

Understanding Importance

Organizations increasingly find that they must rely on effective supply chains, or networks, to compete in the global market and networked economy. In Peter Drucker's (1998) new management paradigms, this concept of business relationships extends beyond traditional enterprise boundaries and seeks to organize entire business processes throughout a value chain of multiple companies.

During the past decades, globalization, outsourcing and information technology have enabled many organizations, such as Dell and Hewlett Packard, to successfully operate solid collaborative supply networks in which each specialized business partner focuses on only a few key strategic activities (Scott, 1993). This inter-organizational supply network can be acknowledged as a new form of organization. However, with the complicated interactions among the players, the network structure fits neither "market" nor "hierarchy" categories (Powell, 1990). It is not clear what kind of performance impacts different supply network structures could have on firms, and little is known about the coordination conditions and trade-offs that may exist among the players. From a systems perspective, a complex network structure can be decomposed into individual component firms (Zhang and Dilts, 2004). Traditionally, companies in a supply network concentrate on the inputs and outputs of the processes, with little concern for the internal management working of other individual players. Therefore, the choice of an internal management control structure is known to impact local firm performance (Mintzberg, 1979).

In the 21st century, changes in the business environment have contributed to the development of supply chain networks. First, as an outcome of globalization and the proliferation of multinational companies, joint ventures, strategic alliances and business partnerships, significant success factors were identified, complementing the earlier "Just-In-Time", "Lean Manufacturing" and "Agile Manufacturing" practices. Second, technological changes, particularly the dramatic fall in information communication costs, which are a significant component of transaction costs, have led to changes in coordination among the members of the supply chain network (Coase, 1998).

Many researchers have recognized these kinds of supply network structures as a new organization form, using terms such as "Keiretsu", "Extended Enterprise", "Virtual Corporation", "Global Production Network", and "Next Generation Manufacturing System". In general, such a structure can be defined as "a group of semi-independent organizations, each with their capabilities, which collaborate in ever-changing constellations to serve one or more markets in order to achieve some business goal specific to that collaboration" (Akkermans, 2001). The security management system for supply chains is described in ISO/IEC 28000 and ISO/IEC 28001 and related standards published jointly by ISO and IEC

Six major movements can be observed in the evolution of supply chain management studies: Creation, Integration, and Globalization (Movahedi et al., 2009), Specialization Phases One and Two, and SCM 2.0.

Creation Era

The term supply chain management was first coined by Keith Oliver in 1982. However, the concept of a supply chain in management was of great importance long before, in the early 20th century, especially with the creation of the assembly line. The characteristics of this era of supply chain management include the need for large-scale changes, re-engineering, downsizing driven by cost reduction programmes, and widespread attention to the Japanese practice of management.

Integration Era

This era of supply chain management studies was highlighted with the development of Electronic Data Interchange (EDI) systems in the 1960s and developed through the 1990s by the introduction of Enterprise Resource Planning (ERP) systems. This era has continued to develop into the 21st century with the expansion of internet-based collaborative systems. This era of supply chain evolution is characterized by both increasing value-adding and cost reductions through integration.

In fact a supply chain can be classified as a Stage 1, 2 or 3 network. In stage 1 type supply chain, various systems such as Make, Storage, Distribution, Material control, etc. are not linked and are independent of each other. In a stage 2 supply chain, these are integrated under one plan and is ERP enabled. A stage 3 supply chain is one in which vertical integration with the suppliers in upstream direction and customers in downstream direction is achieved. An example of this kind of supply chain is Tesco.

Globalization Era

The third movement of supply chain management development, the globalization era, can be characterized by the attention given to global systems of supplier relationships and the expansion of supply chains over national boundaries and into other continents. Although the use of global sources in the supply chain of organizations can be traced back several decades (e.g., in the oil industry), it was not until the late 1980s that a considerable number of organizations started to integrate global sources into their core business. This era is characterized by the globalization of supply chain management in organizations with the goal of increasing their competitive advantage, value-adding, and reducing costs through global sourcing.

Specialization Era (Phase I)

In the 1990s, industries began to focus on "core competencies" and adopted a specialization model. Companies abandoned vertical integration, sold off non-core operations, and outsourced those functions to other companies. This changed management requirements by extending the supply chain well beyond company walls and distributing management across specialized supply chain partnerships.

This transition also re-focused the fundamental perspectives of each respective organization. OEMs became brand owners that needed deep visibility into their supply base. They had to control the entire supply chain from above instead of from within. Contract manufacturers had to manage bills of material with different part numbering schemes from multiple OEMs and support customer requests for work -in-process visibility and vendor-managed inventory (VMI).

The specialization model creates manufacturing and distribution networks composed of multiple, individual supply chains specific to products, suppliers, and customers who work together to design, manufacture, distribute, market, sell, and service a product. The set of partners may change according to a given market, region, or channel, resulting in a proliferation of trading partner environments, each with its own unique characteristics and demands.

Specialization Era (Phase II)

Specialization within the supply chain began in the 1980s with the inception of transportation brokerages, warehouse management, and non-asset-based carriers and has matured beyond transportation and logistics into aspects of supply planning, collaboration, execution and performance management.

At any given moment, market forces could demand changes from suppliers, logistics providers, locations and customers, and from any number of these specialized participants as components of supply chain networks. This variability has significant effects on the supply chain infrastructure, from the foundation layers of establishing and managing the electronic communication between the trading partners to more complex requirements including the configuration of the processes and work flows that are essential to the management of the network itself. Supply chain specialization enables companies to improve their overall competencies in the same way that outsourced manufacturing and distribution has done; it allows them to focus on their core competencies and assemble networks of specific, best-in-class partners to contribute to the overall value chain itself, thereby increasing overall performance and efficiency.

The ability to quickly obtain and deploy this domain-specific supply chain expertise without developing and maintaining an entirely unique and complex competency in house is the leading reason why supply chain specialization is gaining popularity. Outsourced technology hosting for supply chain solutions debuted in the late 1990s and has taken root primarily in transportation and collaboration categories. This has progressed from the Application Service Provider (ASP) model from approximately 1998 through 2003 to the On-Demand model from approximately 2003-2006 to the Software as a Service (SaaS) model currently in focus today.

Supply Chain Management 2.0 (SCM 2.0)

Building on globalization and specialization, the term SCM 2.0 has been coined to describe both the changes within the supply chain itself as well as the evolution of the processes, methods and tools that manage it in this new "era".

Web 2.0 is defined as a trend in the use of the World Wide Web that is meant to increase creativity, information sharing, and collaboration among users. At its core, the common attribute that Web 2.0 brings is to help navigate the vast amount of information available on the Web in order to find what is being sought. It is the notion of a usable pathway. SCM 2.0 follows this notion into supply chain operations. It is the pathway to SCM results, a combination of the processes, methodologies, tools and delivery options to guide companies to their results quickly as the complexity and speed of the supply chain increase due to the effects of global competition, rapid price fluctuations, surging oil prices, short product life cycles, expanded specialization, near-/far- and off-shoring, and talent scarcity.

SCM 2.0 leverages proven solutions designed to rapidly deliver results with the agility to quickly manage future change for continuous flexibility, value and success. This is delivered through competency networks composed of best-of-breed supply chain domain expertise to understand which elements, both operationally and organizationally, are the critical few that deliver the results as well as through intimate understanding of how to manage these elements to achieve desired results. Finally, the solutions are delivered in a variety of options, such as no-touch via business process outsourcing, mid-touch via managed services and software as a service (SaaS), or high touch in the traditional software deployment model.

Role of Business Process Integration

Successful SCM requires a change from managing individual functions to integrating activities into key supply chain processes. An example scenario: the purchasing department places orders as requirements become known. The marketing department, responding to customer demand, communicates with several distributors and retailers as it attempts to determine ways to satisfy this demand. Information shared between supply chain partners can only be fully leveraged through process integration.

Supply chain business process integration involves collaborative work between buyers and suppliers, joint product development, common systems and shared information. According to Lambert and Cooper (2000), operating an integrated supply chain requires a continuous information flow. However, in many companies, management has reached the conclusion that optimizing the product flows cannot be accomplished without implementing a process approach to the business. The key supply chain processes stated by Lambert (2004) are:

- Customer relationship management
- Customer service management
- Demand management style
- Order fulfillment
- Manufacturing flow management
- Supplier relationship management
- Product development and commercialization
- Returns management

Much has been written about demand management. Best-in-Class companies have similar characteristics, which include the following: a) Internal and external collaboration b) Lead time reduction initiatives c) Tighter feedback from customer and market demand d) Customer level forecasting One could suggest other key critical supply business processes which combine these processes stated by Lambert such as:

(a) Customer service management
(b) Procurement
(c) Product development and commercialization
(d) Manufacturing flow management/support
(e) Physical distribution
(f) Outsourcing/partnerships

(g) Performance measurement

(h) Warehousing management

a) Customer Service Management Process

Customer Relationship Management concerns the relationship between the organization and its customers. Customer service is the source of customer information. It also provides the customer with real-time information on scheduling and product availability through interfaces with the company's production and distribution operations. Successful organizations use the following steps to build customer relationships:

- determine mutually satisfying goals for organization and customers
- establish and maintain customer rapport
- produce positive feelings in the organization and the customers

b) Procurement Process

Strategic plans are drawn up with suppliers to support the manufacturing flow management process and the development of new products. In firms where operations extend globally, sourcing should be managed on a global basis. The desired outcome is a win-win relationship where both parties benefit, and a reduction in time required for the design cycle and product development. Also, the purchasing function develops rapid communication systems, such as electronic data interchange (EDI) and Internet linkage to convey possible requirements more rapidly. Activities related to obtaining products and materials from outside suppliers involve resource planning, supply sourcing, negotiation, order placement, inbound transportation, storage, handling and quality assurance, many of which include the responsibility to coordinate with suppliers on matters of scheduling, supply continuity, hedging, and research into new sources or programmes.

c) Product Development and Commercialization

Here, customers and suppliers must be integrated into the product development process in order to reduce time to market. As product life cycles shorten, the appropriate products must be developed and successfully launched with ever shorter time-schedules to remain competitive. According to Lambert and Cooper (2000), managers of the product development and commercialization process must:

1. coordinate with customer relationship management to identify customer-articulated needs;
2. select materials and suppliers in conjunction with procurement, and

3. develop production technology in manufacturing flow to manufacture and integrate into the best supply chain flow for the product/market combination.

d) Manufacturing Flow Management Process

The manufacturing process produces and supplies products to the distribution channels based on past forecasts. Manufacturing processes must be flexible to respond to market changes and must accommodate mass customization. Orders are processes operating on a just-in-time (JIT) basis in minimum lot sizes. Also, changes in the manufacturing flow process lead to shorter cycle times, meaning improved responsiveness and efficiency in meeting customer demand. Activities related to planning, scheduling and supporting manufacturing operations, such as work-in-process storage, handling, transportation, and time phasing of components, inventory at manufacturing sites and maximum flexibility in the coordination of geographic and final assemblies postponement of physical distribution operations.

e) Physical Distribution

This concerns movement of a finished product/service to customers. In physical distribution, the customer is the final destination of a marketing channel, and the availability of the product/service is a vital part of each channel participant's marketing effort. It is also through the physical distribution process that the time and space of customer service become an integral part of marketing, thus it links a marketing channel with its customers (e.g., links manufacturers, wholesalers, retailers).

f) Outsourcing / Partnerships

This is not just outsourcing the procurement of materials and components, but also outsourcing of services that traditionally have been provided in-house. The logic of this trend is that the company will increasingly focus on those activities in the value chain where it has a distinctive advantage, and outsource everything else. This movement has been particularly evident in logistics where the provision of transport, warehousing and inventory control is increasingly subcontracted to specialists or logistics partners. Also, managing and controlling this network of partners and suppliers requires a blend of both central and local involvement. Hence, strategic decisions need to be taken centrally, with the monitoring and control of supplier performance and day-to-day liaison with logistics partners being best managed at a local level.

g) Performance Measurement

Experts found a strong relationship from the largest arcs of supplier and customer integration to market share and profitability. Taking advantage of supplier capabilities and emphasizing a long-term supply chain perspective in customer relationships can both be correlated with firm performance. As logistics competency becomes a more critical factor in creating and maintaining competitive advantage, logistics measurement becomes increasingly important because the difference between profitable and unprofitable operations becomes more narrow. A.T. Kearney Consultants (1985) noted that firms engaging in comprehensive performance measurement realized improvements in overall productivity. According to experts, internal measures are generally collected and analyzed by the firm including

1. Cost
2. Customer Service
3. Productivity measures
4. Asset measurement, and
5. Quality.

External performance measurement is examined through customer perception measures and "best practice" benchmarking, and includes 1) customer perception measurement, and 2) best practice benchmarking.

h) Warehousing Management

As a case of reducing company cost & expenses, warehousing management is carrying the valuable role against operations. In case of perfect storing & office with all convenient facilities in company level, reducing manpower cost, dispatching authority with on time delivery, loading & unloading facilities with proper area, area for service station, stock management system etc.

Components of supply chain management are as follows:

1. Standardization
2. Postponement
3. Customization.

Understanding Theories

Currently there is a gap in the literature available on supply chain management studies: there is no theoretical support for explaining the existence and the boundaries of supply chain management. A few authors such as Halldorsson, et al. (2003), Ketchen and Hult (2006) and Lavassani, et al. (2009) have tried to provide theoretical foundations for different areas related to supply chain by employing organizational theories. These theories include:

- Resource-based view (RBV)
- Transaction Cost Analysis (TCA)
- Knowledge-Based View (KBV)
- Strategic Choice Theory (SCT)
- Agency Theory (AT)
- Institutional theory (InT)
- Systems Theory (ST)
- Network Perspective (NP)
- Materials Logistics Management (MLM)
- Just-in-Time (JIT)
- Material Requirements Planning (MRP)
- Theory of Constraints (TOC)
- Performance Information Procurement Systems (PIPS)
- Performance Information Risk Management System (PIRMS)
- Total Quality Management (TQM)
- Agile Manufacturing
- Time Based Competition (TBC)
- Quick Response Manufacturing (QRM)
- Customer Relationship Management (CRM)
- Requirements Chain Management (RCM)
- Available-to-promise (ATP)
- and many more.

However, the unit of analysis of most of these theories is not the system "supply chain", but another system such as the "firm" or the "supplier/buyer relationship". Among the few exceptions is the relational view, which outlines a theory for considering dyads and networks of firms as a key unit of analysis for explaining superior individual firm performance (Dyer and Singh, 1998).

Role of Supply Chain Centroids

In the study of supply chain management, the concept of centroids has become an important economic consideration. A centroid is a place that has a high proportion of a country's population and a high proportion of its manufacturing, generally within 500 mi (805 km). In the U.S., two major supply chain centroids have been defined, one near Dayton, Ohio and a second near Riverside, California.

The centroid near Dayton is particularly important because it is closest to the population center of the US and Canada. Dayton is within 500 miles of 60% of the population and manufacturing capacity of the U.S., as well as 60 percent of Canada's population. The region includes the Interstate 70/75 interchange, which is one of the busiest in the nation with 154,000 vehicles passing through in a day. Of those, anywhere between 30 percent and 35 percent are trucks hauling goods. In addition, the I-75 corridor is home to the busiest north-south rail route east of the Mississippi.

Tax efficient supply chain management is a business model which considers the effect of tax in design and implementation of supply chain management. As the consequence of globalization, business which is cross-nation should pay different tax rates in different countries. Due to the differences, global players have the opportunity to calculate and optimize supply chain based on tax efficiency legally. It is used as a method of gaining more profit for company which owns global supply chain.

Supply Chain Sustainability

Supply chain sustainability is a business issue affecting an organization's supply chain or logistics network and is frequently quantified by comparison with SECH ratings. SECH ratings are defined as *social, ethical, cultural and health* footprints. Consumers have become more aware of the environmental impact of their purchases and companies' SECH ratings and, along with non-governmental organizations(NGOs), are setting the agenda for transitions to organically-grown foods, anti-sweatshop labor codes and locally-produced goods that support independent and small businesses. Because supply chains frequently account for over 75% of a company's carbon footprint many organizations are exploring how they can reduce this and thus improve their SECH rating.

For example, in July, 2009 the U.S. based Wal-Mart corporation announced its intentions to create a global sustainability index that would rate products according to the environmental and social impact made while the products were manufactured and distributed. The sustainability rating index is intended to create environmental accountability in Wal-Mart's supply chain, and provide the motivation and infrastructure for other retail industry companies to do the same.

More recently, the US Dodd-Frank Wall Street Reform and Consumer Protection Act signed into law by President Obama in July 2010, contained a supply chain sustainability provision in the form of the Conflict Minerals law. This law requires SEC-regulated companies to conduct third party audits of the company supply chains, determine whether any tin, tantalum, tungsten or gold (together referred to as *conflict minerals*) is made of up ore mined/sourced from the Democratic Republic of the Congo (DRC), and create a report (available to the general public and SEC) detailing the supply chain due diligence efforts undertaken and the results of the audit. Of course, the chain of suppliers/vendors to these reporting companies will be expected to provide appropriate supporting information.

Management Components

The SCM components are the third element of the four-square circulation framework. The level of integration and management of a business process link is a function of the number and level, ranging from low to high, of components added to the link (Ellram and Cooper, 1990; Houlihan, 1985). Consequently, adding more management components or increasing the level of each component can increase the level of integration of the business process link. The literature on business process re-engineering, buyer-supplier relationships, and SCM suggests various possible components that must receive managerial attention when managing supply relationships. Lambert and Cooper (2000) identified the following components:

- Planning and control
- Work structure
- Organization structure
- Product flow facility structure
- Information flow facility structure
- Management methods
- Power and leadership structure
- Risk and reward structure
- Culture and attitude.

However, a more careful examination of the existing literature leads to a more comprehensive understanding of what should be the key critical supply chain components, the "branches" of the previous identified supply chain business processes, that is, what kind of relationship the components may have that are related to suppliers and customers. Bowersox and Closs states that the emphasis on cooperation represents the synergism leading to the highest level of joint achievement (Bowersox and Closs, 1996). A primary level channel participant is a business that is willing to participate in the inventory ownership responsibility or assume other aspects of financial risk, thus including primary level components (Bowersox and Closs, 1996).

A secondary level participant (specialized) is a business that participates in channel relationships by performing essential services for primary participants, including secondary level components, which support primary participants. Third level channel participants and components that support the primary level channel participants and are the fundamental branches of the secondary level components may also be included.

Consequently, Lambert and Cooper's framework of supply chain components does not lead to any conclusion about what are the primary or secondary (specialized) level supply chain components. That is, what supply chain components should be viewed as primary or secondary, how should these components be structured in order to have a more comprehensive supply chain structure, and how to examine the supply chain as an integrative one.

Reverse Supply Chain

Reverse logistics is the process of managing the return of goods. Reverse logistics is also referred to as "Aftermarket Customer Services". In other words, any time money is taken from a company's warranty reserve or service logistics budget one can speak of a reverse logistics operation.

Understanding Systems and Value

Supply chain systems configure value for those that organize the networks. Value is the additional revenue over and above the costs of building the network. Co-creating value and sharing the benefits appropriately to encourage effective participation is a key challenge for any supply system. Tony Hines defines value as follows: "Ultimately it is the customer who pays the price for service delivered that confirms value and not the producer who simply adds cost until that point"

Understanding Global Applications

Global supply chains pose challenges regarding both quantity and value:

Supply and value chain trends

- Globalization
- Increased cross border sourcing
- Collaboration for parts of value chain with low-cost providers
- Shared service centers for logistical and administrative functions
- Increasingly global operations, which require increasingly global coordination and planning to achieve global optimums
- Complex problems involve also midsized companies to an increasing degree.

These trends have many benefits for manufacturers because they make possible larger lot sizes, lower taxes, and better environments (culture, infrastructure, special tax zones, sophisticated OEM) for their products. Meanwhile, on top of the problems recognized in supply chain management, there will be many more challenges when the scope of supply chains is global. This is because with a supply chain of a larger scope, the lead time is much longer. Furthermore, there are more issues involved such as multi-currencies, different policies and different laws. The consequent problems include:1. different currencies and valuations in different countries; 2. different tax laws (Tax Efficient Supply Chain Management); 3. different trading protocols; 4. lack of transparency of cost and profit.

Importance of Certification

There are several certification programmes for Supply Chain Management staff development including APICS (the Association for Operations Management), ISCEA (The International Supply Chain Education Alliance) and IOSCM (Institute of Supply Chain Management). APICS' certification is called Certified Supply Chain Professional, or CSCTP, and ISCEA'S certification is called the Certified Supply Chain Manager (CSCM). Another, the Institute for Supply Management, is developing one called the Certified Professional in Supply Management (CPSM) focused on the Procurement and Sourcing areas of Supply Chain Management, also called Supply management.

IMPORTANCE OF SUPPLIER RISK MANAGEMENT

Supplier risk management is an evolving discipline in operations management for manufacturers, retailers, financial services companies and government agencies where the organization is highly dependent on suppliers to achieve business objectives. Outsourcing, globalization, lean supply chain initiatives and supplier rationalization have contributed to a highly fragmented model, where control is often several steps removed from the corporation. While these models have allowed companies to reduce overall costs and expand quickly into new markets, they also expose the company to the risk of a supplier suddenly going bankrupt, closing operations or being acquired.

Main Objectives

To overcome these challenges, companies mitigate supply chain interruptions and reduce risk with strategies and tactics that address supplier-centric risk at multiple stages in the relationship:

- On boarding: Bringing suppliers into the operation with registration that includes:

    - o A centralized supplier registration portal
    - o Integration of third party performance, financial data and predictive indicators into the supplier profile
- Monitoring for stability beyond financial data, including:
    - o Criminal and terrorists (i.e. Office of Foreign Assets Control) ties and operational performance
    - o Visibility into potential disruptions caused by geopolitical threats, acts of nature, etc.
- Cultivating strategic supplier relationships for the long-term:
    - o Leverage supplier scorecards for continuous improvement
    - o Establish and use benchmarks for measuring supplier performance
    - o Creating a system for collaboration and supplier development
- Establish control across the extended enterprise:
    - o Create integrated supplier networks
    - o Extend performance management benchmarks to second and third tier suppliers

Supplier Risk in Recession and Recovery

In 2008-2009, manufacturers experienced the startling speed at which suppliers can move from stability to shutting down operations. The devastating impact of a crucial supplier failure has moved risk management from add-on service to mission-critical. With a new focus on risk management, manufacturers have seen value whether the economy is stagnant or thriving.

With a transparent, accessible and comprehensive set of supplier information, manufacturers have been able to monitor suppliers for behavioral changes which contribute to overall stability, including:

- Changes in the supplier's management team
- EPA violations
- OSHA incidents
- Quality issues
- Noticeable lags in response time to inquiries
- OFAC violations

Changes in any of these conditions can be defined as parameters for raising an alert. For example, a financially stable supplier may in fact be about to lose it CEO to retirement – which may cause issues within the management team. Early visibility into that change gives the manufacturer time to ensure it doesn't negatively affect customers.

Based on the criticality of the supplier and the nature of the alert received, the manufacturer can then choose to take necessary action, such as calling or visiting the supplier, increasing monitoring, or moving towards terminating the relationship with the supplier and finding a replacement.

Main Benefits

Reducing supplier risk can:

- Give insight to manufacturers to create defensive and offensive strategies that turn risk into a competitive advantage.
- Help determine whether or not it is beneficial for a company to conduct a customer intervention and know in advance what the potential outcomes might be for an intervention.
- Improve competitive position in the market.
- Lower supplier costs.
- Position manufacturers to better address customer needs by addressing supplier vulnerabilities before they become apparent.

REFERENCES

Andrew Feller, Dan Shunk, & Tom Callarman (2006). BPTrends, March 2006 - Value Chains Vs. Supply Chains.

David Blanchard (2010), Supply Chain Management Best Practices, 2nd. Edition, John Wiley & Sons.

David Jacoby (2009), Guide to Supply Chain Management: How Getting it Right Boosts Corporate Performance (The Economist Books), Bloomberg Press; 1st edition.

Harland, C.M. (1996) Supply Chain Management, Purchasing and Supply Management, Logistics, Vertical Integration, Materials Management and Supply Chain Dynamics. In: Slack, N (ed.) Blackwell Encyclopedic Dictionary of Operations Management. UK: Blackwell.

Lambert, Douglas M.Supply Chain Management: Processes, Partnerships, Performance, 3rd edition, 2008.

Mentzer, J.T. et. al. (2001): Defining Supply Chain Management, in: *Journal of Business Logistics*, Vol. 22, No. 2, 2001, pp. 1–25.

4

Overview of Production Management

Management is doing things right; leadership is doing the right things.

—Peter F Drucker quotes

PRODUCTION MANAGEMENT

"Production management deals with the decision making related to production process of that the resulting goods and service is produced according to specifications in the amounts and at the scheduled demanded and at minimum cost" – Elwood Butta.

Production involves the step by step convertion of one form of material into another through chemical or mechanical process with a view to enhance the utility of the product or services.

Characteristics Features

1. Production is an organized activity.
2. The system transforms the various inputs into useful outputs.

3. Production system does not operate in isolation from the other organizational systems.
4. There exists a feed back about the activities which is essential to control and improve system proformation.

Production mgmt	*Operation mgmt*
1. It is concerned with manufacturing	1. It is concerned with services
2. Output is tangible	2. Output is intangible
3. In this, job useless labour and more equipment	3. In this, job use more labour and less equipment
4. There is no customer participation	4. Frequent customer participation

Functions of Production Management

1. Production planning
2. Production control
3. Factory building
4. Provision of plant services
5. Plant layout
6. Physical Environment
7. Method study
8. Inventory control
9. Quality control
10. Product department

Different Classification/Types

1. Intermittent production
   - 1.1. Job or unit production
   - 1.2. Batch or quantity production
2. Continuous or mass production
3. Flexible manufacturing system (FMS)
4. Computer Integrated manufacturing (CIM)

Difference between Job or Unit Production and Batch Production

Job Pdn	*Batch Pdn*
1. Job shop production are characterized by manufa-facturing of one or few quantity of products.	1. This production is characterized by the manufacture of limited number of products produced at regular intervals.

Characteristics of Batch Productions

1. Shorter production runs.
2. More number of set ups and hence set up cost.
3. Amount of supervision required is less compared to job order.
4. Plant and machinery are flexible.
5. Higher level of work in process inventory.

Batch production is as a form of manufacturing in which the jobs pass through the functional department in lots or batches and each lot may have a different routing.

Job Production

Job production are characterized by manufacturing of one or few quantity of product is designed and produced as per the specification of customers with in prefixed time and cost.

Characteristics of Job Production

1. High variety of product and low volume.
2. Use of general purpose machines. And facilities.
3. Frequently changing set ups.
4. Process type layouts for arrangement of facilities.
5. Large inventory of materials, tools and parts.

Continuous / Mass Production

Manufacture of discrete parts or assemblies using a continuous process are called mass production. The machineries are arranged in a line or product layout.

Advantages of Mass Production

1. Higher rate of production with reduced cycle time.
2. Higher capacity
3. Less skilled operator can manage the process
4. Low in process inventory
5. Production cost per unit per unit will come down due to economies of scale.

Flexible Manufacturing System (F M S)

A Flexible manufacturing system is a configuration of computer. Controlled, semi-independent workstations where materials are automatically handled and machine loaded. An FMS is a type of flexible manufacturing system that builds on the programmable automation of NC and CNC machines.

Characteristics of FMS

1. It contains several work station, each does different operations.
2. The work station and machines are automated.
3. FMS is a computer control system.
4. Three programme machine, select position and activities the specific tool for each job.

Classification of Production Based on Type of Production & Strategy

1. Make to stork (eg) books, television, airline flight.
2. Make to order (eg) wedding invitations, customer built homes.
3. Assemble to order (eg) computer system, corporate training.

Make to Stock

Make to stock products and services are designed and produced for "standard" Customers in anticipation of demand. This system ensures immediate delivery of good quality, reasonably priced, off the shelf standard products (eg) Books, Televisions, airline flights etc.

Make to Order

Make to order products and services are designed, products and delivered to customer specification in response to customer order. (eg) wedding invitations, custom – built homes.

Assemble to Order

Assemble to order products and services are produced in standard modules to which options are added according to customer specification. (eg) Computer Systems, corporate training etc.

Production and Marketing

- Needs of customer with respect to the company's products and services.
- The demand for the products and the likely market frend for the future period.
- Special features required by customer regarding the products like feedback, performance etc.
- Delivery requirement of the products. Market department requires the following information.
- Production status of the production.

- Performance characteristics of products.
- Delivery schedules.
- Product features and specification.

The product department has to invest in physical facilities, requires raw materials and components parts, etc. Thus Finance department has to make provisions for both long term and short term requirements.

The production department has to furnish the detailed production budgets to finance department.

The personnel department has to keep records of the development of workers, identify their training needs, man power utilization etc. In order to achieve production goals in particular and organisational goals in general, personal deportment has to channelise the skills and efforts of the work fore into constructive outlets to achieve the set objectives.

CIM

Computer Integrated manufacturing is an interdisciplinary science applied to manufacturing. It involves the amalgamation of information science with automated manufacturing.

1. State any four principles of material handling?
   i. Heavy loads must be handled mechanically.
   ii. As for as possible use gravitational force.
   iii. Move the material at constant speed.
   iv. Use trained people at constant speed.
2. What are advantages of using industrial robots in manufacturing:
   i. Speed of manufacturing is high
   ii. Accurate
   iii. Hazardous materials can be handled easily.
   iv. Complex jobs can be done easily.

Costs of Inventory

i. Ordering cost: The cot incurred in placing the order and receiving the order. Eg: Postage charges, telephone charges
ii. Carrying cost: The cost incurred in storing or holding the material.

Buffer Stock

Buffer stock is maintained to avoid following,

i. Price hike

ii. Strike at supplier side,

BOM contains the information to identify each item and the quantity used per unit of the item of which it is a part. It contains not only complete product descriptions, listings, materials, parts and components but also the sequence in which the product is created.

Components of JIT Philosophy

i. People participation and involvement

ii. Total quality control

iii. Just In Time flow

Kanban System

Kanban system is a kind of production system which operates based on the information contained in cards called "kanbans". There are two types of kanbans namely, Withdrawal kanban and production order kanban.

BOR

Bill of Resource is a record of all the required materials. It can met stock and other resources needed for manufacturing. It is prepared based on Master Production Schedule (MPS).

ABC Analysis

ABC analysis is a technique which is used to classify the items in store into A, B and C class items based on demand of the stock. If the stock on hand of a particular item becomes less than or equal to its reorder level, immediately an order is placed for its economical quantity.

Pareto Analysis

Italian scientist Wilfredo Pareto made a study on concentration of wealth. Among the total wealth of the country, 80% of the wealth is concentrated on 20% of the population. This 80/20 relationship is called Pareto analysis.

ROL

Re Order Level deals with when to order to replenish the inventory. ROL is a predetermined point and when the existing stock of inventories reaches this point or falls below it the purchase option is initiated to replenish it.

Principles of Inventory Control

i. Right time

ii. Right quantity
iii. Right Quality
iv. Right place
v. Right people

Materials management is the process of planning, purchasing, receiving, storing of inventory control and scrap and surplus disposal of materials which are required for the production in an organization.

Inventory Control

Inventory control is a systematic procedure for ensuring the availability of items necessary to meet the production requirement at optimum cost. It is concerned with the procurement of raw materials and components and their supplies to the production department.

Reasons of Inventory Control

i. Lead-time
ii. Some products are not available at all time
iii. Benefits while purchasing in bulk.
iv. Price fluctuation

MRP-I

i. Demand for the products
ii. Master production schedule
iii. Bill of material files
iv. Inventory record file
v. Inventory transaction file

AGVs

An automated guided vehicle is a small, driverless, battery-driven truck that moves Materials between operations following instructions from either an on-board or a central computer.

AS/RS

An Automated Storage and Retrieval System is a computer controlled method of storing and retrieving materials and tools using racks, bins and stackers.

E-manufacturing

E-manufacturing is sharing real-time data with trading partners and customers and making decisions about production, through the internet.

Define EOQ

Economic Order Quantity is the quantity at which the total inventory cost is minimum. EOQ can be calculated using the average inventory, carrying cost and ordering cost.

Q-system of Inventory

In this system of inventory, whenever the stock level touches the reorder level, an order is placed for a fixed quantity which is equal to EOQ. It is otherwise called as fixed order quantity system.

P-system of Inventory

Periodic review system is a system of inventory, the stock position is renieved once in a fixed period and an order is placed depending on the stock position, unlike the fixed quantity in the Q system of inventory.

Q-System	*P-System*
1. The quantity to be ordered each time is fixed and normally it is equal to EOQ.	1. Period of ordering the inventory is fixed and the order quantity depends on the stock on hand.
2. It is suitable for low unit cost high volume items.	2. Suitable for high unit volume and less in number items.
3. Normally preferred when supplier puts minimum quantity restriction.	3. Preferred when supplier delivers at fixed periods

Strategic Planning

Strategic planning is the process by which top management determines overall organizational purposes and objectives and how they are achieved. Eg. Defining goal and policy, how will we make the product.

Tactical planning is done over an intermediate term or medium range time horizon by middle management in each function area of management. Eg. How may workers we need should be work overtime.

The lower level management develops operational plans and the planning horizon is (maximum) one year. These plans establish actions that are necessary to achieve operation goals.

Capacity refers to the maximum load an operating unit can handle. The operating unit might be a plant, a department, a machine, a store or a worker. Capacity of a plant is the maximum rate of output the plant can produce.

Capacity planning is necessary when an organization decides to increase it production on introduce new product into the market or to increase the volume of production to gain the advantages of economics scale.

Aggregate planning involves planning the best quantity to produce during time periods in the immediate range horizons (3m to 1 yr) and planning the lowest cost method of providing the adjustable capacity to accumulate the production requirements.

Product planning and development is the process of searching ideas for new products, screening them systematically, converting them into tangible products and introducing he new products into markets. It also involves formulation of product strategies and policies.

- To establish a company wide gain plan for allocating resources.
- To develop an economic strategy for meeting demand.

Inputs and Outputs of Aggregate Planning

The inputs for aggregate planning are demand forecast, capacity constraints, strategic objectives, company policies, financial constraints.

The output for aggregate planning are size of workforce, production per month inventory levels that support the production plan and the number of units subcontracted or cost.

Steps Involved in Aggregate Planning

i. Prepare the sales forecast for each product.
ii. Sumup the individual product or service forecast into one aggregate demand for the factory.
iii. Transform the aggregate demand for each time period into labor, material machines and other elements.
iv. Develop alternative resource schemes for supplying the necessary production capacity to support the cumulative aggregate demand.
v. Select the capacity plan from among alternative consider that satisfy aggregate demand and best meets the objectives of the organization.

Product Development

- Consumer acceptance
- Protection against copying by competitors through patent, copyright, and trademarks.
- Development cost & manufacturing costs
- Complementary products
- Utilizing the by-products and wastages resulting from manufacturing processes.

Stages 'Involved' in New Product Development

- New product strategic development
- Idea generation
- Idea screening and evaluation
- Business analysis
- Product development
- Testing
- Commercialization

Product Design

Product design is concerned with the form and function of a product. Form design involves the determination of what a product would look like (ie) the shape and appearance of the product. Functional design deals with what function the product will perform and how it performs.

Objectives of Product Design

- The overall objective is profit generation in the long-run.
- To achieve the desired product quality
- To reduce the development time and cost to the minimum
- To reduce the cost of the product
- To ensure producibility or manufacturability.

Factors Influencing Product Design

- Customer requirements
- Type of materials used
- Cost/price ratio
- Product quality
- Process capability.

Requirement for an Effective Design Process

1. Match product or service characteristic with customer requirements.
2. To ensure that customers require
3. Reduce the time required to design a new product or service.
4. Minions the revisions necessary to make a design workable.

CAD

CAD is a computer Aided Design. It is a software system that uses computer graphics to assesse in the creation, modification and analysis of a design.

Technologies Used in CAD

The CAD can be used for Geometric modeling, automated Drafting, documentation, Engineering analysis and design analysis.

CAE

Computer Aided Engineering retrieves the description and geometry of a part from a CAD database and subjects it to testing and analysis on the computer screen without physically building a prototype model. Expert systems can be viewed as computerized consultants for decision making that use the collection of facts, knowledge and rules to diagnose the problem and suggest solutions.

Backward Scheduling

Backward Scheduling is the last operation on the job is scheduled first, then the rest of operation. Eg. Assembly type industries

Gantt Load Chart

The Gantt Chart is the visual aid that is commonly used in job shops. It is also used in maintenance and service industries. Gantt Chart are simple to device and easy to understand.

The department has 'n' machines/work center and each center may have more than one machine. The accumulative hours assigned to each work center are plotted on the center. When a center is over loaded it is easy to identify the problem areas and to develop corrective actions by reassigning workloads to alternative machines.

Limitation of Gantt Chart

- The sequence of operation is not considered in detailed. Since the machine are grouped together the weighted time of individual groups and the idle time of machine are not clearly shown.
- The charts do not reflect maintenance and breakdown times.

PERT

- PERT is the name given to in networking approach to planning, monitoring, controlling and evaluation of complex projects.
- PERT consists of a network diagram which is a two dimensional schematic of the relationships between task in a project.
- PERT assumes a probability distribution for the duration of each activity.

Thus completion time estimate for all of the activities are needed.

- To perform PERT analysis on a project, the emphasis is given on the completion of a task rather than the activities required to be performed to reach to a particular event or task. Thus, it is also called an event-oriented technique.
- PERT is used for one-time projects involving activities of non-repetitive nature in which time estimate are uncertain such as redesigning an assembly line or installing a new information system.
- PERT helps in identifying critical areas in a project so that necessary adjustment can be made to meet the scheduled completion date of the project.

Systematic Layout Design Procedure

An organized approach to layout planning has been developed by Muther and has received considerable publicity due to the success derived from its Application is solving a large variety of layout problems. This approach is referred to as systematic layout planning or simply SLP.

Templates

Templates are used to develop plant layout. Templates are made up of Cardboard or colored paper. They are placed on the scaled outline plan of the building. Templates are cutout show the plan of the various facilities like machinery and fittings. They show the actual floor utilization.

Models

Models are prepared on a scale that show the length, breadth and width. Models are easily understood by persons who are not familiar with plant layout Practice. They are made up of wood or plaster of paris. Models are expensive.

ALDEP

ALDEP is Automated Layout Design Programme. It is a construction type algorithm. This algorithm uses basic data on facilities and builds a design by successively placing the departments in the layout. The basic data required for this algorithm are

- Total number of departments
- Area of each departments
- Length and width of layout
- Number of iterations to be performed
- Location and size of each restricted area in the layout if present.

CORELAP

CORELAP is Computerized Relationship Layout Planning. This algorithm is based on Muther's procedure given in Systematic Layout Planning. The input requirements to CORELAP are

- Number of departments and their area.
- Closeness relationship as given by REL-chart
- Weighted ratings for REL-chart entries.

CRAFT

CRAFT is Computerized Relative Allocation of Facilities technique. CRAFT algorithm was originally developed by Armour and Buffa. It is more widely used than ALDEP and CORELAP. It starts with an initial layout and improves the layout by interchanging the departments pairwise so that the transportation cost is minimized.

The CRAFT requirements are

- Initial layout
- Flow data
- Cost per unit distance
- Total number of departments
- Area of departments

Time Study

Time study is considered to be one of the most widely used means of Work study. This was proposed by Frederick Taylor. This technique is used for recording the times and rates of working for the elements of a specified job carried out under specified conditions and for analyzing the data so as to determine the time necessary for carrying out the job at the defined level of performance.

Work Sampling

Work sampling is defined as the technique in which a statistically competent number of instantaneous observations are taken over a period of time of a of machines, processes or workers. Each observations recorded for a particular activity Or delay is a measure of percentage of time observed by the occurrence.

Objectives of Work Measurement

The objectives are

- Comparing alternative method

- Assessing the correct initial manning
- Planning and control
- Realistic costing
- Financial incentive schemes
- Delivery date of goods
- Cost reduction and cost control
- Identifying substandard workers
- Training new employees.

The benefits are

- To develop a basis for comparing alternate methods developed in method study by establishing the work content in each method of doing the job.
- To prepare realistic work schedules by accurate assessment of human work.
- To set standards of performance.
- To compare actual time taken by the worker with allowed time.
- To assist in labour cost estimation.

The techniques of work measurement are:

- Stop watch time study
- Work sampling
- Standard data
- Predetermined Motion Time Study

A Qualified worker is one who is accepted as having necessary physical attributes possessing the required intelligence and education and having acquired the necessary skill and knowledge to carryout the work in hand to satisfactory standards of safety, quantity, quality.

PMTS

PMTS is Predetermined Motion Time System. It is defined as a work measurement technique by which normal or basic times are established for basic 30 human motions and these time values are used to build up the time for a job at a defined level of performance.

The advantages of PMTS as are

- Affords fine analysis and improvement of work methods
- Offers a precise means of recording time, avoiding subjective judgment or bias of the rater.

- Involves no interference in the normal work routine and hence faces little resistance form workers.
- More effective and economical tool for work measurement for repetitive jobs of short duration.

Plant layout and Material handling are closely inter related. An effective layout involves least material handling and less costly material handling equipments. It permits material handling without any loss of time, with minimum delays and least backtracking. The total number of movements and the distances moved are also considerably reduced in properly design plant layout.

REFERENCES

Chris Hendrickson (September 2008). "What Is Construction Project Management?". PM Hut. http://www.pmhut.com/what-is-construction-project-management. Retrieved 2010-07-04.

Stagner, Steve. "Design-Build and Alternative Project Delivery in Texas" (PDF). Texas Council of Engineering Companies.

5

Understanding the Relationships among Logistics, Operations and Supply Chain Management

> Today's leading real-world retailer, Wal-Mart, uses software to power its logistics and distribution capabilities, which it has used to crush its competition.
>
> —*Marc Andreessen*

LOGISTICS MANAGEMENT

It is significant to note that logistics is the management of the flow of goods, information and other resources between the point of origin and the point of consumption in order to meet the requirements of consumers (frequently, and originally, military organizations). Logistics involves the integration of information, transportation, inventory, warehousing, material-handling, and packaging, and occasionally security.

Logistics is a channel of the supply chain which adds the value of time and place utility. Today the complexity of production logistics can be modeled, analyzed, visualized and optimized by plant simulation software.

The term "logistics" comes from the French loger, which means "to lodge" or "to house". It originally referred to the billeting of troops in private dwellings or other housing. Logistics is considered to have originated in the military's need to supply themselves with arms, ammunition and rations as they moved from their base to a forward position. In ancient Greek, Roman and Byzantine empires, there were military officers with the title 'Logistikas' who were responsible for financial and supply distribution matters. The Oxford English dictionary defines logistics as: "The branch of military science having to do with procuring, maintaining and transporting material, personnel and facilities." Another dictionary definition is: "The time-related positioning of resources." As such, logistics is commonly seen as a branch of engineering which creates "people systems" rather than" machine systems."

Military Logistics

ILS Integrated Logistics Support is a discipline used in military industries to ensure an easy supportable system with a robust customer service (logistic) concept at the lowest cost and in line with (often high) reliability, availability, maintainability and other requirements as defined for the project. In military logistics, logistics officers manage how and when to move resources to the places they are needed. In military science, maintaining one's supply lines while disrupting those of the enemy is a crucial—some would say the most crucial—element of military strategy, since an armed force without resources and transportation is defenceless. The defeat of the British in the American War of Independence, and the defeat of the Axis in the African theatre of World War II, have been largely attributed to logistical failure. The historical leaders Hannibal Barca, Alexander the Great, and the Duke of Wellington are considered to have been logistical geniuses. Another field within logistics is called Medical logistics. Medical logistics is the logistics of pharmaceuticals, medical and surgical supplies, medical devices and equipment, and other products needed to support doctors, nurses, and other health and dental care providers. Because its final customers are responsible for the lives and health of their patients, medical logistics is unique in that it seeks to optimize effectiveness rather than efficiency. Medical logistics functions comprise an important part of the health care system: after staff costs, medical supplies are the single most expensive component of health care. To drive costs out of the health-care sector, medical logistics providers are adopting supply chain management theories.

This organizational chart is as follows and separated into three keys areas.

1. Medical Materiel
2. Biomedical Engineering (BMET)) or Clinical Engineering
3. Facilities Management.

These areas are managed by a qualified Director of Logistics. The Director of Logistcs educational background holds some type of accredited graduate degree (MBA or M.S.)

Introduction of Logistics Management

Logistics management is that part of the supply chain which plans, implements and controls the efficient, effective forward and reverse flow and storage of goods, services and related information between the point of origin and the point of consumption in order to meet customer & legal requirements. A professional working in the field of logistics management is called a logistician.

The Chartered Institute of Logistics & Transport (CILT) was established in the United Kingdom in 1919 and was granted the Royal Charter in 1926. The Chartered Institute is one of the professional bodies or institutions, for the logistics & transport sectors, that offers professional qualification or degree in logistics management.

Third-party Logistics

Third-party logistics involves the utilization of external organizations to execute logistics activities that have traditionally been performed within an organization itself. According to this definition, third party logistics includes any form of outsourcing of logistics activities previously performed in-house. If, for example, a company with its own warehousing facilities decides to employ external transportation, this would be an example of third party logistics. Logistics is one of the emerging business area in many countries.

Warehouse Management System and Warehouse Control System

Although there is some functionality overlap, the differences between warehouse management systems (WMS) and warehouse control systems (WCS) can be significant. To put it simply, the WMS plans a weekly activity forecast, based on such factors as statistics, trends, and so forth, whereas a WCS acts like a floor supervisor, working in real time to get the job done by the most effective means. For instance, a WMS can tell the system it's going to need five of SKU A and five of SKU B, hours in advance, but by the time it acts, other considerations may have come into play or there could be a potential logjam on a conveyor. A WCS can prevent that problem by working in real time and adapting to the situation by making a 'last-minute decision' based on current activity and operational status. Working synergistically, WMS and WCS can resolve these issues and maximize efficiency for companies that rely on the effective operation of their warehouse or distribution centre.

Business Logistics

Logistics as a business concept evolved only in the 1950s. This was mainly due to the increasing complexity of supplying one's business with materials and shipping out products in an increasingly globalized supply chain, calling for experts in the field who are called Supply Chain Logisticians. This can be defined as having the right item in the right quantity at the right time at the right place for the right price in the right condition to the right customer and is the science of process and incorporates all industry sectors. The goal of logistics work is to manage the fruition of project life cycles, supply chains and resultant efficiencies.

In business, logistics may have either internal focus (in bound logistics), or external focus (outbound logistics) covering the flow and storage of materials from point of origin to point of consumption. The main functions of a qualified logistician include inventory management, purchasing, transportation, warehousing, consultation and the organizing and planning of these activities. Logisticians combine a professional knowledge of each of these functions so that there is a coordination of resources in an organization. There are two fundamentally different forms of logistics. One optimizes a steady flow of material through a network of transport links and storage nodes. The other coordinates a sequence of resources to carry out some project.

Production Logistics

The term is used for describing logistic processes within an industry. The purpose of production logistics is to ensure that each machine and workstation is being fed with the right product in the right quantity and quality at the right point in time. The issue is not the transportation itself, but to streamline and control the flow through the value adding processes and eliminate non-value adding ones. Production logistics can be applied in existing as well as new plants. Manufacturing in an existing plant is a constantly changing process. Machines are exchanged and new ones added, which gives the opportunity to improve the production logistics system accordingly. Production logistics provides the means to achieve customer response and capital efficiency.

Production logistics is getting more and more important with the decreasing batch sizes. In many industries (e.g. mobile phone) batch size one is the short term aim. This way even a single customer demand can be fulfilled in an efficient way. Track and tracing, which is an essential part of production logistics-due to product safety and product reliability issues-is also gaining importance especially in the automotive and the medical industry.

Professional Logistician

A logistician is a professional logistics practitioner. Professional logisticians are often certified by professional associations. Some universities and academic institutions train students as logisticians, by offering undergraduate and postgraduate programmes.

Liquid Logistics

Liquid Logistics is a special category of logistics that relates to liquid products, and is used extensively in the "Supply Chain for Liquids" discipline. Standard logistics techniques are generally used for discrete or unit products. Liquid products have logistics characteristics that distinguish them from discrete products. Some of the major characteristics of liquid products that impact their logistics handling are:

- Liquids flowing from a higher level to a lower level provide the ability to move the liquids without mechanical propulsion or manual intervention.
- Liquids' adaptation to the shape of the container they are in provides a great deal of flexibility in the design of storage systems and the use of "dead" space for storage.
- The level of a liquid as it has settled in a tank may be used to automatically and continuously know the quantity of liquid in the tank.
- Liquids provide indications through changes in their characteristics that may be sensed and translated into measures of the quality of the liquid.
- Many security and safety risks are significantly reduced or eliminated using liquid logistics techniques. Tools such as liquid level sensors and flow meters can be useful in reducing security risk by providing directly, near real-time and accurate measurements of product's movement and balance along the supply-chain flow. The safety risk is reducing as product movement through the process of supply stream is independent and controlled.
- Liquids may in some cases be "processed" well downstream from the original production facility and thus offer the opportunity for improved efficiencies throughout the supply stream together with more flexibility as to the nature of the product at the point of final usage.

Each of these points represents a differentiation of liquid logistics from logistics techniques used for discrete items. When properly planned for and handled these points of differentiation may lead to business advantages for companies that produce, process, move, or use liquid products.

Logistic Engineering

Logistics Engineering is the scientific organization of the purchase, transport, storage, distribution, and warehousing of materials and finished goods. Logistics is generally a Cost centre service activity, but provides value via improved efficiency and customer satisfaction. It can quickly lose that value if the customer becomes dissatisfied. The end customer can include another process or work centre inside of the manufacturing facility, a warehouse where items are stocked or the final customer who will use the product.

Another much more popular derivative and a complete usage of the logistic term which has appeared in recent years is the supply chain. The supply chain also looks at an efficient chaining of the supply/purchase and distribution sides of an organisation. While Logistics looks at single echelons with the immediate supply and distribution linked up, supply chain looks at multiple echelons/stages, right from procurement of the raw materials to the final distribution of finished goods up to the customer. It is based on the basic premise that the supply and distribution activities if integrated with the manufacturing/logistic activities, can result in better profitability for the organisation. The local minima of total cost of the manufacturing operation is getting replaced by the global minima of total cost of the whole chain, resulting in better profitability for the chain members and hence lower costs for the products.

"Logistics Engineering" as a discipline is also a very important aspect of systems engineering that includes reliability engineering. It is the science and process whereby reliability, maintainability, and availability are designed into products or systems. It includes the supply and physical distribution considerations above as well as more fundamental engineering considerations. For example, if we want to produce a system that is 95% reliable (or improve a system to achieve 95% reliability), a logistics engineer understands that total system reliability can be no greater than the least reliable subsystem or component. Therefore our logistics engineer must consider the reliability of all sub-components or subsystems and modify system design accordingly. If a subsystem is only 50% reliable, one can concentrate on improving the reliability of that subsystem, design in multiple subsystems in parallel (5 in this case would achieve approximately 97% reliability of that subsystem), purchase and store spare subsystems for rapid change out, establish repair capability that would get a failed subsystem back in operation in the required amount of time, and/or choose any combination of those approaches to achieve the optimal cost vs. reliability solution. Then the engineer moves onto the next subsystem.

Logistics Engineers work with complex mathematical models that consider elements such as Mean Time Between Failures (MTBF), Mean Time To Failure (MTTF), Mean Time to Repair (MTTR), Failure Mode and Effects Analysis (FMEA), statistical distributions, queueing theory, and a host of other considerations. Obviously, logistics engineering is a complex science that considers tradeoffs in component/system design, repair capability, training, spares inventory, demand history, storage and distribution points, transportation methods, etc., to ensure the "thing" is where it's needed, when it's needed, and operating the way it's needed all at an acceptable cost.

Performance Metrics

Different performance measures are used to examine the efficiency of an organisation's logistics. The most popular and widely used performance measure is the landed cost. The landed cost is the total cost of purchasing, transporting, warehousing and distributing raw materials, semi-finished and finished goods.

Another performance measure equally important is the end customer fill rate. It is the percentage of customer demand which is satisfied immediately off-the-shelf (from on-site inventory). An alternative to fill rate, is system availability.

In recent years, the United States Department of Defence (DoD) has advocated the use of Performance Based Logistics (PBL) contracts to manage costs for support of weapon systems.

Logistics Management

The term Logistics Management is that part of Supply Chain Management that plans, implements, and controls the efficient, effective, forward, and reverse flow and storage of goods, services, and related information between the point of origin and the point of consumption in order to meet customers' requirements.

Logistics Management Software

Software is used for logistics automation which helps the supply chain industry in automating the work flow as well as management of the system. There are very few generalized software available in the new market in the said topology. This is because there is no rule to generalize the system as well as work flow even though the practice is more or less the same. Most of the commercial companies do use one or the other of the custom solutions. But there are various software solutions that are being used within the departments of logistics. There are a few departments in Logistics, namely: Conventional Department, Container Department, Warehouse, Marine Engineering, Heavy Haulage, etc.

Software used in these departments:

- Conventional department : CVT software/CTMS software
- Container Trucking: CTMS software
- Warehouse : WMS/WCS.

Improving Effectiveness of Logistics Management:

1. Logistical Network
2. Information
3. Transportation
4. Sound Inventory Management
5. Warehousing, Materials Handling & Packaging.

Logistics Officer

A Logistics Officer, known in the past as a Supply Officer, is a member of an armed force responsible for overseeing the supplying of an army, both at home and abroad. Logistics Officers can be stationary on military bases or deployed as an active part of a field army, air wing, or naval force. The responsibilities of Logistics Officers vary, depending on where they are deployed and what tasks they are assigned. In addition, different countries, have different roles for Logistics Officers. The main role of these officers remains the same regardless of where they are stationed; to ensure that the fighting force is supplied with enough food, water, fuel and ammunition to complete the task at hand.

Canada

In Canada, Logistic officers work in five main disciplines, Supply chain, Management, Transportation, Human resource management, Finance and food services. Their main objective is to ensure that all Canadian military operations and training exercises are properly supported.

United States

In the United States, the work of the logistics officer includes providing Strategic, Operational, or Tactical level logistical support and managing the overall logistic processes in support of mission objectives; leveraging existing networks and expanding others; anticipating mission needs and operational requirements and offering alternatives and advice; and evaluating, redesigning and implementing logistics processes for mission support.

United Kingdom

In the United Kingdom, a Logistics Officer in the Royal Air Force is colloquially known as a 'Stacker' (which is an abbreviation of either

'Blanket Stacker' or 'Duvet Stacker'). This is a reference to the traditionally-held perception of the role of the Logistics Officer from the point of view of an Engineering Officer.

Australia

In Australia each of the three independent Services of the Australian Defence Force (ADF) have different definitions for a 'Logistics Officer'. Logistics Officers lead and coordinate planning and execution of the operations support components of the military effects which include the administrative (1) and logistics (4) functions, as well as major enabling support in the capability support dimension of force generation.

Royal Australian Navy (RAN) logisticians are called a Supply Officer, the commissioned element of the Supply Branch. RAN "Loggies" conduct the non-technical component of 1/4 support effects.

Australian Army logisticians are commissioned officers in the Australian Regular Army (ARA) or Army Reserve (ARES) normally drawn from the Ordnance (RAAOC), Transport (RACT), Catering (RAACC), Engineer (RAE), Electrical and Mechanical Engineer (RAEME), or Medical (RAAMC) corps. Army defines engineering as a subset of logistics.

Royal Australian Air Force (RAAF) logisticians are called Logistics Officers (LOG), the commissioned element of the Logistics Employment Group (LEG). As in the RAF they are generally focused on the maintenance of the supply chain (in both Joint and Air environments), equipment governance, catering, movements and transport, the non-technical logistics disciplines. Unlike the Army RAAF "Loggies" work in parallel to RAAF engineers (Aeronautical [AERO], both Ground and Air Electrical [ELECTR], Armament [ARM] and Airfield [AFENG]) who comrise the specialist technical engineering and maintenance components of the RAAF integrated logistics workforce. LOG and ENG personnel (except AFENG) are managed by Logistics Branch-Air Force within Air Force Headquarters (AFHQ). AFENG are managed by the RAAF's Headquarters Combat Support Group. Additionally unlike their Navy and Army counterparts RAAF "Loggies" don't manage administrative, personnel or finance functions which are provided by Administrative Officers (ADMIN) who perform the 1 shop functions of the 1/4 support environment leaving "Loggies" to perform the 4 shop function.

Military supply chain management is a cross-functional approach to procuring, producing and delivering products and services. The broad management scope includes sub-suppliers, suppliers, internal information and funds flow.

Supply

A supply is the procurement, distribution, maintenance while in storage and salvage of supplies, including the determination of kind and quantity of supplies. The producer phase of a military supply extends from determination of procurement schedules to acceptance of finished supplies by the military services. The consumer phase of a military supply extends from receipt of finished supplies by the military services through issue for use or consumption.

Supply Chain

The supply chain is the linked activities associated with providing material from a raw material stage to an end user as a finished good. Supply control is the process by which an item of supply is controlled within the supply system, including requisitioning, receipt, storage, stock control, shipment, disposition, identification, and accounting. The supply point is a location where supplies, services and materiels are located and issued. These locations are temporary and mobile, normally being occupied for up to 72 hours.

Logistics

Military logistics is the science of planning and carrying out the movement and maintenance of armed forces. In its most comprehensive sense, those aspects of military operations that deal with: a. design and development, acquisition, storage, movement, distribution, maintenance, evacuation, and disposition of material; b. movement, evacuation, and hospitalization of personnel; c. acquisition or construction, maintenance, operation and disposition of facilities; and d. acquisition or furnishing of services.

Military Logistics

Military logistics is the art and science of planning and carrying out the movement and maintenance of military forces. In its most comprehensive sense, it is those aspects or military operations that deal with:

- Design, development, acquisition, storage, distribution, maintenance, evacuation, and disposition of materiel.
- Transport of personnel.
- Acquisition or construction, maintenance, operation, and disposition of facilities.
- Acquisition or furnishing of services.
- Medical and health service support.

The word "logistics" is derived from the Greek adjective logistikos meaning "skilled in calculating". The first administrative use of the word was in Roman and Byzantine times when there was a military administrative official with the title Logista. At that time, the word apparently implied a skill involved in mathematical computations.

Research indicates that its first use in relation to an organized military administrative science was by the Swiss writer, Antoine-Henri Jomini, who, in 1838, devised a theory of war on the trinity of strategy, ground tactics, and logistics. The French still use the words logistique and loger with the meaning "to quarter".

The military activity known as logistics probably is as old as war itself. In the early history of man when the first wars were fought, each man had to find his own food, stones, and knotted clubs. Each warrior was responsible for foraging for his own food and firewood.

Not until later, when fighters joined as groups and fighting groups became larger, was there any basis for designating certain men to specialize in providing food and weapons to the combatants. The men who provided support to the fighters constituted the first logistics organization. By the seventeenth century, the French were using a magazine system to keep a network of frontier towns supplied for sieges and to provide for campaigns beyond their borders. The American Civil War saw the introduction of railways for transport of personnel, supplies and heavy field pieces.

During the Seven Weeks War, railways enabled the swift mobilization of the Prussian Army, but the problem of moving supplies from the end of rail lines to units at the front resulted in nearly 18,000 tons trapped on trains unable to be unloaded to ground transport. The Prussian use of railways during the Franco-Prussian War is often cited as a prime example of logistic modernizations, but the advantages of maneuver were often gained by abandoning supply lines that became hopelessly congested with rear-area traffic.

During World War I, unrestricted submarine warfare had a significant impact on the ability of Britain's allies to keep shipping lanes open, while the great size of the German Army proved too much for its railways to support except while immobilized in trench warfare.

Modern Military Logistics

Logistics, occasionally referred to as "combat service support", must address highly uncertain conditions. While perfect forecasts are rarely possible (this is also true in most sciences) forecasts models can reduce uncertainty about what supplies or services will be needed, where and when they will be needed, or the best way to provide them.

Ultimately, responsible officials must make judgments on these matters, sometimes using intuition and scientifically weighing alternatives as the situation requires and permits. Their judgments must be based not only upon professional knowledge of the numerous aspects of logistics itself but also upon an understanding of the interplay of closely related military considerations such as strategy, tactics, intelligence, training, personnel, and finance.

However, case studies have shown that more quantitative, statistical analysis are often a significant improvement on human judgment. One such recent example is the use of Applied Information Economics by the Office of Naval Research and the Marine Corps for forecasting bulk fuel requirements for the battlefield.

In major military conflicts, logistics matters are often crucial in deciding the overall outcome of wars. For instance, tonnage war-the bulk sinking of cargo ships-was a crucial factor in World War II.

The successful Allied anti-submarine campaign and the failure of the German Navy to sink enough cargo in the Second Battle of the Atlantic allowed Britain to stay in the war and establish the second front against the Nazis; by contrast, the successful U.S. submarine campaign against Japanese maritime shipping across Asian waters effectively crippled its economy and its military production capabilities.

More generally, protecting one's own supply lines and attacking those of an enemy is a fundamental military strategy; an example of this as a purely logistical campaign for the military means of implementing strategic policy was the Berlin Airlift.

Military logistics has pioneered a number of techniques that have since become widely deployed in the commercial world. Operations research grew out of WWII military logistics efforts. Likewise, military logistics borrows from methods first introduced to the commercial world.

Distance in Military Affairs

Geographic distance is a key factor in military affairs. The shorter the distance, the greater the ease with which force can be brought to bear upon an opponent.

This is because it is easier to undertake the supply of logistics to a force on the ground as well as engage in bombardment. The continued importance of distance has been subject to academic and political debate, and has influenced US-American overseas basing policy.

Support for Distance in Decline

The view that distance in military affairs was witnessing decreased importance was expressed by Kenneth Boulding in the 1960s. He examined the importance of geographic distance and forward basing for the projection of military power and argued that there was a 20th century revolution undermining the importance of distance. He claimed that there was "a very substantial diminution in the cost of transportation of organized violence of all kinds, especially of organized armed forces" and "an enormous increase in the range of the deadly projectile." A more recent supporter of distance in decline was Doug Bandow who said that technology had reduced the value of proximity.

This view was shared by the Bush Administration which used it as partial justification for the withdrawal of forces from overseas bases in Europe and Asia. In 2004, President George W. Bush announced that US armed forces had become "better able to strike anywhere in the world over great distances". Until put on hold by Defence Secretary Robert M. Gates in late 2007, it was planned that 60–70,000 American troops would be returned to the US by 2014.

Support for the Continued Importance of Distance

There is a counterargument that distance has remained of continued importance in military affairs. The claim is that it affects both logistics and the capacity to attack the opponent from afar.

Reverse Logistics

Reverse logistics stands for all operations related to the reuse of products and materials. It is "the process of planning, implementing, and controlling the efficient, cost effective flow of raw materials, in-process inventory, finished goods and related information from the point of consumption to the point of origin for the purpose of recapturing value or proper disposal. More precisely, reverse logistics is the process of moving goods from their typical final destination for the purpose of capturing value, or proper disposal. Re-manufacturing and refurbishing activities also may be included in the definition of reverse logistics." The reverse logistics process includes the management and the sale of surplus as well as returned equipment and machines from the hardware leasing business. Normally, logistics deal with events that bring the product towards the customer. In the case of reverse, the resource goes at least one step back in the supply chain. For instance, goods move from the customer to the distributor or to the manufacturer.

Business Implications

In today's marketplace, many retailers treat merchandise returns as individual, disjointed transactions. "The challenge for retailers and vendors is to process returns at a proficiency level that allows quick, efficient and cost-effective collection and return of merchandise. Customer requirements facilitate demand for a high standard of service that includes accuracy and timeliness. It's the logistic company's responsibility to shorten the link from return origination to the time of resell." By following returns management best practices, retailers can achieve a returns process that addresses both the operational and customer retention issues associated with merchandise returns.

Further, because of the connection between reverse logistics and customer retention, it has become a key component within Service Lifecycle Management (SLM), a business strategy aimed at retaining customers by bundling even more coordination of a company's services data together to achieve greater efficiency in its operations. Reverse logistics is more than just returns management, it is "activities related to returns avoidance, gatekeeping, disposal and all other after-market supply chain issues".

Returns Management: increasingly being recognized as affecting competitive positioning – provides an important link between marketing and logistics. The broad nature of its cross-functional impact suggests that firms would benefit by improving internal integration efforts. In particular, a firm's ability to react to and plan for the influence of external factors on the returns management process is improved by such internal integration. Third-party logistics providers see that up to 7% of an enterprise's gross sales are captured by return costs. Almost all reverse logistics contracts are customized to fit the size and type of company contracting. The 3PL's themselves realize 12% to 15% profits on this business.

Return of Unsold Goods

In certain industries, goods are distributed to downstream members in the supply chain with the understanding that the goods may be returned for credit if they are not sold. Newspapers and magazines serve as examples. This acts as an incentive for downstream members to carry more stock, because the risk of obsolescence is borne by the upstream supply chain members. However, there is also a distinct risk attached to this logistics concept. The downstream member in the supply chain might exploit the situation by ordering more stock than is required and returning large volumes. In this way, the downstream partner is able to offer high level of service without carrying the risks associated with large inventories. The supplier effectively finances the inventory for the downstream member. It is therefore important to analyze customers' account for hidden cost.

OPERATIONS MANAGEMENT

Basically, operations management is an area of business concerned with the production of goods and services, and involves the responsibility of ensuring that business operations are efficient in terms of using as little resource asaverts inputs (in the forms of materials, labour and energy) into outputs (in the form of goods and services). Operations traditionally refers to the production of goods and services separately, although the distinction between these two main types of operations is increasingly difficult to make as manufacturers tend to merge product and service offerings. More generally, Operations Management aims to increase the content of value-added activities in any given process. Fundamentally, these value-adding creative activities should be aligned with market opportunity for optimal enterprise performance.

According to the U.S. Department of Education, Operations Management [is the field concerned with managing and directing] the physical and/or technical functions of a firm or organization, particularly those relating to development, production, and manufacturing. [Operations Management programmes typically include] instruction in principles of general management, manufacturing and production systems, plant management, equipment maintenance management, production control, industrial labor relations and skilled trades supervision, strategic manufacturing policy, systems analysis, productivity analysis and cost control, and materials planning.

The origins of operations management can be traced back through cultural changes of the 18th, 19th, and 20th centuries, including the Industrial Revolution, the development of interchangeable manufacture, the Waltham-Lowell system, the American system of manufacturing, scientific management, the development of assembly line practice and mass production, and the Toyota Production System. Combined, these ideas allowed for the standardization and continuous improvement of production processes. Key features of these early production systems were the departure from skilled craftsmen to a more thorough division of labor and the transfer of knowledge from within the minds of skilled, experienced workers into the equipment, documentation, and systems. There are scores of people who can be viewed as thought leaders whose life's work laid the foundations for operations management (only some of which have name recognition among the general population). A very cursory list would include (in approximate chronological order) Adam Smith, Jean-Baptiste Vaquette de Gribeauval, Louis de Tousard, Honore Blanc, Eli Whitney, John H. Hall, Simeon North, Frederick Winslow Taylor, Henry Gantt, Henry Ford, Sakichi Toyoda, Alfred Sloan, Frank and Lillian Gilbreth, Tex Thornton and his Whiz Kids team, and W. Edwards Deming and the developers of the Toyota Production System (Taiichi Ohno, Shigeo Shingo, Eiji Toyoda, Kiichiro Toyoda, and others).

Whereas some influences place primary importance on the equipment and too often viewed people as recalcitrant impediments to systems (e.g., Taylor and Ford), over time the need to view production operations as sociotechnical systems, duly considering both humans and machines, was increasingly appreciated and addressed.

Operations research as a sub-discipline gained prominence during World War II, when mathematicians applied analytical tools to optimize operational questions, initially with a military context, and later also within general operations.

Historically, the body of knowledge stemming from industrial engineering formed the basis of the first MBA programmes, and is central to operations management as used across diverse business sectors, industry, consulting and non-profit organizations.

The following organizations support and promote operations management:

- The Association for Operations Management (APICS) which supports the Production and Inventory Management Journal
- European Operations Management Association (EurOMA) which supports the International Journal of Operations & Production Management
- Production and Operations Management Society (POMS) which supports the journal: Production and Operations Management
- Institute for Operations Research and the Management Sciences (INFORMS)
- Institute of Operations Management (UK)
- The Association of Technology, Management, and Applied Engineering (ATMAE).

Business Process Mapping

Business process mapping refers to activities involved in defining exactly what a business entity does, who is responsible, to what standard a process should be completed and how the success of a business process can be determined. Once this is done, there can be no uncertainty as to the requirements of every internal business process. A business process illustration is produced. The first step in gaining control over an organization is to know and understand the basic processes (Deming, 1982; Juran,

1988; Taylor, 1911). ISO 9001 requires a business entity to follow a process approach when managing its business, and to this end creating business process maps will assist. The entity can then work towards ensuring its processes are effective (the right process is followed the first time), and efficient (continually improved to ensure processes use the least amount of resources).

The first structured method for documenting process flow, the flow process chart, was introduced by Frank Gilbreth to members of ASME in 1921 as the presentation "Process Charts—First Steps in Finding the One Best Way". Gilbreth's tools quickly found their way into industrial engineering curricula. In the early 1930s, an industrial engineer, Allan H. Mogensen began training business people in the use of some of the tools of industrial engineering at his Work Simplification Conferences in Lake Placid, New York.

A 1944 graduate of Mogensen's class, Art Spinanger, took the tools back to Procter and Gamble where he developed their Deliberate Methods Change Programme. Another 1944 graduate, Ben S. Graham, Director of Formcraft Engineering at Standard Register Corporation, adapted the flow process chart to information processing with his development of the multi-flow process chart to display multiple documents and their relationships. In 1947, ASME adopted a symbol set derived from Gilbreth's original work as the ASME Standard for Process Charts.

Process mapping has in recent years developed due to software tools that can attach metadata to activities, drivers and triggers to provide a more complete understanding of processes. For example, data elements, KPIs, Times, Volumes, documents, files, databases, compliance applying to an activity can be attached to improve understanding and achieve several business goals simultaneously. Valuable analysis might include identification of duplicated use of data elements, proof or lack of proof of compliance.

The developments mean that process mapping is no longer two-dimensional but multi-dimensional; capable of achieving several important business goals:

- Business process re-engineering
- Regulatory compliance
- Activity analysis
- Service level agreement (SLA) role clarity (RACI)
- Simulation.

Making process maps available using a web-browser only means that communication to, and access by stakeholders, is achievable-thus improving compliance, training and end-to end process understanding. Legislation such as "The Sarbanes-Oxley Act" (also known as SOX) has increased the requirements for improved process understanding and visibility of compliance issues. Quality improvement practitioners have noted that various graphical descriptions of processes can be useful. These include: detailed flow-charts, work flow diagrams and value stream maps. Each map is helpful depending on the process questions and theories being considered.

In these situations process map implies the use of process flow and the current understanding of the causal structure. The purpose of these process maps is to document and stimulate the understanding of y=f(x); where the "y" represents the outputs of a process and x represents the various inputs. These inputs would include sources of noise otherwise described as nuisance variables.

Six Sigma practictioners use the term Business Process Architecture to describe the mapping of business processes as series of cross-functional flowcharts. Under this school of thought, each flowchart is of a certain level (between 0 and 4) based on the amount of detail the flowchart contains. A level 0 flowchart represents the least amount of detail, and usually contains one or two steps, at most. A level 4 flowchart represents the most amount of detail, and can include hundreds of steps. At this level every task, however minor, is represented.

Business Process Modeling

Business process modeling (BPM) in systems engineering and software engineering is the activity of representing processes of an enterprise, so that the current process may be analyzed and improved. BPM is typically performed by business analysts and managers who are seeking to improve process efficiency and quality. The process improvements identified by BPM may or may not require Information Technology involvement, although that is a common driver for the need to model a business process, by creating a process master.

Change management programmes are typically involved to put the improved business processes into practice. With advances in technology from large platform vendors, the vision of BPM models becoming fully executable (and capable of simulations and round-trip engineering) is coming closer to reality every day.

Business process modeling plays an important role in the business process management (BPM) discipline. Since both business process modeling and business process management share the same abbreviation (BPM), these activities are sometimes confused with each other.

BPM addresses the process aspects of a business architecture, leading to an all encompassing enterprise architecture. The relationships of business processes in the context of the rest of the enterprise systems (e.g., data architecture, organizational structure, strategies, etc.) create greater capabilities when analyzing and planning enterprise changes. For example, during a corporate merger it is important to understand the processes of both companies in detail so that management can correctly and efficiently identify and eliminate redundancies in operations

The graphical representation of business process information has proven effective for presenting it to business stakeholders, including business analysts and system developers. Visual modeling languages used to represent business processes include Business Process Modeling Notation (BPMN) and the Unified Modeling Language (UML).

Business process modeling has always been a key aspect of business process reengineering (BPR) and continuous improvement approaches, such as Six Sigma. For routine business activities, BPM tools such as Provision, Intalio, K2 [blackpearl], Axway, Lombardi, Holosofx, Holocentric Modeler and TIBCO are used in order to represent a business process, to run a simulation of the process and for communication purposes. For innovative, adaptive, collaborative human work the techniques of human interaction management are required.

Techniques to model business process such as the flow chart, functional flow block diagram, control flow diagram, Gantt chart, PERT diagram, and IDEF have emerged since the beginning of the 20th century. The Gantt chart were among the first to arrive around 1900, the flow charts in the 1920s, Functional Flow Block Diagram and PERT in the 1950s, Data Flow Diagrams and IDEF in the 1970s. Among the modern methods are Unified Modeling Language and Business Process Modeling Notation. Still these represent just a fraction of the methodologies used over the years to document business processes.

The term "business process modeling" itself was coined in the 1960s in the field of systems engineering by S. Williams in his 1967 article "Business Process Modeling Improves Administrative Control". His idea was that techniques for obtaining a better understanding of physical control systems could be used in a similar way for business processes. It took until the 1990s before the term became popular.

In the 1990s the term "process" became a new productivity paradigm. Companies were encouraged to think in processes instead of functions and procedures. Process thinking looks at the chain of events in the company from purchase to supply, from order retrieval to sales etc.

The traditional modeling tools were developed to picture time and costs, while modern methods focus on cross-function activities. These cross-functional activities have increased severely in number and importance due to the growth of complexity and dependencies. New methodologies such as business process redesign, business process innovation, business process management, integrated business planning among others all "aiming at improving processes across the traditional functions that comprise a company".

In the field of software engineering the term "business process modeling" opposed the common software process modeling, aiming to focus more on the state of the practice during software development. In that time early 1990s all existing and new modeling techniques to picture business processes were considered and called "business process modeling languages."

In the Object Oriented approach, it was considered to be an essential step in the specification of Business Application Systems. Business process modeling became the base of new methodologies, that for example also supported data collection, data flow analysis, process flow diagrams and reporting facilities. Around 1995 the first visually oriented tools for business process modeling and implementation were being presented.

BPM Topics

Business Model

A business model is a framework for creating economic, social, and/or other forms of value. The term' business model' is thus used for a broad range of informal and formal descriptions to represent core aspects of a business, including purpose, offerings, strategies, infrastructure, organizational structures, trading practices, and operational processes and policies.

In the most basic sense, a business model is the method of doing business by which a company can sustain itself. That is, generate revenue. The business model spells-out how a company makes money by specifying where it is positioned in the value chain.

Business Process

A business process is a collection of related, structured activities or tasks that produce a specific service or product (serve a particular goal) for a particular customer or customers. There are three main types of business processes:

1. Management processes, the processes that govern the operation of a system. Typical management processes include "Corporate Governance" and "Strategic Management".

2. Operational processes, processes that constitute the core business and create the primary value stream. Typical operational processes are Purchasing, Manufacturing, Marketing, and Sales.
3. Supporting processes, which support the core processes. Examples include Accounting, Recruitment, Technical support.

A business process can be decomposed into several sub-processes, which have their own attributes, but also contribute to achieving the goal of the super-process. The analysis of business processes typically includes the mapping of processes and sub-processes down to activity level. A business process model is a model of one or more business processes, and defines the ways in which operations are carried out to accomplish the intended objectives of an organization. Such a model remains an abstraction and depends on the intended use of the model. It can describe the workflow or the integration between business processes. It can be constructed in multiple levels.

A workflow is a depiction of a sequence of operations, declared as work of a person, work of a simple or complex mechanism, work of a group of persons, work of an organization of staff, or machines.

Workflow may be seen as any abstraction of real work, segregated in workshare, work split or whatever types of ordering. For control purposes, workflow may be a view on real work under a chosen aspect.

Business Process Modeling Tools

Business process modeling tools provide business users with the ability to model their business processes, implement and execute those models, and refine the models based on as-executed data. As a result, business process modeling tools can provide transparency into business processes, as well as the centralization of corporate business process models and execution metrics.

Modeling and Simulation

Modeling and simulation functionality allows for pre-execution "what-if" modeling and simulation. Post-execution optimization is available based on the analysis of actual as-performed metrics.

Business process modeling diagrams are:

- Use case diagrams created by Ivar Jacobson, 1992. Currently integrated in UML
- Activity diagrams, also currently adopted by UML.

Some business process modeling techniques are:

- Business Process Modeling Notation (BPMN)
- Cognition enhanced Natural language Information Analysis Method (CogNIAM)
- Extended Business Modeling Language (xBML)
- Event-driven process chain (EPC)
- ICAM DEFinition (IDEF0)
- Unified Modeling Language (UML), extensions for business process such as Eriksson-Penker's.

Programming Languages Tools for BPM

BPM suite software provides programming interfaces (web services, application programme interfaces (APIs)) which allow enterprise applications to be built to leverage the BPM engine.

Programming languages that are being introduced for BPM include:

- Architecture of Integrated Information Systems (ARIS) supports EPC,
- Business Process Execution Language (BPEL),
- Web Services Choreography Description Language (WS-CDL).
- XML Process Definition Language (XPDL),
- Java Process Definition Language (JBPM).

Other technologies related to business process modeling include model-driven architecture and service-oriented architecture.

Related Topics

Business Reference Model

A business reference model is a reference model, concentrating on the functional and organizational aspects of an enterprise, service organization or government agency. In general a reference model is a model of something that embodies the basic goal or idea of something and can then be looked at as a reference for various purposes. A business reference model is a means to describe the business operations of an organization, independent of the organizational structure that perform them. Other types of business reference model can also depict the relationship between the business processes, business functions, and the business area's business reference model. These reference models can be constructed in layers, and offer a foundation for the analysis of service components, technology, data, and performance. The most familiar business reference model is the Business Reference Model of the US Federal Government. That model is a function-driven framework for describing the business operations of the Federal Government independent of the agencies that perform them.

The Business Reference Model provides an organized, hierarchical construct for describing the day-to-day business operations of the Federal government. While many models exist for describing organizations-organizational charts, location maps, etc.-this model presents the business using a functionally driven approach.

Business Process Integration

A business model, which may be considered an elaboration of a business process model, typically shows business data and business organizations as well as business processes. By showing business processes and their information flows a business model allows business stakeholders to define, understand, and validate their business enterprise. The data model part of the business model shows how business information is stored, which is useful for developing software code.

Usually a business model is created after conducting an interview, which is part of the business analysis process. The interview consists of a facilitator asking a series of questions to extract information about the subject business process. The interviewer is referred to as a facilitator to emphasize that it is the participants, not the facilitator, who provide the business process information.

Although the facilitator should have some knowledge of the subject business process, but this is not as important as her mastery of a pragmatic and rigorous method interviewing business experts. The method is important because for most enterprises a team of facilitators is needed to collect information across the enterprise, and the findings of all the interviewers must be compiled and integrated once completed.

Business models are developed as defining either the current state of the process, in which case the final product is called the "as is" snapshot model, or a concept of what the process should become, resulting in a "to be" model.

By comparing and contrasting "as is" and "to be" models the business analysts can determine if the existing business processes and information systems are sound and only need minor modifications, or if reengineering is required to correct problems or improve efficiency. Consequently, business process modeling and subsequent analysis can be used to fundamentally reshape the way an enterprise conducts its operations.

Business Process Reengineering

Business process reengineering (BPR) is an approach aiming at improvements by means of elevating efficiency and effectiveness of the processes that exist within and across organizations. The key to business process reengineering is for organizations to look at their business processes from a "clean slate" perspective and determine how they can best construct these processes to improve how they conduct business.

Business process reengineering (BPR) began as a private sector technique to help organizations fundamentally rethink how they do their work in order to dramatically improve customer service, cut operational costs, and become world-class competitors. A key stimulus for reengineering has been the continuing development and deployment of sophisticated information systems and networks. Leading organizations are becoming bolder in using this technology to support innovative business processes, rather than refining current ways of doing work.

Business Process Management

Business process management is a field of management focused on aligning organizations with the wants and needs of clients. It is a holistic management approach that promotes business effectiveness and efficiency while striving for innovation, flexibility and integration with technology. As organizations strive for attainment of their objectives, business process management attempts to continuously improve processes-the process to define, measure and improve your processes – a "process optimization" process.

Lean Manufacturing

Lean manufacturing or lean productions, which is often known simply as "Lean", is a production practice that considers the expenditure of resources for any goal other than the creation of value for the end customer to be wasteful, and thus a target for elimination. Working from the perspective of the customer who consumes a product or service, "value" is defined as any action or process that a customer would be willing to pay for. Basically, lean is centred on preserving value with less work. Lean manufacturing is a generic process management philosophy derived mostly from the Toyota Production System (TPS) (hence the term Toyotism is also prevalent) and identified as "Lean" only in the 1990s. It is renowned for its focus on reduction of the original Toyota seven wastes to improve overall customer value, but there are varying perspectives on how this is best achieved. The steady growth of Toyota, from a small company to the world's largest automaker, has focused attention on how it has achieved this.

Lean manufacturing is a variation on the theme of efficiency based on optimizing flow; it is a present-day instance of the recurring theme in human history toward increasing efficiency, decreasing waste, and using empirical methods to decide what matters, rather than uncritically accepting pre-existing ideas. As such, it is a chapter in the larger narrative that also includes such ideas as the folk wisdom of thrift, time and motion study, Taylorism, the Efficiency Movement, and Fordism. Lean manufacturing is often seen as a more refined version of earlier efficiency efforts, building upon the work of earlier leaders such as Taylor or Ford, and learning from their mistakes.

Lean principles come from the Japanese manufacturing industry. The term was first coined by Bob Hartman in a Fall 1988 article, "Triumph of the Lean Production System," published in the Sloan Management Review and based on his master's thesis at the MIT Sloan School of Management.

Krafcik had been a quality engineer in the Toyota-GM NUMMI joint venture in California before coming to MIT for MBA studies. Krafcik's research was continued by the International Motor Vehicle Programme (IMVP) at MIT, which produced the international best-seller book co-authored by James Womack, Daniel Jones, and Daniel Roos called The Machine That Changed the World. A complete historical account of the IMVP and how the term "lean" was coined is given by Holweg (2007).

For many, Lean is the set of "tools" that assist in the identification and steady elimination of waste (muda). As waste is eliminated quality improves while production time and cost are reduced. Examples of such "tools" are Value Stream Mapping, Five S, Kanban (pull systems), and poka-yoke (error-proofing). There is a second approach to Lean Manufacturing, which is promoted by Toyota, in which the focus is upon improving the "flow" or smoothness of work, thereby steadily eliminating mura ("unevenness") through the system and not upon 'waste reduction' per se. Techniques to improve flow include production leveling, "pull" production (by means of kanban) and the Heijunka box. This is a fundamentally different approach to most improvement methodologies which may partially account for its lack of popularity.

The difference between these two approaches is not the goal itself, but rather the prime approach to achieving it. The implementation of smooth flow exposes quality problems that already existed, and thus waste reduction naturally happens as a consequence. The advantage claimed for this approach is that it naturally takes a system-wide perspective, whereas a waste focus sometimes wrongly assumes this perspective. Both Lean and TPS can be seen as a loosely connected set of potentially competing principles whose goal is cost reduction by the elimination of waste. These principles include: Pull processing, Perfect first-time quality, Waste minimization, Continuous improvement, Flexibility, Building and maintaining a long term relationship with suppliers, Autonomation, Load leveling and Production flow and Visual control.

The disconnected nature of some of these principles perhaps springs from the fact that the TPS has grown pragmatically since 1948 as it responded to the problems it saw within its own production facilities. Thus what one sees today is the result of a 'need' driven learning to improve where each step has built on previous ideas and not something based upon a theoretical framework. Toyota's view is that the main method of Lean is not the tools, but the reduction of three types of waste: muda ("non-value-adding work"), muri ("overburden"), and mura ("unevenness"), to expose problems systematically and to use the tools where the ideal cannot be achieved. From this perspective, the tools are workarounds adapted to different situations, which explains any apparent incoherence of the principles above.

Also known as the flexible mass production, the TPS has two pillar concepts: Just-in-time (JIT) or "flow", and "autonomation" (smart automation). Adherents of the Toyota approach would say that the smooth flowing delivery of value achieves all the other improvements as side-effects. If production flows perfectly then there is no inventory; if customer valued features are the only ones produced, then product design is simplified and effort is only expended on features the customer values. The other of the two TPS pillars is the very human aspect of autonomation, whereby automation is achieved with a human touch. The "human touch" here meaning to automate so that the machines/systems are designed to aid humans in focusing on what the humans do best. This aims, for example, to give the machines enough intelligence to recognize when they are working abnormally and flag this for human attention. Thus, in this case, humans would not have to monitor normal production and only have to focus on abnormal, or fault, conditions.

Lean implementation is therefore focused on getting the right things to the right place at the right time in the right quantity to achieve perfect work flow, while minimizing waste and being flexible and able to change. These concepts of flexibility and change are principally required to allow production leveling, using tools like SMED, but have their analogues in other processes such as research and development (R&D). The flexibility and ability to change are within bounds and not open-ended, and therefore often not expensive capability requirements. More importantly, all of these concepts have to be understood, appreciated, and embraced by the actual employees who build the products and therefore own the processes that deliver the value. The cultural and managerial aspects of Lean are possibly more important than the actual tools or methodologies of production itself. There are many examples of Lean tool implementation without sustained benefit, and these are often blamed on weak understanding of Lean throughout the whole organization. Lean aims to make the work simple enough to understand, do and manage. To achieve these three goals at once there is a belief held by some that Toyota's mentoring process (loosely called Senpai and Kohai), is one of the best ways to foster Lean Thinking up and down the organizational structure. This is the process undertaken by Toyota as it helps its suppliers improve their own production.

The closest equivalent to Toyota's mentoring process is the concept of "Lean Sensei", which encourages companies, organizations, and teams to seek outside, third-party experts, who can provide unbiased advice and coaching. There have been recent attempts to link Lean to Service Management, perhaps one of the most recent and spectacular of which was London Heathrow Airport's Terminal 5. This particular case provides a graphic example of how care should be taken in translating successful practices from one context (production) to another (services), expecting the same results.

In this case the public perception is more of a spectacular failure, than a spectacular success, resulting in potentially an unfair tainting of the lean manufacturing philosophies.

The avoidance and then lateral removal of waste has a long history, and as such this history forms much of the basis of the philosophy now known as "Lean". In fact many of the concepts now seen as key to lean have been discovered and rediscovered over the years by others in their search to reduce waste.

Most of the basic goals of lean manufacturing are common sense, and documented examples can be seen as early as Benjamin Franklin. Poor Richard's Almanac says of wasted time, "He that idly loses 5s. worth of time, loses 5s., and might as prudently throw 5s. into the river."

He added that avoiding unnecessary costs could be more profitable than increasing sales: "A penny saved is two pence clear. A pin a-day is a groat a-year. Save and have." Again Franklin's The Way to Wealth says the following about carrying unnecessary inventory. "You call them goods; but, if you do not take care, they will prove evils to some of you. You expect they will be sold cheap, and, perhaps, they may [be bought] for less than they cost; but, if you have no occasion for them, they must be dear to you. Remember what Poor Richard says, 'Buy what thou hast no need of, and ere long thou shalt sell thy necessaries.' In another place he says, 'Many have been ruined by buying good penny worths'."

Henry Ford cited Franklin as a major influence on his own business practices, which included Just-in-time manufacturing. The concept of waste being built into jobs and then taken for granted was noticed by motion efficiency expert Frank Gilbreth, who saw that masons bent over to pick up bricks from the ground. The bricklayer was therefore lowering and raising his entire upper body to pick up a 2.3 kg (5 lb.) brick, and this inefficiency had been built into the job through long practice.

Introduction of a non-stooping scaffold, which delivered the bricks at waist level, allowed masons to work about three times as quickly, and with less effort.

Frederick Winslow Taylor, the father of scientific management, introduced what are now called standardization and best practice deployment. In his *Principles of Scientific Management,* (1911), Taylor said: "And whenever a workman proposes an improvement, it should be the policy of the management to make a careful analysis of the new method, and if necessary conduct a series of experiments to determine accurately the relative merit of the new suggestion and of the old standard. And whenever the new method is found to be markedly superior to the old, it should be adopted as the standard for the whole establishment."

Taylor also warned explicitly against cutting piece rates (or, by implication, cutting wages or discharging workers) when efficiency improvements reduce the need for raw labor: "...after a workman has had the price per piece of the work he is doing lowered two or three times as a result of his having worked harder and increased his output, he is likely entirely to lose sight of his employer's side of the case and become imbued with a grim determination to have no more cuts if soldiering [marking time, just doing what he is told] can prevent it." Shigeo Shingo, the best-known exponent of single minute exchange of die (SMED) and error-proofing or poka-yoke, cites Principles of Scientific Management as his inspiration.

American industrialists recognized the threat of cheap offshore labor to American workers during the 1910s, and explicitly stated the goal of what is now called lean manufacturing as a countermeasure. Henry Towne, past President of the American Society of Mechanical Engineers, wrote in the Foreword to Frederick Winslow Taylor's Shop Management (1911), "We are justly proud of the high wage rates which prevail throughout our country, and jealous of any interference with them by the products of the cheaper labor of other countries. To maintain this condition, to strengthen our control of home markets, and, above all, to broaden our opportunities in foreign markets where we must compete with the products of other industrial nations, we should welcome and encourage every influence tending to increase the efficiency of our productive processes."

Henry Ford continued this focus on waste while developing his mass assembly manufacturing system. Charles Buxton Going wrote in 1915:

Ford's success has startled the country, almost the world, financially, industrially, mechanically. It exhibits in higher degree than most persons would have thought possible the seemingly contradictory requirements of true efficiency, which are: constant increase of quality, great increase of pay to the workers, repeated reduction in cost to the consumer. And with these appears, as at once cause and effect, an absolutely incredible enlargement of output reaching something like one hundredfold in less than ten years, and an enormous profit to the manufacturer.

Ford, in My Life and Work (1922), provided a single-paragraph description that encompasses the entire concept of waste:

> I believe that the average farmer puts to a really useful purpose only about 5%. of the energy he expends.... Not only is everything done by hand, but seldom is a thought given to a logical arrangement. A farmer doing his chores will walk up and down a rickety ladder a dozen times. He will carry water for years instead of putting in a few lengths of pipe. His whole idea, when there is extra work to do, is to hire extra men. He thinks of putting money into improvements as an expense.... It is waste motion— waste effort— that makes farm prices high and profits low.

Poor arrangement of the workplace—a major focus of the modern kaizen—and doing a job inefficiently out of habit—are major forms of waste even in modern workplaces. Ford also pointed out how easy it was to overlook material waste. A former employee, Harry Bennett, wrote:

One day when Mr. Ford and I were together he spotted some rust in the slag that ballasted the right of way of the D. T. & I [railroad]. This slag had been dumped there from our own furnaces. 'You know,' Mr. Ford said to me, 'there's iron in that slag. You make the crane crews who put it out there sort it over, and take it back to the plant.'

In other words, Ford saw the rust and realized that the steel plant was not recovering all of the iron. Ford's early success, however, was not sustainable. As James Womack and Daniel Jones pointed out in "Lean Thinking", what Ford accomplished represented the "special case" rather than a robust lean solution. The major challenge that Ford faced was that his methods were built for a steady-state environment, rather than for the dynamic conditions firms increasingly face today. Although his rigid, top-down controls made it possible to hold variation in work activities down to very low levels, his approach did not respond well to uncertain, dynamic business conditions; they responded particularly badly to the need for new product innovation.

This was made clear by Ford's precipitous decline when the company was forced to finally introduce a follow-on to the Model T.

Design for Manufacture (DFM) also is a Ford concept. Ford said in My Life and Work (the same reference describes just in time manufacturing very explicitly):

> ...entirely useless parts [may be]—a shoe, a dress, a house, a piece of machinery, a railroad, a steamship, an airplane. As we cut out useless parts and simplify necessary ones, we also cut down the cost of making.... But also it is to be remembered that all the parts are designed so that they can be most easily made.

This standardization of parts was central to Ford's concept of mass production, and the manufacturing "tolerances", or upper and lower dimensional limits that ensured interchangeability of parts became widely applied across manufacturing. Decades later, the renowned Japanese quality guru, Genichi Taguchi, demonstrated that this "goal post" method of measuring was inadequate. He showed that "loss" in capabilities did not begin only after exceeding these tolerances, but increased as described by the Taguchi Loss Function at any condition exceeding the nominal condition. This became an important part of W. Edwards Deming's quality movement of the 1980s, later helping to develop improved understanding of key areas of focus such as cycle time variation in improving manufacturing quality and efficiencies in aerospace and other industries. While Ford is renowned for his production line it is often not recognized how much effort he put into removing the fitters' work to make the production line possible. Until Ford, a car's components always had to be fitted or reshaped by a skilled engineer at the point of use, so that they would connect properly. By enforcing very strict specification and quality criteria on component manufacture, he eliminated this work almost entirely, reducing manufacturing effort by between 60-90%. However, Ford's mass production system failed to incorporate the notion of "pull production" and thus often suffered from over-production.

Toyota's development of ideas that later became Lean may have started at the turn of the 20th century with Sakichi Toyoda, in a textile factory with looms that stopped themselves when a thread broke, this became the seed of autonomation and Jidoka. Toyota's journey with JIT may have started back in 1934 when it moved from textiles to produce its first car. Kiichiro Toyoda, founder of Toyota, directed the engine casting work and discovered many problems in their manufacture. He decided he must stop the repairing of poor quality by intense study of each stage of the process. In 1936, when Toyota won its first truck contract with the Japanese government, his processes hit new problems and he developed the "Kaizen" improvement teams.

Levels of demand in the Post War economy of Japan were low and the focus of mass production on lowest cost per item via economies of scale therefore had little application. Having visited and seen supermarkets in the USA, Taiichi Ohno recognised the scheduling of work should not be driven by sales or production targets but by actual sales. Given the financial situation during this period, over-production had to be avoided and thus the notion of Pull (build to order rather than target driven Push) came to underpin production scheduling.

It was with Taiichi Ohno at Toyota that these themes came together. He built on the already existing internal schools of thought and spread their breadth and use into what has now become the Toyota Production System (TPS). It is principally from the TPS, but now including many other sources, that Lean production is developing. Norman Bodek wrote the following in his foreword to a reprint of Ford's Today and Tomorrow:

> I was first introduced to the concepts of just-in-time (JIT) and the Toyota production system in 1980. Subsequently I had the opportunity to witness its actual application at Toyota on one of our numerous Japanese study missions. There I met Mr. Taiichi Ohno, the system's creator. When bombarded with questions from our group on what inspired his thinking, he just laughed and said he learned it all from Henry Ford's book."

It is the scale, rigour and continuous learning aspects of the TPS which have made it a core of Lean.

Types of Wastes

While the elimination of waste may seem like a simple and clear subject it is noticeable that waste is often very conservatively identified. This then hugely reduces the potential of such an aim. The elimination of waste is the goal of Lean, and Toyota defined three broad types of waste: muda, muri and mura; it should be noted that for many Lean implementations this list shrinks to the last waste type only with corresponding benefits decrease. To illustrate the state of this thinking Shigeo Shingo observed that only the last turn of a bolt tightens it—the rest is just movement. This ever finer clarification of waste is key to establishing distinctions between value-adding activity, waste and non-value-adding work. Non-value adding work is waste that must be done under the present work conditions. One key is to measure, or estimate, the size of these wastes, to demonstrate the effect of the changes achieved and therefore the movement toward the goal.

The "flow" (or smoothness) based approach aims to achieve JIT, by removing the variation caused by work scheduling and thereby provide a driver, rationale or target and priorities for implementation, using a variety of techniques. The effort to achieve JIT exposes many quality problems that are hidden by buffer stocks; by forcing smooth flow of only value-adding steps, these problems become visible and must be dealt with explicitly. Muri is all the unreasonable work that management imposes on workers and machines because of poor organization, such as carrying heavy weights, moving things around, dangerous tasks, even working significantly faster than usual. It is pushing a person or a machine beyond its natural limits.

This may simply be asking a greater level of performance from a process than it can handle without taking shortcuts and informally modifying decision criteria. Unreasonable work is almost always a cause of multiple variations. To link these three concepts is simple in TPS and thus Lean. Firstly, muri focuses on the preparation and planning of the process, or what work can be avoided proactively by design. Next, mura then focuses on how the work design is implemented and the elimination of fluctuation at the scheduling or operations level, such as quality and volume.

Muda is then discovered after the process is in place and is dealt with reactively. It is seen through variation in output. It is the role of management to examine the muda, in the processes and eliminate the deeper causes by considering the connections to the muri and mura of the system. The muda and mura inconsistencies must be fed back to the muri, or planning, stage for the next project.

A typical example of the interplay of these wastes is the corporate behaviour of "making the numbers" as the end of a reporting period approaches.

Demand is raised to 'make plan', increasing (mura), when the "numbers" are low which causes production to try to squeeze extra capacity from the process which causes routines and standards to be modified or stretched. This stretch and improvisation leads to muri-style waste which leads to downtime, mistakes and backflows and waiting, thus the muda of waiting, correction and movement.

The original seven muda are:

- Transportation (moving products that is not actually required to perform the processing)
- Inventory (all components, work in process and finished product not being processed)
- Motion (people or equipment moving or walking more than is required to perform the processing)
- Waiting (waiting for the next production step)
- Overproduction (production ahead of demand)

- Over Processing (resulting from poor tool or product design creating activity)
- Defects (the effort involved in inspecting for and fixing defects).

Later an eighth waste was defined by Womack et al. (2003); it was described as manufacturing goods or services that do not meet customer demand or specifications. Many others have added the "waste of unused human talent" to the original seven wastes. These wastes were not originally a part of the seven deadly wastes defined by Taiichi Ohno in TPS, but were found to be useful additions in practice. For a complete listing of the "old" and "new" wastes see Bicheno and Holweg (2009). Some of these definitions may seem rather idealistic, but this tough definition is seen as important and they drove the success of TPS. The clear identification of non-value-adding work, as distinct from wasted work, is critical to identifying the assumptions behind the current work process and to challenging them in due course.

Breakthroughs in SMED and other process changing techniques rely upon clear identification of where untapped opportunities may lie if the processing assumptions are challenged.

The discipline required to implement Lean and the disciplines it seems to require are so often counter-cultural that they have made successful implementation of Lean a major challenge. Some would say that it was a major challenge in its manufacturing 'heartland' as well. Implementations under the Lean label are numerous and whether they are Lean and whether any success or failure can be laid at Lean's door is often debatable.

Individual examples of success and failure exist in almost all spheres of business and activity and therefore cannot be taken as indications of whether Lean is particularly applicable to a specific sector of activity. It seems clear from the "successes" that no sector is immune from beneficial possibility. Lean is about more than just cutting costs in the factory. One crucial insight is that most costs are assigned when a product is designed. Often an engineer will specify familiar, safe materials and processes rather than inexpensive, efficient ones. This reduces project risk, that is, the cost to the engineer, while increasing financial risks, and decreasing profits. Good organizations develop and review checklists to review product designs.

Companies must often look beyond the shop-floor to find opportunities for improving overall company cost and performance. At the system engineering level, requirements are reviewed with marketing and customer representatives to eliminate those requirements which are costly. Shared modules may be developed, such as multipurpose power supplies or shared mechanical components or fasteners. Requirements are assigned to the cheapest discipline. For example, adjustments may be moved into software, and measurements away from a mechanical solution to an electronic solution. Another approach is to choose connection or power-transport methods that are cheap or that used standardized components that become available in a competitive market.

An Example Program

In summary, an example of a lean implementation programme could be:

With a tools-based approach

- Senior management to agree and discuss their lean vision
- Management brainstorm to identify project leader and set objectives
- Communicate plan and vision to the workforce
- Ask for volunteers to form the Lean Implementation team (5-7 works best, all from different departments)
- Appoint members of the Lean Manufacturing Implementation Team
- Train the Implementation Team in the various lean tools-make a point of trying to visit other non competing businesses which have implemented lean
- Select a Pilot Project to implement – 5S is a good place to start
- Run the pilot for 2–3 months-evaluate, review and learn from your mistakes
- Roll out pilot to other factory areas
- Evaluate results, encourage feedback
- Stabilize the positive results by teaching supervisors how to train the new standards you've developed with TWI methodology (Training Within Industry).

Once you are satisfied that you have a habitual programme, consider introducing the next lean tool. Select the one which will give you the biggest return for your business.

With a muri or flow based approach:

- Sort out as many of the visible quality problems as you can, as well as downtime and other instability problems, and get the internal scrap acknowledged and its management started.

- Make the flow of parts through the system or process as continuous as possible using workcells and market locations where necessary and avoiding variations in the operators work cycle
- Introduce standard work and stabilise the work pace through the system
- Start pulling work through the system, look at the production scheduling and move toward daily orders with kanban cards
- Even out the production flow by reducing batch sizes, increase delivery frequency internally and if possible externally, level internal demand
- Improve exposed quality issues using the tools

Lean Leadership

The role of the leaders within the organization is the fundamental element of sustaining the progress of lean thinking. Experienced kaizen members at Toyota, for example, often bring up the concepts of Senpai, Kohai, and Sensei, because they strongly feel that transferring of Toyota culture down and across Toyota can only happen when more experienced Toyota Sensei continuously coach and guide the less experienced lean champions. Unfortunately, most lean practitioners in North America focus on the tools and methodologies of lean, versus the philosophy and culture of lean. Some exceptions include Shingijitsu Consulting out of Japan, which is made up of ex-Toyota managers, and Lean Sensei International based in North America, which coaches lean through Toyota-style cultural experience. One of the dislocative effects of Lean is in the area of key performance indicators (KPI). The KPIs by which a plant/ facility are judged will often be driving behaviour, because the KPIs themselves assume a particular approach to the work being done. This can be an issue where, for example a truly Lean, Fixed Repeating Schedule (FRS) and JIT approach is adopted, because these KPIs will no longer reflect performance, as the assumptions on which they are based become invalid. It is a key leadership challenge to manage the impact of this KPI chaos within the organization.

A set of performance metrics which is considered to fit well in a Lean environment is Overall Equipment Effectiveness, or OEE. Similarly, commonly used accounting systems developed to support mass production are no longer appropriate for companies pursuing Lean. Lean Accounting provides truly Lean approaches to business management and financial reporting. After formulating the guiding principles of its lean manufacturing approach in the Toyota Production System (TPS) Toyota formalized in 2001 the basis of its lean management: the key managerial values and attitudes needed to sustain continuous improvement in the long run. These core management principles are articulated around the twin pillars of Continuous Improvement (relentless elimination of waste) and Respect for People (engagement in long term relationships based on continuous improvement and mutual trust). This formalization stems from problem solving.

As Toyota expanded beyond its home base for the past 20 years, it hit the same problems in getting TPS properly applied that other western companies have had in copying TPS. Like any other problem, it has been working on trying a series of countermeasures to solve this particular concern. These countermeasures have focused on culture: how people behave, which is the most difficult challenge of all. Without the proper behavioural principles and values, TPS can be totally misapplied and fail to deliver results. As one sensei said, one can create a Buddha image and forget to inject soul in it. As with TPS, the values had originally been passed down in a master-disciple manner, from boss to subordinate, without any written statement on the way.

And just as with TPS, it was internally argued that formalizing the values would stifle them and lead to further misunderstanding. But as Toyota veterans eventually wrote down the basic principles of TPS, Toyota set to put the Toyota Way into writing to educate new joiners.

Continuous Improvement breaks down into three basic principles:

1. *Challenge:* Having a long term vision of the challenges one needs to face to realize one's ambition (what we need to learn rather than what we want to do and then having the spirit to face that challenge). To do so, we have to challenge ourselves every day to see if we are achieving our goals.
2. *Kaizen:* Good enough never is, no process can ever be thought perfect, so operations must be improved continuously, striving for innovation and evolution.
3. *Genchi Genbutsu:* Going to the source to see the facts for oneself and make the right decisions, create consensus, and make sure goals are attained at the best possible speed.

Respect For People is less known outside of Toyota, and essentially involves two defining principles:

1. Respect Taking every stakeholders' problems seriously, and making every effort to build mutual trust. Taking responsibility for other people reaching their objectives. Thought provoking, I find. As a manager, I must take responsibility for my subordinates reaching the target I set for them.

2. *Teamwork:* This is about developing individuals through team problem-solving. The idea is to develop and engage people through their contribution to team performance. Shop floor teams, the whole site as team, and team Toyota at the outset.

Differences from TPS

Whilst Lean is seen by many as a generalization of the Toyota Production System into other industries and contexts there are some acknowledged differences that seem to have developed in implementation.

1. Seeking profit is a relentless focus for Toyota exemplified by the profit maximization principle (Price – Cost = Profit) and the need, therefore, to practice systematic cost reduction (through TPS or otherwise) to realize benefit. Lean implementations can tend to de-emphasise this key measure and thus become fixated with the implementation of improvement concepts of "flow" or "pull". However, the emergence of the "value curve analysis" promises to directly tie lean improvements to bottom-line performance measuments.
2. Tool orientation is a tendency in many programmes to elevate mere tools (standardized work, value stream mapping, visual control, etc.) to an unhealthy status beyond their pragmatic intent. The tools are just different ways to work around certain types of problems but they do not solve them for you or always highlight the underlying cause of many types of problems. The tools employed at Toyota are often used to expose particular problems that are then dealt with, as each tool's limitations or blindspots are perhaps better understood.

   So, for example, Value Stream Mapping focuses upon material and information flow problems (a title built into the Toyota title for this activity) but is not strong on Metrics, Man or Method. Internally they well know the limits of the tool and understood that it was never intended as the best way to see and analyze every waste or every problem related to quality, downtime, personnel development, cross training related issues, capacity bottlenecks, or anything to do with profits, safety, metrics or morale, etc. No one tool can do all of that. For surfacing these issues other tools are much more widely and effectively used.
3. Management technique rather than change agents has been a principle in Toyota from the early 1950s when they started emphasizing the development of the production manager's and supervisors' skills set in guiding natural work teams and did not rely upon staff-level change agents to drive improvements.

This can manifest itself as a "Push" implementation of Lean rather than "Pull" by the team itself. This area of skills development is not that of the change agent specialist, but that of the natural operations work team leader. Although less prestigious than the TPS specialists, development of work team supervisors in Toyota is considered an equally, if not more important, topic merely because there are tens of thousands of these individuals. Specifically, it is these manufacturing leaders that are the main focus of training efforts in Toyota since they lead the daily work areas, and they directly and dramatically affect quality, cost, productivity, safety, and morale of the team environment.

In many companies implementing Lean the reverse set of priorities is true. Emphasis is put on developing the specialist, while the supervisor skill level is expected to somehow develop over time on its own.

Lean Services

Lean, as a concept or brand, has captured the imagination of many in different spheres of activity. Examples of these from many sectors are listed below.

Lean principles have been successfully applied to call centre services to improve live agent call handling. By combining Agent-assisted Voice solutions and Lean's waste reduction practices, a company reduced handle time, reduced between agent variability, reduced accent barriers, and attained near perfect process adherence. Lean principles have also found application in software application development and maintenance and other areas of information technology (IT). More generally, the use of Lean in IT has become known as Lean IT.

A study conducted on behalf of the Scottish Executive, by Warwick University, in 2005/06 found that Lean methods were applicable to the public sector, but that most results had been achieved using a much more restricted range of techniques than Lean provides. The challenge in moving Lean to services is the lack of widely available reference implementations to allow people to see how directly applying lean manufacturing tools and practices can work and the impact it does have. This makes it more difficult to build the level of belief seen as necessary for strong implementation. However, some research does relate widely recognized examples of success in retail and even airlines to the underlying principles of lean.

Despite this, it remains the case that the direct manufacturing examples of 'techniques' or 'tools' need to be better 'translated' into a service context to support the more prominent approaches of implementation, which has not yet received the level of work or publicity that would give starting points for implementors.

The upshot of this is that each implementation often 'feels its way' along as must the early industrial engineers of Toyota. This places huge importance upon sponsorship to encourage and protect these experimental developments.

Lean Goals

The four goals of Lean manufacturing systems are to:

- Improve quality: To stay competitive in today's marketplace, a company must understand its customers' wants and needs and design processes to meet their expectations and requirements.
- Eliminate waste: Waste is any activity that consumes time, resources, or space but does not add any value to the product or service. There are seven types of waste:
    1. Transport (unnecessary movement of materials)
    2. Inventory (excess inventory not directly required for current orders)
    3. Motion (extra steps taken by employees because of inefficient layout)
    4. Waiting (periods of inactivity)
    5. Overproduction (occurs when production should have stopped)
    6. Over Processing (rework and reprocessing)
    7. Defects (do not conform to specifications or expectations).

Taking the first letter of each waste, the acronym "TIM WOOD" is formed. This is a common way to remember the wastes.

- Reduce time: Reducing the time it takes to finish an activity from start to finish is one of the most effective ways to eliminate waste and lower costs.
- Reduce total costs: To minimize cost, a company must produce only to customer demand. Overproduction increases a company's inventory costs because of storage needs.

Steps to Achieve Lean Systems

The following steps should be implemented to create the ideal lean manufacturing system:

1. Design a simple manufacturing system
2. Recognize that there is always room for improvement
3. Continuously improve the lean manufacturing system design.

Design a Simple Manufacturing System

A fundamental principle of lean manufacturing is demand-based flow manufacturing. In this type of production setting, inventory is only pulled through each production centre when it is needed to meet a customer's order. The benefits of this goal include:

- decreased cycle time
- less inventory
- increased productivity
- increased capital equipment utilization.

The core of lean is founded on the concept of continuous product and process improvement and the elimination of non-value added activities.

"The Value adding activities are simply only those things the customer is willing to pay for, everything else is waste, and should be eliminated, simplified, reduced, or integrated" (Rizzardo, 2003).

Improving the flow of material through new ideal system layouts at the customer's required rate would reduce waste in material movement and inventory.

A continuous improvement mindset is essential to reach a company's goals. The term "continuous improvement" means incremental improvement of products, processes, or services over time, with the goal of reducing waste to improve workplace functionality, customer service, or product performance (Suzaki, 1987).

Stephen Shortell (Professor of Health Services Management and Organisational Behaviour – Berkeley University, California) states:

> "For improvement to flourish it must be carefully cultivated in a rich soil bed (a receptive organisation), given constant attention (sustained leadership), assured the right amounts of light (training and support) and water (measurement and data) and protected from damaging."

Measure

A set of performance metrics which is considered to fit well in a Lean environment is overall equipment effectiveness, or OEE.

Understanding Six Sigma

Six Sigma is a business management strategy originally developed by

Motorola, USA in 1981. As of 2010, it enjoys widespread application in many sectors of industry, although its application is not without controversy.

Six Sigma seeks to improve the quality of process outputs by identifying and removing the causes of defects (errors) and minimizing variability in manufacturing and business processes. It uses a set of quality management methods, including statistical methods, and creates a special infrastructure of people within the organization ("Black Belts", "Green Belts", etc.) who are experts in these methods. Each Six Sigma project carried out within an organization follows a defined sequence of steps and has quantified targets.

These targets can be financial (cost reduction or profit increase) or whatever is critical to the customer of that process (cycle time, safety, delivery, etc.). The term six sigma originated from terminology associated with manufacturing, specifically terms associated with statistical modelling of manufacturing processes. The maturity of a manufacturing process can be described by a sigma rating indicating its yield, or the percentage of defect-free products it creates. A six-sigma process is one in which 99.99966% of the products manufactured are free of defects, compared to a one-sigma process in which only 31% are free of defects. Motorola set a goal of "six sigmas" for all of its manufacturing operations and this goal became a byword for the management and engineering practices used to achieve it.

Six Sigma originated as a set of practices designed to improve manufacturing processes and eliminate defects, but its application was subsequently extended to other types of business processes as well. In Six Sigma, a defect is defined as any process output that does not meet customer specifications, or that could lead to creating an output that does not meet customer specifications.

Bill Smith first formulated the particulars of the methodology at Motorola in 1986. Six Sigma was heavily inspired by six preceding decades of quality improvement methodologies such as quality control, TQM, and Zero Defects, based on the work of pioneers such as Shewhart, Deming, Juran, Ishikawa, Taguchi and others.

Like its predecessors, Six Sigma doctrine asserts that:

- Continuous efforts to achieve stable and predictable process results (i.e., reduce process variation) are of vital importance to business success.
- Manufacturing and business processes have characteristics that can be measured, analyzed, improved and controlled.

- Achieving sustained quality improvement requires commitment from the entire organization, particularly from top-level management.

Features that set Six Sigma apart from previous quality improvement initiatives include:

- A clear focus on achieving measurable and quantifiable financial returns from any Six Sigma project.
- An increased emphasis on strong and passionate management leadership and support.
- A special infrastructure of "Champions," "Master Black Belts," "Black Belts," "Yellow Belts", etc. to lead and implement the Six Sigma approach.
- A clear commitment to making decisions on the basis of verifiable data, rather than assumptions and guesswork.

In fact, the term "Six Sigma" comes from a field of statistics known as process capability studies. Originally, it referred to the ability of manufacturing processes to produce a very high proportion of output within specification. Processes that operate with "six sigma quality" over the short term are assumed to produce long-term defect levels below 3.4 defects per million opportunities (DPMO). Six Sigma's implicit goal is to improve all processes to that level of quality or better.

Six Sigma is a registered service mark and trademark of Motorola Inc. As of 2006 Motorola reported over US$17 billion in savings from Six Sigma.

Other early adopters of Six Sigma who achieved well-publicized success include Honeywell (previously known as Allied Signal) and General Electric, where Jack Welch introduced the method. By the late 1990s, about two-thirds of the Fortune 500 organizations had begun Six Sigma initiatives with the aim of reducing costs and improving quality.

In recent years, some practitioners have combined Six Sigma ideas with lean manufacturing to yield a methodology named Lean Six Sigma.

Methods

Six Sigma projects follow two project methodologies inspired by Deming's Plan-Do-Check-Act Cycle. These methodologies, composed of five phases each, bear the acronyms DMAIC and DMADV.

- DMAIC is used for projects aimed at improving an existing business process. DMAIC is pronounced as "duhmayick".

- DMADV is used for projects aimed at creating new product or process designs. DMADV is pronounced as "duhmadvee".

DMAIC

The DMAIC project methodology has five phases:

- Define the problem, the voice of the customer, and the project goals, specifically.
- Measure key aspects of the current process and collect relevant data.
- Analyze the data to investigate and verify cause-and-effect relationships. Determine what the relationships are, and attempt to ensure that all factors have been considered. Seek out root cause of the defect under investigation.
- Improve or optimize the current process based upon data analysis using techniques such as design of experiments, poka yoke or mistake proofing, and standard work to create a new, future state process. Set up pilot runs to establish process capability.
- Control the future state process to ensure that any deviations from target are corrected before they result in defects. Control systems are implemented such as statistical process control, production boards, and visual workplaces and the process is continuously monitored.

DMADV

The DMADV project methodology, also known as DFSS ("Design For Six Sigma"), features five phases:

- Define design goals that are consistent with customer demands and the enterprise strategy.
- Measure and identify CTQs (characteristics that are Critical To Quality), product capabilities, production process capability, and risks.
- Analyze to develop and design alternatives, create a high-level design and evaluate design capability to select the best design.
- Design details, optimize the design, and plan for design verification. This phase may require simulations.
- Verify the design, set up pilot runs, implement the production process and hand it over to the process owner(s).

Quality Management Tools and Methods Used in Six Sigma

Within the individual phases of a DMAIC or DMADV project, Six

Sigma utilizes many established quality-management tools that are also used outside of Six Sigma. The following table shows an overview of the main methods used.

- 5 Whys
- Analysis of variance
- ANOVA Gauge R&R
- Axiomatic design
- Business Process Mapping
- Catapult exercise on variability
- Cause & effects diagram (also known as fishbone or Ishikawa diagram)
- Chi-square test of independence and fits
- Control chart
- Correlation
- Cost-benefit analysis
- CTQ tree
- Design of experiments
- Failure mode and effects analysis (FMEA)
- Histograms
- Homoscedasticity
- Quality Function Deployment (QFD)
- Pareto chart
- Pick chart
- Process capability
- Quantitative marketing research through use of Enterprise Feedback Management (EFM) systems
- Regression analysis
- Root cause analysis
- Run charts
- SIPOC analysis (Suppliers, Inputs, Process, Outputs, Customers)
- Stratification
- Taguchi methods
- Taguchi Loss Function
- TRIZ.

Implementation Roles

One key innovation of Six Sigma involves the "professionalizing" of quality management functions. Prior to Six Sigma, quality management in practice was largely relegated to the production floor and to statisticians in a separate quality department. Formal Six Sigma programmes borrow martial arts ranking terminology to define a hierarchy (and career path) that cuts across all business functions. Six Sigma identifies several key roles for its successful implementation.

- Executive Leadership includes the CEO and other members of top management. They are responsible for setting up a vision for Six Sigma implementation. They also empower the other role holders with the freedom and resources to explore new ideas for breakthrough improvements.
- Champions take responsibility for Six Sigma implementation across the organization in an integrated manner. The Executive Leadership draws them from upper management. Champions also act as mentors to Black Belts.
- Master Black Belts, identified by champions, act as in-house coaches on Six Sigma. They devote 100% of their time to Six Sigma. They assist champions and guide Black Belts and Green Belts. Apart from statistical tasks, they spend their time on ensuring consistent application of Six Sigma across various functions and departments.
- Black Belts operate under Master Black Belts to apply Six Sigma methodology to specific projects. They devote 100% of their time to Six Sigma. They primarily focus on Six Sigma project execution, whereas Champions and Master Black Belts focus on identifying projects/functions for Six Sigma.
- Green Belts, the employees who take up Six Sigma implementation along with their other job responsibilities, operate under the guidance of Black Belts.
- Yellow Belts, trained in the basic application of Six Sigma management tools, work with the Black Belt throughout the project stages and are often the closest to the work.

Role of the 1.5 Sigma Shift

Experience has shown that in the long term, processes usually do not perform as well as they do in the short. As a result, the number of sigmas that will fit between the process mean and the nearest specification limit may well drop over time, compared to an initial short-term study. To account for this real-life increase in process variation over time, an empirically-based 1.5 sigma shift is introduced into the calculation.

According to this idea, a process that fits six sigmas between the process mean and the nearest specification limit in a short-term study will in the long term only fit 4.5 sigmas – either because the process mean will move over time, or because the long-term standard deviation of the process will be greater than that observed in the short term, or both.

Hence the widely accepted definition of a six sigma process as one that produces 3.4 defective parts per million opportunities (DPMO). This is based on the fact that a process that is normally distributed will have 3.4 parts per million beyond a point that is 4.5 standard deviations above or below the mean (one-sided capability study).

So the 3.4 DPMO of a "Six Sigma" process in fact corresponds to 4.5 sigmas, namely 6 sigmas minus the 1.5 sigma shift introduced to account for long-term variation. This takes account of special causes that may cause a deterioration in process performance over time and is designed to prevent underestimation of the defect levels likely to be encountered in real-life operation.

Sigma Levels

The table below gives long-term DPMO values corresponding to various short-term sigma levels. Note that these figures assume that the process mean will shift by 1.5 sigma toward the side with the critical specification limit. In other words, they assume that after the initial study determining the short-term sigma level, the long-term C_{pk} value will turn out to be 0.5 less than the short-term C_{pk} value. So, for example, the DPMO figure given for 1 sigma assumes that the long-term process mean will be 0.5 sigma beyond the specification limit (C_{pk} = –0.17), rather than 1 sigma within it, as it was in the short-term study (C_{pk} = 0.33). Note that the defect percentages only indicate defects exceeding the specification limit to which the process mean is nearest. Defects beyond the far specification limit are not included in the percentages.

Sigma level	*DPMO*	*Percent defective*	*Percentage yield*	*Short-term C_{pk}*	*Long-term C_{pk}*
1	691,462	69%	31%	0.33	–0.17
2	308,538	31%	69%	0.67	0.17
3	66,807	6.7%	93.3%	1.00	0.5
4	6,210	0.62%	99.38%	1.33	0.83
5	233	0.023%	99.977%	1.67	1.17
6	3.4	0.00034%	99.99966%	2.00	1.5
7	0.019	0.0000019%	99.9999981%	2.33	1.83

Noted quality expert Joseph M. Juran has described Six Sigma as "a basic version of quality improvement", stating that "[t]here is nothing new there. It includes what we used to call facilitators. They've adopted more flamboyant terms, like belts with different colors. I think that concept has merit to set apart, to create specialists who can be very helpful. Again, that's not a new idea. The American Society for Quality long ago established certificates, such as for reliability engineers."

The use of "Black Belts" as itinerant change agents has (controversially) fostered a cottage industry of training and certification. Critics argue there is overselling of Six Sigma by too great a number of consulting firms, many of which claim expertise in Six Sigma when they only have a rudimentary understanding of the tools and techniques involved.

Potential Negative Effects

A Fortune article stated that "of 58 large companies that have announced Six Sigma programmes, 91 percent have trailed the S&P 500 since". The statement is attributed to "an analysis by Charles Holland of consulting firm Qualpro (which espouses a competing quality-improvement process)." The summary of the article is that Six Sigma is effective at what it is intended to do, but that it is "narrowly designed to fix an existing process" and does not help in "coming up with new products or disruptive technologies." Advocates of Six Sigma have argued that many of these claims are in error or ill-informed. A Business Week article says that James McNerney's introduction of Six Sigma at 3M may have had the effect of stifling creativity. It cites two Wharton School professors who say that Six Sigma leads to incremental innovation at the expense of blue-sky work. This phenomenon is further explored in the book, Going Lean, which describes a related approach known as lean dynamics and provides data to show that Ford's "6 Sigma" programme did little to change its fortunes.

While 3.4 defects per million opportunities might work well for certain products/processes, it might not operate optimally or cost effectively for others. A pacemaker process might need higher standards, for example, whereas a direct mail advertising campaign might need lower standards. The basis and justification for choosing 6 (as opposed to 5 or 7, for example) as the number of standard deviations is not clearly explained. In addition, the Six Sigma model assumes that the process data always conform to the normal distribution. The calculation of defect rates for situations where the normal distribution model does not apply is not properly addressed in the current Six Sigma literature.

The statistician Donald J. Wheeler has dismissed the 1.5 sigma shift as "goofy" because of its arbitrary nature. Its universal applicability is seen as doubtful.

The 1.5 sigma shift has also become contentious because it results in stated "sigma levels" that reflect short-term rather than long-term performance: a process that has long-term defect levels corresponding to 4.5 sigma performance is, by Six Sigma convention, described as a "6 sigma process."

The accepted Six Sigma scoring system thus cannot be equated to actual normal distribution probabilities for the stated number of standard deviations, and this has been a key bone of contention about how Six Sigma measures are defined. The fact that it is rarely explained that a "6 sigma" process will have long-term defect rates corresponding to 4.5 sigma performance rather than actual 6 sigma performance has led several commentators to express the opinion that Six Sigma is a confidence trick.

Certification

In the United States. Six Sigma certification for both green and black belts is offered by the Institute of Industrial Engineers and by the American Society for Quality.

6

Understanding the Theory of Constraints and Role of Customer Relationship Management

The goal as a company is to have customer service that is not just the best but legendary.

—*Sam Walton, Founder of Wal-Mart*

THEORY OF CONSTRAINTS

It is pertinent to note that Theory of Constraints (TOC) is a management philosophy developed by Dr. Eliyahu Moshe Goldratt. According to Goldratt the strength of any chain, process, or system is dependent upon its weakest link. TOC is systemic and strives to identify constraints to system success and to effect the changes necessary to remove them. Dr. Goldratt and the TOC became widely known with the 1984 publication of Goldratt's novel The Goal.

In early 1979 Goldratt introduced a software-based manufacturing scheduling programme known as Optimized Production Timetables (OPT), changed in 1982 to Optimized Production Technology. With the publication of The Goal, Goldratt used his Socratic teaching style to educate the world about managing bottlenecks (constraints) and his new ideas about performance. The Goal, is a love story set in the manufacturing industry (thrice revised) detailing the tribulations of a plant manager named Alex Rogo. Rogo is faced with the shutdown of his hometown manufacturing plant.

Goldratt uses Rogo's predicament to introduce his principles, which result not only in the rescue of Rogo's plant, but also in the salvation of Rogo's marriage. Goldratt himself appears in the book as a character known as Jonah, Rogo's old college professor. Goldratt used three additional novels to refine and develop the principles set forth in The Goal. It's Not Luck, a sequel to The Goal, addresses changing markets and introduces a number of methods of logical thinking that are used to make decisions, solve problems, and resolve conflict. The Critical Chain depicts a situation whereby TOC principles are effectively utilized in project management. Necessary But Not Sufficient contains Goldratt's most holistic expression of TOC and deals with the role of technology in organizations. Goldratt also produced a number of nonliterary works that espouse his ideas. The Race, introduced the concept of the drum-buffer-rope and buffer management. Essays on the Theory of Constraints, What Is This Thing Called Theory of Constraints and How Should It Be Implemented? and The Haystack Syndrome: Sifting Information Out of the Data Ocean were used, among other publications, to introduce the thinking processes and other TOC concepts.

Main Components

Theory of constraints consists of separate, but related processes and interrelated concepts, including the following: the performance measures and five focusing steps, logical thinking processes, and logistics. According to Goldratt there are three key performance measurements to evaluate: throughput, inventory and operating expense. TOC emphasizes the use of these three global operational measures rather than local measures (e.g., efficiency and utilization). Goldratt places the greatest importance on increasing throughput. Throughput is defined as the rate at which the system generates money through sales, not through production.

Goods are not considered an asset until sold. This contradicts the common accounting practice of listing inventory as an asset even if it may never be sold. Goldratt has advocated a new accounting model as an alternative to traditional cost accounting procedures and measures. Inventory is defined as the money invested in goods that the firm intends to sell or material that the firm intends to convert into salable items. The concept of value-added and overhead are not considered. Operating expense includes all the money the firm spends converting inventory into throughput. The objective of the firm, therefore, is to increase throughput and/or decrease inventory and operating expense in such a way as to increase profit, return on investment, and cash flow (more global measures).

In The Goal, Alex explains to Jonah that his plant's use of a robot has resulted in a thirty six percent improvement in one area. Jonah then asks if Alex is now able to ship more products, and if he has fired any employees or reduced inventory as a result (in other words, whether increased throughput, reduced operating expense, or reduced inventory resulted). When the reply was no, Jonah questions how there can be any real improvement; and of course, there can't. Increasing throughput and/ or decreasing inventory or operating expense should lead to the accomplishment of the firm's goal: to make money now as well as in the future. Anything that prevents a firm from reaching this goal is labelled as a constraint. Constraints may appear in the form of capacity, material, logistics, the market (demand), behavior, or even management policy.

TOC thinking regards all progress toward the goal of making money as relating directly to management attention toward the constraint(s). The marginal value of time at a constraint resource is said to be equal to the throughput rate of the product processed at the constraint, while the marginal value of time at a nonconstraint resource is said to be negligible.

Five Focusing Steps

The five focusing steps are a tool Goldratt developed to help systems deal with constraints. These steps ensure improvement efforts remains on track towards system-level improvements. Dettmer believes that these are collectively the most important aspect of TOC. TOC's five focusing steps are:

1. Identify the system's constraint(s).
2. Decide how to exploit the system's constraint(s).
3. Subordinate everything else to the decisions made in Step 2.
4. Elevate the system's constraint(s)
5. If a constraint is broken in Step 4, go back to Step 1, but do not allow inertia to cause a new constraint.

The orientation of TOC is toward the output of the entire system, rather than a look at a discrete unit or component. The five focusing steps assist with identifying the largest constraint that overshadows all of the others. These steps constitute an iterative process. As soon as one constraint is strengthened, the next weakest link becomes the priority constraint and should be addressed. Thus, a process of ongoing system improvement is applied to the business practice of the firm.

Logical Thinking Process

Goldratt introduced a staged logical thinking process to be used in conjunction with the five focusing steps. The thinking process assists with working through the change process by identifying the following: what to change, what to change to, and how to effect the change. The thinking processes consist of logic tools used to identify problems, then develop and implement solutions. These tools include effect-cause-effect (ECE) diagramming and its components: negative branch reservations, the current reality tree, the future reality tree, the prerequisite tree, the transition tree, the evaporating cloud, the negative branch reservation, and the ECE audit process. These tools allow an organization to analyze and to verbalize cause and effect.

The following is a brief description of the thinking process. A current reality tree, a cause-effect diagram, is drawn in order to discover the problems. These problems are known as undesirable effects. The cause of an undesirable effect is known as a root cause. The first goal is to find the causes of these undesirable effects. Each statement in a current reality tree that is not a derivative of another must be a root cause. If you build a tree that is comprehensive enough, at least one root cause will lead to most of the undesirable effects. This particular root cause is labelled a core problem, the major improvement target. The fewer root causes responsible for the undesirable effects, the better. The solution to this core problem is apparently not readily available. If it were, then the problem would have already been solved. Some conflict, therefore, must exist that prevents an immediate solution. This conflict becomes evident upon the construction of an evaporating cloud.

An evaporating cloud is a conflict-resolution tool. The process begins with a statement of the desired objective, one that is the opposite of the core problem. Then, the prerequisites necessary to achieve the requirements are listed. Any conflicts and assumptions that exist between the prerequisites are verbalized. For example, if one objective is to increase profit, then the requirements may be to improve the product and to decrease expenses. Prerequisites for each, respectively, might be to increase expenditures on capital equipment and to decrease expenditures, two obviously conflicting elements. The best solution is to remove the conflict; a compromise is not desirable. The next move involves finding an injection, a breakthrough idea that will evaporate the cloud. The "evaporating" refers to the tool's ability to dissipate conflict and to create a win-win solution. Usually, the original injection is not sufficient to fully solve the problem, but additional needed injections become clear when building the future reality tree.

A future reality tree is another cause-effect diagram. The tree starts with the proposed solution to the core problem and delineates the injection(s) and the ensuing desirable effects. The future reality tree is a "what if." It provides the opportunity to evaluate and to improve a solution before it is implemented. It is noted that one should be careful not to allow the solution to cause new undesirable effects. A prerequisite tree describes the implementation of the injection(s) and is composed of an obstacle and an intermediate objective. This diagram breaks the implementation tasks into smaller increments, noting expected obstacles and intermediate objectives whose accomplishments will overcome the obstacles. The intermediate objectives are sequenced, displaying the necessary order of accomplishment and determining which ones can be achieved in parallel. This tool is powerful in that it does not ignore the obstacles. It uses them, rather, as the main vehicle for this phase.

Finally, a transition tree or implementation plan is constructed. This element presents a detailed description of the gradually evolving change envisioned. This task forces one to carefully examine which actions are really needed and if they are sufficient to guarantee the required change.

The thinking-process tools are powerful resources when used effectively. They have found successful use in the logistics and medicine areas of the United States Air Force, in primary education, and in the service sector. James Cox and Michael Spencer, both college professors and "Jonahs," state in The Constraints Management Handbook that the thinking processes may be the most important management tools developed this century.

Logistics

Logistics in TOC include drum-buffer-rope scheduling, buffer management, and VAT analysis.

Drum-buffer-rope

Drum-buffer-rope is a TOC production application and the name given to the method used to schedule the flow of materials in a TOC facility. Srikanth and Umble (1997), define each component as follows:

- Drum. The drum is the constraint and therefore sets the pace for the entire system. The drum must reconcile the customer requirements with the system's constraints. In simpler terms, the drum is the rate or pace of production set by the system's constraint.
- Buffer. A buffer includes time or materials that support throughput and/or due date performance. A buffer establishes some protection against uncertainty so that the system can maximize throughput. A time buffer is the additional planned lead time allowed, beyond the required setup and run times, for materials to reach a specified point in the product flow. Strategically placed, time buffers are designed to protect the system throughput from the internal disruptions that are inherent in any process. A stock buffer is defined as inventories of specific products that are held in finished, partially finished, or raw material form, in order to fill customer orders in less than the normal lead-time. Stock buffers are designed to improve the responsiveness of the system to specific market conditions.

- Rope. The rope is a schedule for releasing raw materials to the floor. The rope is devised according to the drum and the buffer. The rope ensures that non-capacity constraint resources are subordinate to the constraint. Restated, the rope is a communication process from the constraint to the gating operation that checks or limits material released into the system to support the constraint.

Buffer Management

Buffer management provides the means by which the schedule is managed on the shop floor. Buffer management is a process in which all expediting in a shop is motivated by what is scheduled to be in the buffers (constraint, shipping, and assembly buffers). Buffers can be maintained at the constraint, convergent points, divergent points, and shipping points. By expediting this material into the buffers, the system helps to avoid idleness at the constraint and missed customer due dates. Also, the causes of items missing from the buffer are identified, and the frequency of occurrences is used to prioritize improvement activities.

Vat Analysis

VAT analysis determines the general flow of parts and products from raw materials to finished products. It conceptualizes an organization in terms of the interaction of its individual component parts, both products and processes. Three general categories of production structures result from this standpoint, each necessitating a unique approach to management planning and control. The logical structure is the sequence of operations through which each product must pass in order to manufacture and assemble a product or product family. A V logical structure starts with one or a few raw materials, and the product expands into a number of different products as it flows through its routings. The shape of an A logical structure is dominated by converging points. Many raw materials are fabricated and assembled into a few finished projects. A T logical structure consists of numerous similar finished products assembled from common assemblies and sub-assemblies. The graph shows the general appearance of each structure. Once the general parts flow is determined, the system control points (gating operations, convergent points, divergent points, constraints, and shipping points) can be identified and managed. This determination focuses management's attention on a few control points where buffers can be used to protect and to maximize throughput.

Five control points are used to manage the process: (1) the constraint, (2) the points of divergence (where a part or material is diverted to different routes in order to make different products), (3) the points of convergence (where two or more parts are combined in subassembly), (4) the gating operation (releases work into the shop), and (5) the shipping operation.

The shape of the structure determines which control points are utilized to manage production. A T structure focuses attention on the constraint and the gating operation. The five-step focusing process is used to manage the constraint with a buffer placed before the constraint to absorb variations in the process. The output from the gating operation is tied to the constraint; that is, since the constraint controls the amount of throughput; the gating operation cannot process more than the constraint.

A V structure also uses a buffer to protect the constraint and the gating operation releases orders at the same rate as the constraint as seen in the T structure. However, an additional control point exists in the V structure, the divergent point. The divergent point is controlled by a schedule derived from the shipping schedule. This derivation prevents misallocation of material to a product not currently in demand.

The A structure also manages the constraint and gating operation in a fashion similar to the T structure. Any diverging points are scheduled in accordance with the shipping schedule. In addition, an assembly buffer is used to maintain the flow into the convergent points. An additional schedule based on the shipping schedule (similar to that used in the V structure) is used to keep capacity from being misallocated to the wrong order. By using VAT analysis, significant improvements in the production process can result.

The unexpected and enormous success of The Goal, initially published in a small run of 3,000 copies and has now sold more than 2 million copies, and further development of TOC has lead many organizations to put TOC theory into practice. Over the past two decades a growing number of books, articles, and dissertations have appeared elaborating on Dr. Goldratt's philosophy and providing examples of TOC principles in use. Followers of Goldratt's philosophy, those who have completed an extensive training course conducted by Goldratt's educational firm, the Avraham Y. Goldratt Institute, refer to themselves as Jonahs. TOC materials are available in multiple languages and formats, including videotapes, audiotapes, and computer software.

Integrated Business Planning

Integrated business planning (IBP) refers to the technologies, applications and processes of connecting the planning function across the enterprise to improve organizational alignment and financial performance. IBP accurately represents a holistic model of the company in order to link strategic planning and operational planning with financial planning.

By deploying a single model across the enterprise and leveraging the organization's information assets, corporate executives, business unit heads and planning managers use IBP to evaluate plans and activities based on the true economic impact of each consideration.

History of IBP

The roots of IBP date back to 1996 where Dr. Robert Whitehair, working at the University of Massachusetts, developed technology for capturing and exploiting expert knowledge. Dr. Whitehair worked in close collaboration with several colleagues, including Professor Igor Budyachevsky of the Russian Academy of Science, to develop a technology now called COR (Constraint Oriented Reasoning). COR technology was used to capture expert knowledge; then embed it in applications that allow users to leverage it through a natural language interface. Using grant funding from corporate giants such as Chase, DuPont, General Electric, Price water house Coopers, Shell and the Williams Company, Dr. Whitehair captured expert knowledge from numerous disciplines and introduced an application for business analysis that empowered decision makers.

Components of IBP

As illustrated right, planning is integrated across the enterprise, which enables decision makers to identify the activities that deliver the greatest financial impact across the company. Recent developments and successes in the areas of business intelligence and performance management are accelerating the adoption of integrated business planning.

While IBP has been a vision for many years; the technology required for modeling, optimization and scaling was non-existent. Dr. Robert C. Whitehair of River Logic, considered to be the father of IBP, used constraint-oriented reasoning (COR) and knowledge-based rules engines to generate mathematical representations of planning constraints and variables; thereby making IBP a reality. Dr. Whitehair, working in collaboration with scientists in the U.S. and the Russian Academy of Science, solved the problem of scaling real-life situations in mathematical equivalents. Today, IBP software easily runs thousands of analyses of a mathematical representation of ~1,000,000 equations, each in excess of 1,000,000 variables, in a typical solve. In broad terms, the use of mathematical representations and extensive knowledge bases enable users to build the massive, multivariable models required for Integrated Business Planning.

Analyses

Companies use IBP to translate insight into financial impact by providing analyses such as: Identification of top financial (profit) drivers

- Answers to "what-if" questions
- Simulation
- Optimization to any variable or ratio, including balance sheet, profitability, NPV, cash flow, etc.
- Intelligent sensitivity analysis
- Modeling infeasibilities
- Understanding of unique performance driver relationships
- Opportunity costs and marginal economic value.

Benefits

IBP transforms planning into a decisive competitive advantage by:

- Providing an integrated planning platform across marketing, operations and finance
- Generating a holistic understanding of performance drivers
- Quantifying the financial impact and inter dependencies across planning alternatives
- Optimizing strategic planning and resource allocation
- Balancing sales and operations planning for profitability
- Quantifying financial risk
- Increasing business flexibility.

IBP Applications

IBP has been used to successfully model and integrate the planning efforts in a number of applications, including:

- Product profitability
- Customer profitability
- Capital expenditures
- Manufacturing operations
- Supply chain
- Business processes (human and information-based)
- Business policy
- Market demand curves
- Competitive strategy.

Manufacturing Resources Planning

Manufacturing resource planning, also known as MRP II, is a method for the effective planning of a manufacturer's resources. MRP II is composed of several linked functions, such as business planning, sales and operations planning, capacity requirements planning, and all related support systems. The output from these MRP II functions can be integrated into financial reports, such as the business plan, purchase commitment report, shipping budget, and inventory projections. It has the capability of specifically addressing operational planning and financial planning, and has simulation capability that allows its users to conduct sensitivity analyses (answering "what if" questions).

The earliest form of manufacturing resource planning was known as material requirements planning (MRP). This system was vastly improved upon until it no longer resembled the original version. The newer version was so fundamentally different from MRP, that a new term seemed appropriate. Oliver Wight coined the acronym MRP II for manufacturing resource planning.

In order to best understand MRP II, one must have a basic understanding of MRP, so we will begin with a look at MRP and then expand into MRP II.

Material Requirements Planning

Material requirements planning (MRP) is a computer-based, time-phased system for planning and controlling the production and inventory function of a firm from the purchase of materials to the shipment of finished goods. All MRP systems are computer based since the detail involved and the inherent burden of computation make manual use prohibitive. MRP is time phased because it not only determines what and how much needs to be made or purchased, but also when.

Material requirements planning first appeared in the early 1970s and was popularized by a book of the same name by Joseph Orlicky. Its use was quickly heralded as the new manufacturing panacea, but enthusiasm slowed somewhat when firms began to realize the difficulty inherent in its implementation. The MRP system is composed of three primary modules, all of which function as a form of input. These are the master production schedule, the bill-of-materials, and the inventory status file. Each module serves a unique purpose that is inter-related with the purpose of the other modules, and produces several forms of usable output.

Master Production Schedule

The master production schedule (MPS) is basically the production schedule for finished goods. This schedule is usually derived from current orders, plus any forecast requirements. The MPS is divided into units of time called "buckets." While any time frame may be utilized, usually days or weeks is appropriate. The MPS is also said to be the aggregate plan "disaggregated." In other words, the plan for goods to be produced in aggregate is broken down into its individual units or finished goods.

Bill-of-materials

The bill-of-materials is a file made up of bills-of-material (BOM). Each BOM is a hierarchical listing of the type and number of parts needed to produce one unit of finished goods. Other information, such as the routings (the route through the system that individual parts take on the way to becoming a finished good), alternate routings, or substitute materials may be also be contained with the BOM. A tool known as a product structure tree is used to clarify the relationship among the parts making up each unit of finished goods. How a product structure tree for a rolling cart might appear on a bill-of-material. This cart consists of a top that is pressed from a sheet of steel; a frame formed from four steel bars; and a leg assembly consisting of four legs, each with a caster attached. Each caster is made up of a wheel, a ball bearing, an axle, and a caster frame. The bill-of-material can be used to determine the gross number of component parts needed to manufacturer a given number of finished goods. Since a gross number is determined, safety stock can be reduced because component parts may be shared by any number of finished goods (this is known as commonality). The process of determining gross requirements of components is termed the "explosion" process, or "exploding" the bill-of-material. Assuming we need 100 rolling carts, we can use our example product structure tree to compute the gross requirements for each rolling cart component. We can easily see that in order to produce 100 rolling carts, we would need 100 tops, which would require 100 sheets of steel; 100 leg assemblies, which would require 400 legs and 400 casters (requiring 400 wheels, 400 ball bearings, 400 axles, and 400 caster frames); and 100 frames, which would require 400 bars.

Inventory Status File

The inventory status file, or inventory records file, contains a count of the on-hand balance of every part held in inventory. In addition, the inventory status file contains all pertinent information regarding open orders and the lead time (the time that elapses between placing an order and actually receiving it) for each item. Open orders are purchase orders (orders for items purchased outside the firm) or shop orders (formal instructions to the plant floor to process a given number of parts by a given date) that have not been completely satisfied. In other words, they are items that have been ordered, but are yet to be received.

The MRP Process

The MRP logic starts at the MPS, where it learns the schedule for finished goods (how many and when). It takes this information to the

BOM where it "explodes" the gross requirements for all component parts. The MRP package then takes its knowledge of the gross requirements for all components parts to the inventory status file, where the on-hand balances are listed. It then subtracts the on-hand balances and open orders from the gross requirements for components yielding the net requirements for each component. Of course, we now know not only how many components are needed but when they are needed in order to complete the schedule for finished goods on time. By subtracting the lead time from the due date for each part, we now see when an order must be placed for each part so that it can be received in time to avoid a delay in the MPS. A manual version of MRP for a part with requirements of 100 in period 3 and 250 in period 6 and with a two-period lead time. Notice that in order for the firm to meet demand on time (the MPS), they must place an order for 25 in Period 1 and an order for 200 in Period 4. The reader should be aware that this is an overly simplified version of MRP, which does not include such relevant factors as lot sizing and safety stock.

Expanding Into MRP II

With MRP generating the material and schedule requirements necessary for meeting the appropriate sales and inventory demands, more than the obvious manufacturing resources for supporting the MRP plan was found to be needed. Financial resources would have to be generated in varying amounts and timing. Also, the process would require varying degrees of marketing resource support. Production, marketing, and finance would be operating without complete knowledge or even regard for what the other functional areas of the firm were doing. In the early 1980s MRP was expanded into a much broader approach. This new approach, manufacturing resource planning (MRP II), was an effort to expand the scope of production resource planning and to involve other functional areas of the firm in the planning process, most notably marketing and finance, but also engineering, personnel, and purchasing. Incorporation of other functional areas allows all areas of the firm to focus on a common set of goals. It also provides a means for generating a variety of reports to help managers in varying functions monitor the process and make necessary adjustments as the work progresses.

When finance knows which items will be purchased and when products will be delivered, it can accurately project the firm's cash flows. In addition, personnel can project hiring or layoff requirements, while marketing can keep track of up-to-the-minute changes in delivery times, lead times, and so on. Cost accounting information is gathered, engineering input is recorded, and distribution requirements planning is performed.

An MRP II system also has a simulation capability that enables its users to conduct sensitivity analyses or evaluate a variety of possible scenarios. The MRP II system can simulate a certain decision's impact throughout the organization, and predict its results in terms of customer orders, due dates, or other "what if" outcomes. Being able to answer these "what if" questions provides a firmer grasp of available options and their potential consequences.

As with MRP, MRP II requires a computer system for implementation because of its complexity and relatively large scale. Pursuit of MRP or MRP II in a clerical fashion would prove far too cumbersome to ever be useful.

In addition to its efficient performance of the data processing and file handling, a computer also allows the system to run remarkably quick, providing near-immediate results and reports when asked to simulate a decision.

Classes of Firms Using MRP and MRP II

MRP and MRP II users are classified by the degree to which they utilize the various aspects of these systems. Class D companies have MRP working in their data processing area, but utilize little more than the inventory status file and the master production schedule, both of which may be poorly used and mismanaged. Typically, these firms are not getting much return for the expense incurred by the system.

Class C firms use their MRP system as an inventory ordering technique but make little use of its scheduling capabilities.

Class B companies utilize the basic MRP system (MPS, BOM, and Inventory file) with the addition of capacity requirements planning and a shop floor control system. Class B users have not incorporated purchasing into the system and do not have a management team that uses the system to run the business, but rather see it as a production and inventory control system.

Class A firms are said use the system in a closed loop mode. Their system consists of the basic MRP system, plus capacity planning and control, shop floor control, and vendor scheduling systems. In addition, their management uses the system to run the business. The system provides the game plan for sales, finance, manufacturing, purchasing, and engineering. Management then can use the system's report capability to monitor accuracy in the BOM, the inventory status file, and routing, as well as monitor the attainment of the MPS and capacity plans.

Class A firms have also tied in the financial system and have developed the system's simulation capabilities to answer "what if" questions. Because everyone is using the same numbers (e.g., finance and production), management has to work with only one set of numbers to run the business.

Developments

With the advent of lean manufacturing and just-in-time (JIT), MRP and MRP II have fallen into disfavour with some firms, with some feeling that the systems are obsolete. However, research has found that in certain environments with advance demand information, MRP-type push strategies yield better performance in term of inventories and service levels than did JIT's kanban-based pull strategies.

A further extension of MRP and MRP II has been developed to improve resource planning by broadening the scope of planning to include more of the supply chain. The Gartner Group of Stamford, Connecticut, coined the term "enterprise resource planning" (ERP) for this system. The authors of Manufacturing Planning and Control for Supply Chain Management note that MRP and ERP have become so entrenched in businesses that they no longer provide a source of competitive advantage. They feel that a sustaining competitive advantage will now require that manufacturing planning and control (MPC) systems to cross organizational boundaries and coordinate company units that have traditionally worked independently.

CUSTOMER RELATIONSHIP MANAGEMENT

It is pertinent to note that customer relationship management (CRM) is a widely implemented model for managing a company's interactions with customers, clients, and sales prospects. It involves using technology to organize, automate, and synchronize business processes—principally sales activities, but also those for marketing, customer service, and technical support.

The overall goals are to find, attract, and win new clients; nurture and retain those the company already has; entice former clients back into the fold; and reduce the costs of marketing and client service. Customer relationship management describes a company-wide business strategy including customer-interface departments as well as other departments. Measuring and valuing customer relationships is critical to implementing this strategy.

Main Advantages

A Customer Relationship Management system may be chosen because it is thought to provide the following advantages:

- Quality and efficiency
- Decrease in overall costs
- Decision support
- Enterprise ability
- Customer Attentions
- Increase profitability
- Improved planning
- Improved product development.

Challenges

It must be remembered that successful development, implementation, use and support of customer relationship management systems can provide a significant advantage to the user, but often there are obstacles that obstruct the user from using the system to its full potential. Instances of a CRM attempting to contain a large, complex group of data can become cumbersome and difficult to understand for ill-trained users.

The lack of senior management sponsorship can also hinder the success of a new CRM system. Stakeholders must be identified early in the process and a full commitment is needed from all executives before beginning the conversion. But the challenges faced by the company will last longer for the convenience of their customers. Additionally, an interface that is difficult to navigate or understand can hinder the CRM's effectiveness, causing users to pick and choose which areas of the system to be used, while others may be pushed aside. This fragmented implementation can cause inherent challenges, as only certain parts are used and the system is not fully functional.

The increased use of customer relationship management software has also led to an industry-wide shift in evaluating the role of the developer in designing and maintaining its software. Companies are urged to consider the overall impact of a viable CRM software suite and the potential for good or bad in its use. In fact, tools and workflows can be complex, especially for large businesses. Previously these tools were generally limited to simple CRM solutions which focused on monitoring and recording interactions and communications. Software solutions then expanded to embrace deal tracking, territories, opportunities, and the sales pipeline itself. Next came the advent of tools for other client-interface business functions, as described below.

These tools have been, and still are, offered as on-premises software that companies purchase and run on their own IT infrastructure.

One of the largest challenges that customer relationship management systems face is poor usability. With a difficult interface for a user to navigate, implementation can be fragmented or not entirely complete.

The importance of usability in a system has developed over time. Customers are likely not as patient to work through malfunctions or gaps in user safety, and there is an expectation that the usability of systems should be somewhat intuitive: "it helps make the machine an extension of the way I think — not how it wants me to think."

In fact, an intuitive design can prove most effective in developing the content and layout of a customer relationship management system. Two 2008 case studies show that the layout of a system provides a strong correlation to the ease of use for a system and that it proved more beneficial for the design to focus on presenting information in a way that reflected the most important goals and tasks of the user, rather than the structure of the organization. This "ease of service" is paramount for developing a system that is usable. In many cases, the growth of capabilities and complexities of systems has hampered the usability of a customer relationship management system. An overly complex computer system can result in an equally complex and non-friendly user interface, thus not allowing the system to work as fully intended. This bloated software can appear sluggish and/or overwhelming to the user, keeping the system from full use and potential. A series of 1998 research indicates that each item added to an information display can significantly affect the overall experience of the user.

Often, poor usability can lead to implementations that are fragmented — isolated initiatives by individual departments to address their own needs. Systems that start disunited usually stay that way: [siloed thinking] and decision processes frequently lead to separate and incompatible systems, and dysfunctional processes. A fragmented implementation can negate any financial benefit associated with a customer relationship management system, as companies choose not to use all the associated features factored when justifying the investment.

Instead, it is important that support for the CRM system is companywide. The challenge of fragmented implementations may be mitigated with improvements in late-generation CRM systems.

Business Reputation

Building and maintaining a strong business reputation has become increasingly challenging. The outcome of internal fragmentation that is observed and commented upon by customers is now visible to the rest of the world in the era of the social customer; in the past, only employees or partners were aware of it. Addressing the fragmentation requires a shift in philosophy and mindset in an organization so that everyone considers the impact to the customer of policy, decisions and actions.

Human response at all levels of the organization can affect the customer experience for good or ill. Even one unhappy customer can deliver a body blow to a business. Some developments and shifts have made companies more conscious of the life-cycle of a customer relationship management system. Companies now consider the possibility of brand loyalty and persistence of its users to purchase updates, upgrades and future editions of software.

Additionally, CRM systems face the challenge of producing viable financial profits, with a 2002 study suggesting that less than half of CRM projects are expected to provide a significant return on investment. Poor usability and low usage rates lead many companies to indicate that it was difficult to justify investment in the software without the potential for more tangible gains.

Security, Privacy and Data Security Concerns

One function of CRM is to collect information about clients. It is important to consider the customers' need for privacy and data security. Close attention should be paid to relevant laws and regulations. Vendors may need to reassure clients that their data not be shared with third parties without prior consent, and that illegal access can be prevented. A large challenge faced by developers and users is found in striking a balance between ease of use in the CRM interface and suitable and acceptable security measures and features.

Corporations investing in CRM software do so expecting a relative ease of use while also requiring that customer and other sensitive data remain secure. This balance can be difficult, as many believe that improvements in security come at the expense of system usability. Research and study show the importance of designing and developing technology that balances a positive user interface with security features that meet industry and corporate standards.

A 2002 study shows, however, that security and usability can coexist harmoniously. In many ways, a secure CRM system can become more usable. Researchers have argued that, in most cases, security breaches are the result of user-error (such as unintentionally downloading and executing a computer virus). In these events, the computer system acted as it should in identifying a file and then, following the user's orders to execute the file, exposed the computer and network to a harmful virus. Researchers argue that a more usable system creates less confusion and lessens the amount of potentially harmful errors, in turn creating a more secure and stable CRM system. Technical writers can play a large role in developing content management systems that are secure and easy to use.

A series of 2008 research shows that CRM systems, among others, need to be more open to flexibility of technical writers, allowing these professionals to become content builders. These professionals can then gather information and use it at their preference, developing a system that allows users to easily access desired information and is secure and trusted by its users.

Sales Force Automation

Sales force automation (SFA) involves using software to streamline all phases of the sales process, minimizing the time that sales representatives need to spend on each phase. This allows a business to use fewer sales representatives to manage their clients. At the core of SFA is a contact management system for tracking and recording every stage in the sales process for each prospective client, from initial contact to final disposition. Many SFA applications also include insights into opportunities, territories, sales forecasts and workflow automation.

Marketing

CRM systems for marketing help the enterprise identify and target potential clients and generate leads for the sales team. A key marketing capability is tracking and measuring multichannel campaigns, including email, search, social media, telephone and direct mail. Metrics monitored include clicks, responses, leads, deals, and revenue. Alternatively, Prospect Relationship Management (PRM) solutions offer to track customer behaviour and nurture them from first contact to sale, often cutting out the active sales process altogether. In a web-focused marketing CRM solution, organizations create and track specific web activities that help develop the client relationship. These activities may include such activities as free downloads, online video content, and online web presentations.

Customer Service and Support

CRM software provides a business with the ability to create, assign and manage requests made by customers. An example would be Call Center software which helps to direct a customer to the agent who can best help them with their current problem. Recognizing that this type of service is an important factor in attracting and retaining customers, organizations are increasingly turning to technology to help them improve their clients' experience while aiming to increase efficiency and minimize costs. CRM software can also be used to identify and reward loyal customers which in turn will help customer retention. Even so, a 2009 study revealed that only 39% of corporate executives believe their employees have the right tools and authority to solve client problems.

Creating and scheduling appointments with customers is a central activity of most customer oriented businesses. Sales, customer support, and service personnel regularly spend a portion of their time getting in touch with customers and prospects through a variety of means to agree on a time and place for meeting for a sales conversation or to deliver customer service. Appointment CRM is a relatively new CRM platform category in which an automated system is used to offer a suite of suitable appointment times to a customer via e-mail or through a web site. An automated process is used to schedule and confirm the appointment, and place it on the appropriate person's calendar. Appointment CRM systems can be an origination point for a sales lead and are generally integrated with sales and marketing CRM systems to capture and store the interaction.

Analytics

Relevant analytics capabilities are often interwoven into applications for sales, marketing, and service. These features can be complemented and augmented with links to separate, purpose-built applications for analytics and business intelligence. Sales analytics let companies monitor and understand client actions and preferences, through sales forecasting and data quality. Marketing applications generally come with predictive analytics to improve segmentation and targeting, and features for measuring the effectiveness of online, offline, and search marketing campaigns.

Web analytics have evolved significantly from their starting point of merely tracking mouse clicks on Web sites. By evaluating "buy signals," marketers can see which prospects are most likely to transact and also identify those who are bogged down in a sales process and need assistance. Marketing and finance personnel also use analytics to assess the value of multi-faceted programmes as a whole.

It must be remembered that these types of analytics are increasing in popularity as companies demand greater visibility into the performance of call centers and other service and support channels, in order to correct problems before they affect satisfaction levels. Support-focused applications typically include dashboards similar to those for sales, plus capabilities to measure and analyze response times, service quality, agent performance, and the frequency of various issues.

Integrated/Collaborative

Departments within enterprises — especially large enterprises —

tend to function with little collaboration. More recently, the development and adoption of these tools and services have fostered greater fluidity and cooperation among sales, service, and marketing. This finds expression in the concept of collaborative systems that use technology to build bridges between departments.

For example, feedback from a technical support center can enlighten marketers about specific services and product features clients are asking for. Reps, in their turn, want to be able to pursue these opportunities without the burden of re-entering records and contact data into a separate SFA system.

Small Business

For small business, basic client service can be accomplished by a contact manager system: an integrated solution that lets organizations and individuals efficiently track and record interactions, including emails, documents, jobs, faxes, scheduling, and more. These tools usually focus on accounts rather than on individual contacts.

They also generally include opportunity insight for tracking sales pipelines plus added functionality for marketing and service. As with larger enterprises, small businesses may find value in online solutions, especially for mobile and telecommuting workers.

Social Media

Social media sites like Twitter, LinkedIn, Facebook and Google Plus are amplifying the voice of people in the marketplace and are having profound and far-reaching effects on the ways in which people buy. Customers can now research companies online and then ask for recommendations through social media channels, as well as share opinions and experiences on companies, products and services.

As social media is not as widely moderated or censored as mainstream media, individuals can say anything they want about a company or brand, positive or negative.

Increasingly, companies are looking to gain access to these conversations and take part in the dialogue. More than a few systems are now integrating to social networking sites. Social media promoters cite a number of business advantages, such as using online communities as a source of high-quality leads and a vehicle for crowd sourcing solutions to client-support problems. Companies can also leverage client stated habits and preferences to "Hypertargeting" their sales and marketing communications. Some analysts take the view that business-to-business marketers should proceed cautiously when weaving social media into their business processes.

These observers recommend careful market research to determine if and where the phenomenon can provide measurable benefits for client interactions, sales and support. It is stated that people feel their interactions are peer-to-peer between them and their contacts, and resent company involvement, sometimes responding with negatives about that company.

Non-Profit and Membership-Based

Systems for non-profit and membership-based organizations help track constituents and their involvement in the organization. Capabilities typically include tracking the following: fund-raising, demographics, membership levels, membership directories, volunteering and communications with individuals.

Horizontal Vs. Vertical

Horizontal CRM manufacturers offer the same non-specialized base product across all industries. They tend to be cheaper, least common denominator solutions. For example, a bakery would get the same product as a bank. Vertical CRM manufacturers offer specialized, specific industry or pain-point CRM solutions. In general, horizontal CRM solutions are less costly up front, and more costly in the future, due to the fact that companies must tailor them for their particular industry and business model. On the other hand, Vertical CRM solutions tend to be more costly up front and less costly down the road because they already incorporate best practices that are specific to an industry and business model. Major CRM vendors offer horizontal CRM solutions. In order to tailor a horizontal CRM solution, companies may use industry templates to overlay some generic best practices by industry on top of the horizontal CRM solution.

Horizontal CRM vendors may also rely on value added reseller networks of systems integrators to build vertical solutions and sell them as 3rd party add-ons or to come in and customize the solution to fit into a particular scenario. Vertical CRM vendors focus on a particular industry. As a general rule of thumb in CRM, it is ten times as costly to build a vertical solution from a horizontal software programme than it is to find a particular vertical solution that is already tailored to your business model and industry.

Strategy

For larger-scale enterprises, a complete and detailed plan is required to obtain the funding, resources, and company-wide support that can make the initiative of choosing and implementing a system successfully.

Benefits must be defined, risks assessed, and cost quantified in three general areas:

- *Processes:* Though these systems have many technological components, business processes lie at its core. It can be seen as a more client-centric way of doing business, enabled by technology that consolidates and intelligently distributes pertinent information about clients, sales, marketing effectiveness, responsiveness, and market trends. Therefore, a company must analyze its business workflows and processes before choosing a technology platform; some will likely need re-engineering to better serve the overall goal of winning and satisfying clients. Moreover, planners need to determine the types of client information that are most relevant, and how best to employ them.
- *People:* For an initiative to be effective, an organization must convince its staff that the new technology and workflows will benefit employees as well as clients. Senior executives need to be strong and visible advocates who can clearly state and support the case for change. Collaboration, teamwork, and two-way communication should be encouraged across hierarchical boundaries, especially with respect to process improvement.
- *Technology:* In evaluating technology, key factors include alignment with the company's business process strategy and goals, including the ability to deliver the right data to the right employees and sufficient ease of adoption and use. Platform selection is best undertaken by a carefully chosen group of executives who understand the business processes to be automated as well as the software issues. Depending upon the size of the company and the breadth of data, choosing an application can take anywhere from a few weeks to a year or more.

Implementation

Increases in revenue, higher rates of client satisfaction, and significant savings in operating costs are some of the benefits to an enterprise. Proponents emphasize that technology should be implemented only in the context of careful strategic and operational planning. Implementations almost invariably fall short when one or more facets of this prescription are ignored:

- *Poor planning:* Initiatives can easily fail when efforts are limited to choosing and deploying software, without an accompanying rationale, context, and support for the workforce. In other instances, enterprises simply automate flawed client-facing processes rather than redesign them according to best practices.

- *Poor integration:* For many companies, integrations are piecemeal initiatives that address a glaring need: improving a particular client-facing process or two or automating a favored sales or client support channel. Such "point solutions" offer little or no integration or alignment with a company's overall strategy. They offer a less than complete client view and often lead to unsatisfactory user experiences.
- *Toward a solution:* overcoming siloed thinking. Experts advise organizations to recognize the immense value of integrating their client-facing operations. In this view, internally focused, department-centric views should be discarded in favor of reorienting processes toward information-sharing across marketing, sales, and service. For example, sales representatives need to know about current issues and relevant marketing promotions before attempting to cross-sell to a specific client. Marketing staff should be able to leverage client information from sales and service to better target campaigns and offers. And support agents require quick and complete access to a client's sales and service history.

Adoption Issues

Historically, the landscape is littered with instances of low adoption rates. Many of the challenges listed above offer a glimpse into some of the obstacles that corporations implementing a CRM suite face; in many cases time, resources and staffing do not allow for the troubleshooting necessary to tackle an issue and the system is shelved or sidestepped instead. Why is it so difficult sometimes to get employees up to date on rapidly developing new technology?

Essentially, your employees need to understand how the system works, as well as understand the clients and their needs. No doubt this process is time consuming, but it is well worth the time and effort, as you will be better able to understand and meet the needs of your clients. CRM training needs to cover two types of information: relational knowledge and technological knowledge.

Statistics

In 2003, a Gartner report estimated that more than $1 billion had been spent on software that was not being used. More recent research indicates that the problem, while perhaps less severe, is a long way from being solved. According to *CSO Insights*, less than 40 percent of 1,275 participating companies had end-user adoption rates above 90 percent. Additionally, many corporations only use CRM systems on a partial or fragmented basis, thus missing opportunities for effective marketing and efficiency. In a 2007 survey from the UK, four-fifths of senior executives reported that their biggest challenge is getting their staff to use the systems they had installed.

Further, 43 percent of respondents said they use less than half the functionality of their existing system; 72 percent indicated they would trade functionality for ease of use; 51 percent cited data synchronization as a major issue; and 67 percent said that finding time to evaluate systems was a major problem. With expenditures expected to exceed $11 billion in 2010, enterprises need to address and overcome persistent adoption challenges.

It must be remembered that the amount of time needed for the development and implementation of a customer relationship management system can prove costly to the implementation as well. Research indicates that implementation timelines that are greater than 90 days in length run an increased risk in the CRM system failing to yield successful results.

Specialists offer these recommendations for boosting adoptions rates and coaxing users to blend these tools into their daily workflow:

Additionally, researchers found the following themes were common in systems that users evaluated favorably. These positive evaluations led to the increased use and more thorough implementation of the CRM system. Further recommendations include

- *Breadcrumb Trail:* This offers the user a path, usually at the top of a web or CRM page, to return to the starting point of navigation. This can prove useful for users who might find themselves lost or unsure how they got to the current screen in the CRM.
- *Readily available search engine boxes:* Research shows that users are quick to seek immediate results through the use of a search engine box. A CRM that uses a search box will keep assistance and immediate results quickly within the reach of a user.
- *Help Option Menu:* An outlet for quick assistance or frequently asked questions can provide users with a lifeline that makes the customer relationship management software easier to use. Researchers suggest making this resource a large component of the CRM during the development stage.

A larger theme is found in that the responsiveness, intuitive design and overall usability of a system can influence the users' opinions and preferences of systems.

Researchers noted a strong correlation between the design and layout of a user interface and the perceived level of trust from the user. The researchers found that users felt more comfortable on a system evaluated as usable and applied that comfort and trust into increased use and adoption.

One of the largest issues surrounding the implementation and adoption of a CRM comes in the perceived lack of technical and user support in using the system. Individual users — and large corporations — find themselves equally stymied by a system that is not easily understood. Technical support in the form of a qualified and comprehensive help menu can provide significant improvement in implementation when providing focused, context-specific information.

Data show that CRM users are often unwilling to consult a help menu if it is not easily accessible and immediate in providing assistance. A 1998 case study found that users would consult the help menu for an average of two or three screens, abandoning the assistance if desired results weren't found by that time. Researchers believe that help menus can provide assistance to users through introducing additional screenshots and other visual and interactive aids. A 2004 case study concluded that the proper use of screenshots can significantly support a user's "developing a mental model of the program" and help in "identifying and locating window elements and objects."

This research concluded that screen shots allowed users to "learn more, make fewer mistakes, and learn in a shorter time frame," which can certainly assist in increasing the time frame for full implementation of a CRM system with limited technical or human support.

Experts have identified five characteristics to make a help menu effective:

- "context-specific" — the help menu contains only the information relevant to the topic that is being discussed or sought
- "useful" — in conjunction with being context-specific, the help menu must be comprehensive in including all of the information that the user seeks
- "obvious to invoke" — the user must have no trouble in locating the help menu or how to gain access to its contents
- "non-intrusive" — the help menu must not interfere with the

user's primary path of work and must maintain a distance that allows for its use only when requested

- "easily available" — the information of the help menu must be accessible with little or few steps required

Development

Thoughtful and thorough development can avoid many of the challenges and obstacles faced in using and implementing a customer relationship management system. With shifts in competition and the increasing reliance by corporations to use a CRM system, development of software has become more important than ever. Technical communicators can play a significant role in developing software that is usable and easy to navigate.

Clarity

One of the largest issues in developing a usable customer relationship management system comes in the form of clear and concise presentation. Developers are urged to consider the importance of creating software that is easy to understand and without unnecessary confusion, thus allowing a user to navigate the system with ease and confidence.

Strong writing skills can prove extremely beneficial for software development and creation. A 1998 case study showed that software engineering majors who successfully completed a technical writing course created capstone experience projects that were more mindful of end user design than the projects completed by their peers. The case study yielded significant results:

- Students who completed the technical writing course submitted capstone projects that contained more vivid and explicit detail in writing than their peers who did not complete the course. Researchers note that the students appeared to weigh multiple implications on the potential user, and explained their decisions more thoroughly than their peers.
- Those participating in the writing course sought out test users more frequently to add a perspective outside their own as developer. Students appeared sensitive of the user's ability to understand the developed software.
- The faculty member overseeing the capstone submissions felt that students who did not enroll in the technical writing class were at a significant disadvantage when compared to their peers who did register for the course.

In the case study, researchers argue for the inclusion of technical writers in the development process of software systems. These professionals can offer insight into usability in communication for software projects. Technical writing can help build a unified resource for successful documentation, training and execution of customer relationship management systems.

It must be remembered that in many circumstances, test users play a significant role in developing software. These users offer software developers an outside perspective of the project, often helping developers gain insight into potential areas of trouble that might have been overlooked or passed over because of familiarity with the system. Test users can also provide feedback from a targeted audience: a software development team creating a customer relationship management software system for higher education can have a user with a similar profile explore the technology, offering opportunities to cater the further development of the system.

Test users help developers discover which areas of the software perform well, and which areas require further attention. Research notes that test users can prove to be most effective in providing developers a structured overview of the software creation. These users can provide a fresh perspective that can reflect on the state of the CRM development without the typically narrow or invested focus of a software developer.

Interestingly, 2007 study suggests some important steps are needed in creating a quality and effective test environment for software development. In this case study, researchers observed a Danish software company in the midst of new creating new software with usability in mind. The study found these four observations most appropriate:

- The developers must make a conscious effort and commitment to the test user. Researchers note that the company had dedicated specific research space and staff focused exclusively on usability.
- Usability efforts must carry equal concern in the eyes of developers as other technology-related concerns in the creation stage. The study found that test users became discouraged when items flagged as needing attention were marked as lower priority by the software developers.
- Realistic expectations from both test users and software developers help maintain a productive environment. Researchers note that developers began to limit seeking input from test users after the test users suggested remedies the developers felt were improbable, leading the developers to believe consulting the test users would only prove to be more work.
- Developers must make themselves available to test users and colleagues alike throughout the creation process of a software system.

The researchers note that some of the best instances of usability adjustments can be made through casual conversation, and that often usability is bypassed by developers because these individuals never think to consult test users. Allowing users to test developing products can have its limits in effectiveness, as the culture of the industry and desired outcomes can affect the effect on CRM creation, as a 2008 case study suggests that the responsiveness of test users can vary dramatically depending on the industry and field of the user.

Research suggests that test users can rate the importance or severity of potential software issues in a significantly different fashion than software developers. Similarly so, researchers note the potential for costly delay if developers spend too much time attempting to coerce hesitant test users from participating. Additionally, involving too many test users can prove cumbersome and delay the development of a CRM system. Additional research notes that test users may be able to identify an area that proves challenging in a software system, but might have difficulty explaining the outcome. A related 2007 case study noted that test users were able to describe roughly a third of the usability problems. Further, the language used by test users in many circumstances proves to be quite general and lacking the specific nature needed by developers to enact real change.

Related Trends

Many CRM vendors offer Web-based tools (cloud computing) and software as a service (SaaS), which are accessed via a secure Internet connection and displayed in a Web browser. These applications are sold as subscriptions, with customers not needing to invest in purchasing and maintaining IT hardware, and subscription fees are a fraction of the cost of purchasing software outright.

The trend towards cloud-based CRM has forced traditional providers to move into the "cloud" through acquisitions of smaller providers: Oracle purchased RightNow in October 2011 and SAP acquired SuccessFactors in December 2011. Salesforce.com pioneered the concept of delivering enterprise applications through a web browser and paved the way for future cloud companies to deliver software over the web. Salesforce.com continues to be the leader amongst providers in cloud CRM systems.

The era of the "social customer" refers to the use of social media (Twitter, Facebook, LinkedIn, Yelp, customer reviews in Amazon, etc.) by customers in ways that allow other potential customers to glimpse real world experience of current customers with the seller's products and services. This shift increases the power of customers to make purchase decisions that are informed by other parties sometimes outside of the control of the seller or seller's network. In response, CRM philosophy and strategy has shifted to encompass social networks and user communities, podcasting, and personalization in addition to internally generated marketing, advertising and webpage design. With the spread of self-initiated customer reviews, the user experience of a product or service requires increased attention to design and simplicity, as customer expectations have risen. CRM as a philosophy and strategy is growing to encompass these broader components of the customer relationship, so that businesses may anticipate and innovate to better serve customers, referred to as "Social CRM".

Another related development is vendor relationship management, or VRM, which is the customer-side counterpart of CRM: tools and services that equip customers to be both independent of vendors and better able to engage with them. VRM development has grown out of efforts by ProjectVRM at Harvard's Berkman Center for Internet & Society and Identity Commons' Internet Identity Workshops, as well as by a growing number of startups and established companies. VRM was the subject of a cover story in the May 2010 issue of *CRM* Magazine.

In 2001 Doug Laney coined the term 'Extended Relationship Management' (XRM). He defined XRM as the principle and practice of applying CRM disciplines and technologies to other core enterprise constituents, including primary partners, employees and suppliers as well as other secondary allies such as government, press, and industry consortia.

REFERENCES

Jonathan Coulter and Andrew W. Shepherd, Inventory Credit – An approach to developing agricultural markets, FAO, Rome, 1995

Kaplan, Robert S. and Bruns, W. Accounting and Management: A Field Study Perspective (Harvard Business School Press, 1987).

Maher, Lanen and Rahan, Fundamentals of Cost Accounting, 1st Edition (McGraw-Hill 2005).

Maskell & Baggaley (December 19, 2003). "Practical Lean Accounting". *Productivity Press, New York, NY.*

7

Focus on Purchasing-Oriented Aspects Other Issues and Challenges

> Purchasing the Bobcats is the culmination of my post-playing career goal of becoming the majority owner of an NBA franchise.
>
> —*Michael Jordan*

PURCHASING

It is pertinent to note that purchasing refers to a business or organization attempting for acquiring goods or services to accomplish the goals of the enterprise. Though there are several organizations that attempt to set standards in the purchasing process, processes can vary greatly between organizations. Typically the word "purchasing" is not used interchangeably with the word "procurement", since procurement typically includes Expediting, Supplier Quality, and Traffic and Logistics (T&L) in addition to Purchasing.

Basically, purchasing managers/directors, and procurement managers/directors guide the organization's acquisition procedures and standards. Most organizations use a three-way check as the foundation of their purchasing programmes. This involves three departments in the organization completing separate parts of the acquisition process. The three departments do not all report to the same senior manager to prevent unethical practices and lend credibility to the process.

These departments can be purchasing, receiving; and accounts payable or engineering, purchasing and accounts payable; or a plant manager, purchasing and accounts payable. Combinations can vary significantly, but a purchasing department and accounts payable are usually two of the three departments involved. When the receiving department is not involved, it's typically called a two-way check or two-way purchase order. In this situation, the purchasing department issues the purchase order receipt not required. When an invoice arrives against the order, the accounts payable department will then go directly to the requestor of the purchase order to verify that the goods or services were received. This is typically what is done for goods and services that will bypass the receiving department.

A few examples are software delivered electronically, NRE work (non reoccurring engineering services), consulting hours, etc. Historically, the purchasing department issued purchase orders for supplies, services, equipment, and raw materials. Then, in an effort to decrease the administrative costs associated with the repetitive ordering of basic consumable items, "blanket" or "master" agreements were put into place.

These types of agreements typically have a longer duration and increased scope to maximize the quantities of scale concept. When additional supplies were required, a simple release would be issued to the supplier to provide the goods or services. Another method of decreasing administrative costs associated with repetitive contracts for common material, is the use of company credit cards, also known as "Purchasing Cards" or simply "P-Cards". P-card programmes vary, but all of them have internal checks and audits to ensure appropriate use. Purchasing managers realized once contracts for the low dollar value consumables are in place, procurement can take a smaller role in the operation and use of the contracts.

There is still oversight in the forms of audits and monthly statement reviews, but most of their time is now available to negotiate major purchases and setting up of other long term contracts. These contracts are typically renewable annually. This trend away from the daily procurement function (tactical purchasing) resulted in several changes in the industry. The first was the reduction of personnel. Purchasing departments were now smaller. There was no need for the army of clerks processing orders for individual parts as in the past. Another change was the focus on negotiating contracts and procurement of large capital equipment. Both of these functions permitted purchasing departments to make the biggest financial contribution to the organization. A new terms and job title emerged – Strategic sourcing and Sourcing Managers. These professionals not only focused on the bidding process and negotiating with suppliers, but the entire supply function. In these roles they were able to add value and maximize savings for organizations.

This value was manifested in lower inventories, less personnel, and getting the end product to the organization's consumer quicker. Purchasing manager's success in these roles resulted in new assignments outside to the traditional purchasing function – logistics, materials management, distribution, and warehousing. More and more purchasing managers were becoming Supply Chain Managers handling additional functions of their organizations operation. Purchasing managers were not the only ones to become Supply Chain Managers.

Logistic managers, material managers, distribution managers, etc. all rose the broader function and some had responsibility for the purchasing functions now. In accounting, purchases is the amount of goods a company bought throughout this year. it is also refers to information as to the kind,quality,quantity and cost of goods bought that should be maintained. They are added to inventory. Purchases are offset by Purchase Discounts and Purchase Returns and Allowances. When it should be added depends on the Free On Board (FOB) policy of the trade.

For the purchaser, this new inventory is added on shipment if the policy was FOB shipping point, and the seller remove this item from its inventory. On the other hand, the purchaser added this inventory on receipt if the policy was FOB destination, and the seller remove this item from its inventory when it was delivered.

Goods bought for the purpose other than direct selling, such as for Research and Development, are added to inventory and allocated to Research and Development expense as they are used. On a side note, equipments bought for Research and Development are not added to inventory, but are capitalized as assets.

Acquisition Process

The revised acquisition process for major systems in industry and defence is shown in the next figure. Then the purchase has to clear all the materials. The process is defined by a series of phases during which technology is defined and matured into viable concepts, which are subsequently developed and readied for production, after which the systems produced are supported in the field. The process allows for a given system to enter the process at any of the development phases. For example, a system using unproven technology would enter at the beginning stages of the process and would proceed through a lengthy period of technology maturation, while a system based on mature and proven technologies might enter directly into engineering development or, conceivably, even production. The process itself includes four phases of development:

- Concept and Technology Development: is intended to explore alternative concepts based on assessments of operational needs, technology readiness, risk, and affordability.
- Concept and Technology Development phase begins with concept

exploration. During this stage, concept studies are undertaken to define alternative concepts and to provide information about capability and risk that would permit an objective comparison of competing concepts.

- System Development and Demonstration phase. This phase could be entered directly as a result of a technological opportunity and urgent user need, as well as having come through concept and technology development.
- The last, and longest, phase is the Sustainment and Disposal phase of the programme. During this phase all necessary activities are accomplished to maintain and sustain the system in the field in the most cost-effective manner possible.

Selection of Bidders

This is the process where the organization identifies potential suppliers for specified supplies, services or equipment. These suppliers' credentials and history are analyzed, together with the products or services they offer. The bidder selection process varies from organization to organization, but can include running credit reports, interviewing management, testing products, and touring facilities. This process is not always done in order of importance, but rather in order of expense.

Often purchasing managers research potential bidders obtaining information on the organizations and products from media sources and their own industry contacts. Additionally, purchasing might send Request for Information (RFI) to potential suppliers to help gather information. Engineering would also inspect sample products to determine if the company or organisation can produce products they need. If the bidder passes both of these stages engineering may decide to do some testing on the materials to further verify quality standards. These tests can be expensive and involve significant time of multiple technicians and engineers.

Engineering management must make this decision based on the cost of the products they are likely to procure, the importance of the bidders' product to production, and other factors. Credit checks, interviewing management, touring plants as well as other steps could all be utilized if engineering, manufacturing, and supply chain managers decide they could help their decision and the cost is justifiable.

Other organizations might have minority procurement goals to consider in selection of bidders. Organizations identify goals in the use of companies owned and operated by certain ethnicities or women owned business enterprises. Significant utilizing of minority suppliers may qualify the firm as a potential bidder for a contract with a company or governmental entity looking to increase their minority supplier programmes. This selection process can include or exclude international suppliers depending on organizational goals and criteria. Companies looking to increase their pacific rim supplier base may exclude suppliers from the Americas, Europe, and Australia.

Other organizations may be looking to purchase domestically to ensure a quicker response to orders as well as easier collaboration on design and production. Organizational goals will dictate the criteria for the selection process of bidders. It is also possible that the product or service being procured is so specialized that the number of bidders are limited and the criteria must be very wide to permit competition. If only one firm can meet the specifications for the product then the purchasing managers must consider utilizing a "Sole Source" option or work with engineering to broaden the specifications if the project will permit alteration in the specifications.

The sole source option is the part of the selection of bidders that acknowledges there is sometimes only one reasonable supplier for some services or products. This can be because of the limited applications for the product cannot support more than one manufacturer, proximity of the service provided, or the products are newly designed or invented and competition is not yet available.

Bidding Process

This is the process an organization utilizes to procure goods, services or equipment. Processes vary significantly from the stringent to the very informal. Large corporations and governmental entities are most likely to have stringent and formal processes. These processes can utilize specialized bid forms that require specific procedures and detail. The very stringent procedures require bids to be open by several staff from various departments to ensure fairness and impartiality.

Responses are usually very detailed. Bidders not responding exactly as specified and following the published procedures can be disqualified. Smaller private businesses are more likely to have less formal procedures. Bids can be in the form of an email to all of the bidders specifying products or services. Responses by bidders can be detailed or just the proposed dollar amount. Most bid processes are multi-tiered. Acquisitions under a specified dollar amount can be "user discretion" permitting the request or to choose who ever they want. This level can be as low as $100 or as high as $10,000 depending on the organization. The rationale is the savings realized by processing these request the same as expensive items is minimal and does not justify the time and expense. Purchasing departments watch for abuses of the user discretion privilege.

Acquisitions in a mid range can be processed with a slightly more formal process. This process may involve the user providing quotes from three separate suppliers. Purchasing may be asked or required to obtain the quotes. The formal bid process starts as low as $10,000 or as high as $100,000 depending on the organization. The bid usually involves a specific form the bidder fills out and must be returned by a specified deadline. Depending of the commodity being purchased and the organization the bid may specify a weighted evaluation criterion. Other bids would be evaluated at the discretion of purchasing or the end users. Some bids could be evaluated by a cross-functional committee. Other bids may be evaluated by the end user or the buyer in Purchasing. Especially in small, private firms the bidders could be evaluated on criteria or factors that have little if anything to do with the actual bid. Examples of these factors are history of the bidder with the company, history of the bidder with the company's senior management at other firms, and bidder's breadth of products.

Technical Evaluation

Technical evaluations, evaluations of the technical suitability of the quoted goods or services, if required, are normally performed prior to the commercial evaluation. During this phase of the procurement process, a technical representative of the company (usually an engineer) will review the proposal and designate each bidder as either technically acceptable or technically unacceptable.

Commercial Evaluation

Cost of Money is calculated by multiplying the applicable currency interest rate multiplied by the amount of money paid prior to the receipt of the Goods. If the money was to have remained in the buyer's account, interest would be drawn. That interest is essentially an additional cost associated with such Progress or Milestone payments.

The manufacturing location is taken into consideration during the evaluation stage primarily to calculate freight costs and regional issues which may be considered. For instance, in Europe it is common for factories to close during the month of August for Summer holiday. Labor agreements may also be taken into consideration and may be drawn into the evaluation if the particular region is known to frequent labor unions.

The manufacturing lead-time is the time from the placement of the order (or time final drawings are submitted by the Buyer to the Seller) until the goods are manufactured and prepared for delivery. Lead-times vary by commodity and can range from several days to years.

Transportation time is evaluated while comparing the delivery of goods to the Buyer's required use-date. If Goods are shipped from a remote port, with infrequent vessel transportation, the transportation time could exceed the schedule and adjustments would need to be made. Delivery Charges - the charge for the Goods to be delivered to a stated point. Bid Validity Packing Bid Adjustments Terms and Conditions Seller's Services Standards Organizations Financial Review Payment Currency Risk Analysis - market volatility, financial stress within the bidders Testing

Negotiating

Negotiating is a key skillset in the Purchasing field. One of the goals of Purchasing Agents is to acquire goods per the most advantageous terms of the buying entity (or simply, the "Buyer"). Purchasing Agents typically attempt to decrease costs while meeting the Buyer's other requirements such as an on-time delivery, compliance to the commercial terms and conditions (including the warranty, the transfer of risk, assignment, auditing rights, confidentiality, remedies, etc.).

Good negotiators, those with high levels of documented "cost savings", receive a premium within the industry relative to their compensation. Depending on the employment agreement between the Purchasing Agent (Buyer) and the employer, Buyer's cost savings can result in the creation of value to the business, and may result in a flat-rate bonus, or a percentage payout to the Purchasing Agent of the documented cost savings.

Purchasing Departments, while they can be considered as a support function of the key business, are actually revenue generating departments. For example, if the company needs to buy $30 million USD of widgets and the Purchasing Department secures the widgets for $25M USD, the Purchasing Department would have saved the company $5M USD. That savings could exceed the annual budget of the department, which in effect would pay the department's overhead - the employee's salaries, computers, office space, etc.

Post-award administration typically consists of making minor changes, additions or subtractions, that in some way change the terms of the agreement or the Seller's Scope of Supply. Such changes are often minor, but for auditing purposes must be documented into the existing agreement. Examples include increasing the quantity of a Line Item or changing the metallurgy of a particular component.

WHOLESALE

Wholesaling, jobbing, or distributing is defined as the sale of goods or merchandise to retailers, to industrial, commercial, institutional, or other professional business users, or to other wholesalers and related subordinated services. In general, it is the sale of goods to anyone other than a standard consumer.

According to the United Nations Statistics Division, "wholesale" is the resale (sale without transformation) of new and used goods to retailers, to industrial, commercial, institutional or professional users, or to other wholesalers, or involves acting as an agent or broker in buying merchandise for, or selling merchandise to, such persons or companies. Wholesalers frequently physically assemble, sort and grade goods in large lots, break bulk, repack and redistribute in smaller lots. While wholesalers of most products usually operate from independent premises, wholesale marketing for foodstuffs can take place at specific wholesale markets where all traders are congregated.

Traditionally, wholesalers were closer to the markets they supplied than the source from which they got the products.

However, with the advent of the internet and E-procurement there are an increasing number of wholesalers located nearer manufacturing bases in China, Taiwan, and Southeast Asia. For example, Chinavasion, Ownta, Salehoo, and Modbom. These companies offer drop shipping services to companies and individuals.

In the banking industry "wholesale" usually refers to wholesale banking, providing tailored services to large customers, in contrast with retail banking, providing standardized services to large numbers of smaller customers.

Taxes

Often, wholesalers are not required to charge their buyers sales tax, but they sometimes decide or are required to charge a special wholesale tax.

ROLE OF DEMAND CHAIN

It is pertinent to note that the demand chain is that part of the value chain which drives demand. Analysing the firm's activities as a linked chain is a tried and tested way of revealing value creation opportunities. The business economist Michael Porter of Harvard Business School pioneered this value chain approach: "the value chain disaggregates the firm into its strategically relevant activities in order to understand the costs and existing potential sources of differentiation" .

It is the micro mechanism at the level of the firm that equalizes supply and demand at the macro market level. Early applications in distribution, manufacturing and purchasing collectively gave rise to a subject known as the supply chain. Old supply chains have been transformed into faster, cheaper and more reliable modern supply chains as a result of investment in information technology, cost-analysis and process-analysis.

Marketing, sales and service are the other half of the value-chain, which collectively drive and sustain demand, and are known as the Demand Chain. Progress in transforming the demand side of business is behind the supply side, but there is growing interest today in transforming demand chains.

Demand Chain Challenges

At present, there appear to be four main challenges to progress in transforming Demand Chains and making them faster, leaner and better:

- Linking Demand and Supply Chains
- Demand Chain Information Systems
- Demand Chain Process Re-Engineering
- Demand Chain Resource Distribution and Optimisation.

Issue of Linking Demand and Supply Chains

In fact, challenge of linking demand and supply chains has occupied many supply chain specialists in recent years; and concepts such as "demand-driven supply chains", customer-driven supply chains and sales and operations planning have attracted attention and become the subject of conferences and seminars. The core problem from the supply chain perspective is getting good demand plans and forecasts from the people driving demand: marketing, sales promotions, new product developments etc.

The aim is to minimise out-of-stock (OOS) situations and excessive cost of supply due to spiky demand. Much attention has been drawn to the bullwhip effect. This occurs when demand patterns are extremely volatile, usually as a result of sales promotions, and it has the unintended consequences of driving up supply chain costs and service issues, due to supply capacity being unable to meet the spiky demand pattern and the entire chain becoming unstable as a consequence .

While the aim of linking the chains is clearly sensible, most of the people involved so far come from the supply side, and there has been a noticeable lack of input to these debates from Marketing and Sales specialists.

Progress in modernising marketing and sales processes and information systems has also been slow; these systems and processes have been an obstacle to linking the two chains.

Demand Chain Information Systems

Information about activities and costs is an essential resource for improving value chain performance. Such information is nowadays readily available for the supply chain, due to the widespread implementation of ERP technology (systems such as SAP), and these systems have been instrumental in the transformation of supply chain performance.

Demand chain IT development has focused on database marketing and CRM systems . Demand driving activities and associated costs are still recorded in an inconsistent manner, mostly on spreadsheets and even then the quality of the information tends to be incomplete and inaccurate .

Recently, however, Marketing Resource Management systems have become available to plan, track and measure activities and costs as an embedded part of marketing workflows.

> "MRM is a set of processes and capabilities that aim to enhance your ability to orchestrate and optimize the use of internal and external marketing resources...The desire to deal with increased marketing complexity, along with a mandate to do more with less, are the primary drivers behind the growth of MRM".

Implementation of MRM systems often reveals process issues that must be tackled, as Gartner have observed:

> "All too often, large enterprises lack documented or standardized marketing processes — resulting in misalignments, inconsistencies and wasted effort. Marketing personnel frequently rotate job responsibilities. Along with thwarting progress toward best practices and processes, this disarray contributes to a loss of corporate memory and key lessons learned. The elongated learning curve affects new or transferred employees as they struggle to find information or have to relearn what the organization, in effect, already "knows."

Demand Chain Process Improvement

Processes in the demand chain are often less well-organised and disciplined than their supply side equivalents. This arises partly from the absence of an agreed framework for analysing the demand chain process.

Professors Philip Kotler and Robert Shaw have recently proposed such a framework . Describing it as the "Idea to Demand Chain" they say:

> "The I2D process can be pictured as shown in Exhibit 1; it is the mirror image of the supply chain, and contains all the activities that result in demand being stimulated. Yet unlike the supply chain, which has successfully delivered economies of scale through process simplification and process control, marketing's demand chain is primitive and inefficient. In many firms it is fragmented, obscured by departmental boundaries, invisible and unmanaged."

Demand Chain Budget Segmentation, Targeting and Optimization

In fact, demand chain budgets for marketing, sales and service expenditure are substantial. Maximising their impact on shareholder value has become an important financial goal for decision makers. Developing a shared language across marketing and finance is one the challenges to achieving this goal. Segmentation is the initial thing to decide. From a strategic finance perspective "segments are responsibility centers for which a separate measure of revenues and costs is obtained". From a marketing perspective "segmentation is the act of dividing the market into distinct groups of buyers who might require separate products and/or marketing mixes". An important challenge for decision makers is how to align these two marketing and finance perspectives on segmentation.

Targeting of the budget is the final thing to decide. From the marketing perspective the challenge is how "to optimally allocate a given marketing budget to various target markets" . From a finance perspective the problem is one of resource and budget allocation "determining the right quantity of resources to implement the value maximising strategy" .

Optimization provides the technical basis for targeting decisions. Whilst mathematical optimization theory has been in existence since the 1950s, its application to marketing only began in the 1970s , and lack of data and computer power were limiting factors until the 1990s.

Since 2000, applying maths to budget segmentation, targeting and optimization has become more commonplace. In the UK the IPA Awards have documented over 1000 cases of modelling over 15 years, as part of their award process. The judging criteria are rigorous and not a matter of taste or fashion. Entrants must prove beyond all reasonable doubt that the marketing is profitable . It enables marketing to be brought centre stage in four important ways

It is to be noted first that it translates the language of marketing and sales into the language of the boardroom. Finance and profits are the preferred language of the modern executive suite. Marketing and sales strategies have to be justified in terms of their ability to increase the financial value of the business. It provides a bridge between marketing and the other functions. Second, it strengthens demand chain accountability.

In Marketing Departments awareness, preference and satisfaction are often tracked as alternative objectives to shareholder value. In Sales Departments, sales promotion spending is often used to boost volumes, even when the result is unprofitable . Optimization modelling can assess these practices and support more rigorous accountability methods. Third, it provides a counter-argument to the arbitrary cutting of demand-chain budgets. Return on marketing investment models can help demonstrate where financial impact of demand driving activities is positive and negative, and so help support fact-based budgeting. Finally, demand-chain profitability modelling encourages a strategic debate. Because long-term cashflow and NPV calculations can show the shareholder value effect of marketing, sales and service, strong arguments can be made for putting the Demand Chain on an equal footing to the Supply Chain.

DEMAND CHAIN MANAGEMENT

Demand chain management (DCM) is the management of upstream and downstream relationships between suppliers and customers to deliver the best value to the customer at the least cost to the demand chain as a whole. The term demand chain management is used to denote the concept commonly referred to as supply chain management, however with special regard to the customer pull. In that sense, demand chain management software tools bridge the gap between the customer relationship management and the supply chain management. The organization's supply chain processes are managed to deliver best value according to the demand of the customers.

A study of the university in Wageningen (the Netherlands) sees DCM as an extension of supply chain management, due to its incorporation of the market orientation perspective on its concept. While the term "demand-driven supply chain or network" denotes a set of concepts, the term "demand-driven execution" or DDE is used to express the means of achieving those concepts.

Demand-Driven Supply Network

A *Demand-driven supply network (DDSN)* is one method of supply chain management which involves building supply chains in response to demand signals. The main force of DDSN is that it is driven by customers demand. In comparison with the traditional supply chain, DDSN uses the pull technique. It gives DDSN market opportunities to share more information and to collaborate with others in the supply chain. DDSN uses a capability model that consist of four levels. The first level is *Reacting*, the second level is *Anticipating*, the third level is *Collaborating* and the last level is *Orchestrating*. The first two levels focus on the internal supply chain while the last two levels concentrate on external relations throughout the Extended Enterprise.

Competitive Advantages

To create sustainable competitive advantages with DDSN, companies have to do deal with three conditions: *Alignment* (create shared incentives), *Agility* (respond quickly to short-term change) and *Adaptability* (adjust design of the supply chain).

Misconceptions

There are five commonly made misconceptions of demand driven (DDSN):.

1. Companies might think they are demand driven because they have a good forecast of their company.
2. They have implemented lean manufacturing.
3. They have great data on all their customers.
4. They think it is a technology project and the corporate forecast is a demand visibility signal.
5. They have a better view of customers demand.

An important component of DDSN is DDM ("real-time" demand driven manufacturing). DDM gives customers the opportunity to say what they want, where and when.

Demand-Driven Execution

Demand chain management is the same as supply chain management, but with emphasis on consumer pull vs. supplier push. The demand chain begins with customers, then funnels through any resellers, distributors, and other business partners who help sell the company's products and services. The demand chain includes both direct and indirect sales forces. Customers demand is hard to detect because out of stock situations (OOS) falsify data collected from POS-Terminals. According to studies of Corsten/Gruen (2002, 2008) the OOS-rate is about 8%. For products under sales promotion OOS rates up to 30% exist. Reliable information about demand is necessary for DCM therefore lowering OOS is a main factor for successful DCM.

Corsten and Gruen describe key factors for lowering OOS-rates:

- data accuracy
- forecast and order accuracy
- order quantity

- replenishment
- Capacity (time supply)
- Capacity (Packout) and Planogram Compliance
- Shelf Replenishment.

Implementation of system supported processes leads to the new technology Extreme Transaction Processing described by Gartner Research. This technology allows to process the huge amount of data (POS, RFID) in real time providing information for store managers, shelve managers and the supply chain.

IMPORTANCE OF INVENTORY

Inventory means a list compiled for some formal purpose, such as the details of an estate going to probate, or the contents of a house let furnished. This remains the prime meaning in British English. In the USA and Canada the term has developed from a list of goods and materials to the goods and material available in stock by a business; and this has become the primary meaning of the term in North American English, equivalent to the term "stock" in British English. In accounting, inventory or stock is considered an asset.

Inventory Management

Infact, inventory management is primarily about specifying the shape and percentage of stocked goods. It is required at different locations within a facility or within many locations of a supply network to precede the regular and planned course of production and stock of materials. The scope of inventory management concerns the fine lines between replenishment lead time, carrying costs of inventory, asset management, inventory forecasting, inventory valuation, inventory visibility, future inventory price forecasting, physical inventory, available physical space for inventory, quality management, replenishment, returns and defective goods, and demand forecasting.

Balancing these competing requirements leads to optimal inventory levels, which is an on-going process as the business needs shift and react to the wider environment. Inventory management involves a retailer seeking to acquire and maintain a proper merchandise assortment while ordering, shipping, handling, and related costs are kept in check. It also involves systems and processes that identify inventory requirements, set targets, provide replenishment techniques, report actual and projected inventory status and handle all functions related to the tracking and management of material.

This would include the monitoring of material moved into and out of stockroom locations and the reconciling of the inventory balances. It also may include ABC analysis, lot tracking, cycle counting support, etc. Management of the inventories, with the primary objective of determining/controlling stock levels within the physical distribution system, functions to balance the need for product availability against the need for minimizing stock holding and handling costs.

Infact, inventory management is primarily about specifying the size and placement of stocked goods. Inventory management is required at different locations within a facility or within multiple locations of a supply network to protect the regular and planned course of production against the random disturbance of running out of materials or goods.

The scope of inventory management also concerns the fine lines between replenishment lead time, carrying costs of inventory, asset management, inventory forecasting, inventory valuation, inventory visibility, future inventory price forecasting, physical inventory, available physical space for inventory, quality management, replenishment, returns and defective goods and demand forecasting.

The Reasons for Keeping Stock

There are three basic reasons for keeping an inventory:

(a) *Time* - The time lags present in the supply chain, from supplier to user at every stage, requires that you maintain certain amounts of inventory to use in this lead time. However, in practice, inventory is to be maintained for consumption during 'variations in lead time'. Lead time itself can be addressed by ordering that many days in advance.

(b) *Uncertainty* - Inventories are maintained as buffers to meet uncertainties in demand, supply and movements of goods.

(c) *Economies of scale* - Ideal condition of "one unit at a time at a place where a user needs it, when he needs it" principle tends to incur lots of costs in terms of logistics. So bulk buying, movement and storing brings in economies of scale, thus inventory.

Remarkably, all these stock reasons can apply to any owner or product.

Special Terms used in Dealing with Inventory

- *Stock Keeping Unit* (SKU) is a unique combination of all the components that are assembled into the purchasable item. Therefore, any change in the packaging or product is a new SKU. This level of detailed specification assists in managing inventory.

- *Stockout* means running out of the inventory of an SKU.
- "New old stock" (sometimes abbreviated NOS) is a term used in business to refer to merchandise being offered for sale that was manufactured long ago but that has never been used. Such merchandise may not be produced anymore, and the new old stock may represent the only market source of a particular item at the present time.

Typology

1. Buffer/safety stock
2. Cycle stock (Used in batch processes, it is the available inventory, excluding buffer stock)
3. De-coupling (Buffer stock held between the machines in a single process which serves as a buffer for the next one allowing smooth flow of work instead of waiting the previous or next machine in the same process)
4. Anticipation stock (Building up extra stock for periods of increased demand - e.g. ice cream for summer)
5. Pipeline stock (Goods still in transit or in the process of distribution - have left the factory but not arrived at the customer yet).

Examples

While accountants often discuss inventory in terms of goods for sale, organizations - manufacturers, service-providers and not-for-profits - also have inventories (fixtures, furniture, supplies, etc.) that they do not intend to sell. Manufacturers', distributors', and wholesalers' inventory tends to cluster in warehouses. Retailers' inventory may exist in a warehouse or in a shop or store accessible to customers. Inventories not intended for sale to customers or to clients may be held in any premises an organization uses. Stock ties up cash and, if uncontrolled, it will be impossible to know the actual level of stocks and therefore impossible to control them.

While the reasons for holding stock were covered earlier, most manufacturing organizations usually divide their "goods for sale" inventory into:

- Raw materials - materials and components scheduled for use in making a product.
- Work in process, WIP - materials and components that have began their transformation to finished goods.
- Finished goods - goods ready for sale to customers.
- Goods for resale - returned goods that are salable.

Manufacturing

A canned food manufacturer's materials inventory includes the ingredients to form the foods to be canned, empty cans and their lids (or coils of steel or aluminum for constructing those components), labels, and anything else (solder, glue, etc.) that will form part of a finished can. The firm's work in process includes those materials from the time of release to the work floor until they become complete and ready for sale to wholesale or retail customers. This may be vats of prepared food, filled cans not yet labeled or sub-assemblies of food components. It may also include finished cans that are not yet packaged into cartons or pallets. Its finished good inventory consists of all the filled and labeled cans of food in its warehouse that it has manufactured and wishes to sell to food distributors (wholesalers), to grocery stores (retailers), and even perhaps to consumers through arrangements like factory stores and outlet centers.

Principle of Inventory Proportionality

Inventory proportionality is the goal of demand-driven inventory management. The primary optimal outcome is to have the same number of days' (or hours', etc.) worth of inventory on hand across all products so that the time of runout of all products would be simultaneous. In such a case, there is no "excess inventory," that is, inventory that would be left over of another product when the first product runs out. Excess inventory is sub-optimal because the money spent to obtain it could have been utilized better elsewhere, i.e. to the product that just ran out.

The secondary goal of inventory proportionality is inventory minimization. By integrating accurate demand forecasting with inventory management, replenishment inventories can be scheduled to arrive just in time to replenish the product destined to run out first, while at the same time balancing out the inventory supply of all products to make their inventories more proportional, and thereby closer to achieving the primary goal. Accurate demand forecasting also allows the desired inventory proportions to be dynamic by determining expected sales out into the future; this allows for inventory to be in proportion to expected short-term sales or consumption rather than to past averages, a much more accurate and optimal outcome. Integrating demand forecasting into inventory management in this way also allows for the prediction of the "can fit" point when inventory storage is limited on a per-product basis.

The technique of inventory proportionality is most appropriate for inventories that remain unseen by the consumer, as opposed to "keep full" systems where a retail consumer would like to see full shelves of the product they are buying so as not to think they are buying something old, unwanted or stale; and differentiated from the "trigger point" systems where product is reordered when it hits a certain level; inventory proportionality is used effectively by just-in-time manufacturing processes and retail applications where the product is hidden from view.

One early example of inventory proportionality used in a retail application in the United States was for motor fuel. Motor fuel (e.g. gasoline) is generally stored in underground storage tanks. The motorists do not know whether they are buying gasoline off the top or bottom of the tank, nor need they care. Additionally, these storage tanks have a maximum capacity and cannot be overfilled. Finally, the product is expensive. Inventory proportionality is used to balance the inventories of the different grades of motor fuel, each stored in dedicated tanks, in proportion to the sales of each grade. Excess inventory is not seen or valued by the consumer, so it is simply cash sunk (literally) into the ground. Inventory proportionality minimizes the amount of excess inventory carried in underground storage tanks. This application for motor fuel was first developed and implemented by Petrolsoft Corporation in 1990 for Chevron Products Company. Most major oil companies use such systems today.

> It is interesting to note that the use of inventory proportionality in the United States is thought to have been inspired by Japanese just-in-time parts inventory management made famous by Toyota Motors in the 1980s.

High-level Inventory Management

It seems that around 1880 there was a change in manufacturing practice from companies with relatively homogeneous lines of products to horizontally integrated companies with unprecedented diversity in processes and products. Those companies (especially in metalworking) attempted to achieve success through economies of scope - the gains of jointly producing two or more products in one facility. The managers now needed information on the effect of product-mix decisions on overall profits and therefore needed accurate product-cost information. A variety of attempts to achieve this were unsuccessful due to the huge overhead of the information processing of the time. However, the burgeoning need for financial reporting after 1900 created unavoidable pressure for financial accounting of stock and the management need to cost manage products became overshadowed. In particular, it was the need for audited accounts that sealed the fate of managerial cost accounting. The dominance of financial reporting accounting over management accounting remains to this day with few exceptions, and the financial reporting definitions of 'cost' have distorted effective management 'cost' accounting since that time. This is particularly true of inventory.

Hence, high-level financial inventory has these two basic formulas, which relate to the accounting period:

1. Cost of Beginning Inventory at the start of the period + inventory purchases within the period + cost of production within the period = cost of goods available
2. Cost of goods available " cost of ending inventory at the end of the period = cost of goods sold

The benefit of these formulae is that the first absorbs all overheads of production and raw material costs into a value of inventory for reporting. The second formula then creates the new start point for the next period and gives a figure to be subtracted from the sales price to determine some form of sales-margin figure.

Manufacturing management is more interested in *inventory turnover ratio* or *average days to sell inventory* since it tells them something about relative inventory levels.

Inventory turnover ratio (also known as inventory turns) = cost of goods sold / Average Inventory = Cost of Goods Sold / ((Beginning Inventory + Ending Inventory) / 2) and its inverse

Average Days to Sell Inventory = Number of Days a Year / Inventory Turnover Ratio = 365 days a year / Inventory Turnover Ratio

This ratio estimates how many times the inventory turns over a year. This number tells how much cash/goods are tied up waiting for the process and is a critical measure of process reliability and effectiveness. So a factory with two inventory turns has six months stock on hand, which is generally not a good figure (depending upon the industry), whereas a factory that moves from six turns to twelve turns has probably improved effectiveness by 100%. This improvement will have some negative results in the financial reporting, since the 'value' now stored in the factory as inventory is reduced.

While these accounting measures of inventory are very useful because of their simplicity, they are also fraught with the danger of their own assumptions. There are, in fact, so many things that can vary hidden under this appearance of simplicity that a variety of 'adjusting' assumptions may be used. These include:

- Specific Identification
- Weighted Average Cost
- Moving-Average Cost
- FIFO and LIFO.

Inventory Turn is a financial accounting tool for evaluating inventory and it is not necessarily a management tool. Inventory management should be forward looking. The methodology applied is based on historical cost of goods sold. The ratio may not be able to reflect the usability of future production demand, as well as customer demand.

Business models, including Just in Time (JIT) Inventory, Vendor Managed Inventory (VMI) and Customer Managed Inventory (CMI), attempt to minimize on-hand inventory and increase inventory turns. VMI and CMI have gained considerable attention due to the success of third-party vendors who offer added expertise and knowledge that organizations may not possess.

Accounting for Inventory

Each country has its own rules about accounting for inventory that fit with their financial-reporting rules.

For example, organizations in the U.S. define inventory to suit their needs within US Generally Accepted Accounting Practices (GAAP), the rules defined by the Financial Accounting Standards Board (FASB) (and others) and enforced by the U.S. Securities and Exchange Commission (SEC) and other federal and state agencies. Other countries often have similar arrangements but with their own accounting standards and national agencies instead.

It is intentional that financial accounting uses standards that allow the public to compare firms' performance, cost accounting functions internally to an organization and potentially with much greater flexibility. A discussion of inventory from standard and Theory of Constraints-based (throughput) cost accounting perspective follows some examples and a discussion of inventory from a financial accounting perspective. The internal costing/valuation of inventory can be complex. Whereas in the past most enterprises ran simple, one-process factories, such enterprises are quite probably in the minority in the 21st century. Where 'one process' factories exist, there is a market for the goods created, which establishes an independent market value for the good.

Today, with multistage-process companies, there is much inventory that would once have been finished goods which is now held as 'work in process' (WIP). This needs to be valued in the accounts, but the valuation is a management decision since there is no market for the partially finished product. This somewhat arbitrary 'valuation' of WIP combined with the allocation of overheads to it has led to some unintended and undesirable results.

Financial Accounting

An organization's inventory can appear a mixed blessing, since it counts as an asset on the balance sheet, but it also ties up money that could serve for other purposes and requires additional expense for its protection. Inventory may also cause significant tax expenses, depending on particular countries' laws regarding depreciation of inventory, as in Thor Power Tool Company v. Commissioner.

Inventory appears as a current asset on an organization's balance sheet because the organization can, in principle, turn it into cash by selling it. Some organizations hold larger inventories than their operations require in order to inflate their apparent asset value and their perceived profitability. In addition to the money tied up by acquiring inventory, inventory also brings associated costs for warehouse space, for utilities, and for insurance to cover staff to handle and protect it from fire and other disasters, obsolescence, shrinkage (theft and errors), and others.

Such holding costs can mount up: between a third and a half of its acquisition value per year. Businesses that stock too little inventory cannot take advantage of large orders from customers if they cannot deliver. The conflicting objectives of cost control and customer service often pit an organization's financial and operating managers against its sales and marketing departments. Salespeople, in particular, often receive sales-commission payments, so unavailable goods may reduce their potential personal income.

This conflict can be minimised by reducing production time to being near or less than customers' expected delivery time. This effort, known as "Lean production" will significantly reduce working capital tied up in inventory and reduce manufacturing costs.

By helping the organization to make better decisions, the accountants can help the public sector to change in a very positive way that delivers increased value for the taxpayer's investment. It can also help to incentivise progress and to ensure that reforms are sustainable and effective in the long term, by ensuring that success is appropriately recognized in both the formal and informal reward systems of the organization.

To say that they have a key role to play is an understatement. Finance is connected to most, if not all, of the key business processes within the organization. It should be steering the stewardship and accountability systems that ensure that the organization is conducting its business in an appropriate, ethical manner. It is critical that these foundations are firmly laid. So often they are the litmus test by which public confidence in the institution is either won or lost.

Finance should also be providing the information, analysis and advice to enable the organizations' service managers to operate effectively. This goes beyond the traditional preoccupation with budgets – how much have we spent so far, how much do we have left to spend? It is about helping the organization to better understand its own performance. That means making the connections and understanding the relationships between given inputs – the resources brought to bear – and the outputs and outcomes that they achieve. It is also about understanding and actively managing risks within the organization and its activities.

FIFO vs. LIFO Accounting

When a merchant buys goods from inventory, the value of the inventory account is reduced by the cost of goods sold (COGS). This is simple where the CoG has not varied across those held in stock; but where it has, then an agreed method must be derived to evaluate it. For commodity items that one cannot track individually, accountants must choose a method that fits the nature of the sale. Two popular methods that normally exist are: FIFO and LIFO accounting (first in - first out, last in - first out). FIFO regards the first unit that arrived in inventory as the first one sold. LIFO considers the last unit arriving in inventory as the first one sold.

Which method an accountant selects can have a significant effect on net income and book value and, in turn, on taxation. Using LIFO accounting for inventory, a company generally reports lower net income and lower book value, due to the effects of inflation. This generally results in lower taxation. Due to LIFO's potential to skew inventory value, UK GAAP and IAS have effectively banned LIFO inventory accounting.

Standard cost accounting uses ratios called efficiencies that compare the labour and materials actually used to produce a good with those that the same goods would have required under "standard" conditions. As long as actual and standard conditions are similar, few problems arise. Unfortunately, standard cost accounting methods developed about 100 years ago, when labor comprised the most important cost in manufactured goods. Standard methods continue to emphasize labor efficiency even though that resource now constitutes a (very) small part of cost in most cases.

Standard cost accounting can hurt managers, workers, and firms in several ways. For example, a policy decision to increase inventory can harm a manufacturing manager's performance evaluation. Increasing inventory requires increased production, which means that processes must operate at higher rates. When (not if) something goes wrong, the process takes longer and uses more than the standard labor time. The manager appears responsible for the excess, even though s/he has no control over the production requirement or the problem.

In adverse economic times, firms use the same efficiencies to downsize, rightsize, or otherwise reduce their labor force. Workers laid off under those circumstances have even less control over excess inventory and cost efficiencies than their managers.

Many financial and cost accountants have agreed for many years on the desirability of replacing standard cost accounting. They have not, however, found a successor.

Eliyahu M. Goldratt developed the Theory of Constraints in part to address the cost-accounting problems in what he calls the "cost world." He offers a substitute, called throughput accounting, that uses throughput (money for goods sold to customers) in place of output (goods produced that may sell or may boost inventory) and considers labor as a fixed rather than as a variable cost. He defines inventory simply as everything the organization owns that it plans to sell, including buildings, machinery, and many other things in addition to the categories listed here. Throughput accounting recognizes only one class of variable costs: the truly variable costs, like materials and components, which vary directly with the quantity produced

Finished goods inventories remain balance-sheet assets, but labor-efficiency ratios no longer evaluate managers and workers. Instead of an incentive to reduce labor cost, throughput accounting focuses attention on the relationships between throughput (revenue or income) on one hand and controllable operating expenses and changes in inventory on the other. Those relationships direct attention to the constraints or bottlenecks that prevent the system from producing more throughput, rather than to people - who have little or no control over their situations.

National Accounts

Inventories also play an important role in national accounts and the analysis of the business cycle. Some short-term macroeconomic fluctuations are attributed to the inventory cycle.

Distressed Inventory

Also known as distressed or expired stock, distressed inventory is inventory whose potential to be sold at a normal cost has passed or will soon pass. In certain industries it could also mean that the stock is or will soon be impossible to sell. Examples of distressed inventory include products that have reached their expiry date, or have reached a date in advance of expiry at which the planned market will no longer purchase them (e.g. 3 months left to expiry), clothing that is defective or out of fashion, music that is no longer popular and old newspapers or magazines.

It also includes computer or consumer-electronic equipment that is obsolete or discontinued and whose manufacturer is unable to support it. One current example of distressed inventory is the VHS format.

In 2001, Cisco wrote off inventory worth US $2.25 billion due to duplicate orders. This is one of the biggest inventory write-offs in business history.

Inventory Credit

Inventory credit refers to the use of stock, or inventory, as collateral to raise finance. Where banks may be reluctant to accept traditional collateral, for example in developing countries where land title may be lacking, inventory credit is a potentially important way of overcoming financing constraints. This is not a new concept; archaeological evidence suggests that it was practiced in Ancient Rome.

Obtaining finance against stocks of a wide range of products held in a bonded warehouse is common in much of the world. It is, for example, used with Parmesan cheese in Italy.

Inventory credit on the basis of stored agricultural produce is widely used in Latin American countries and in some Asian countries. A precondition for such credit is that banks must be confident that the stored product will be available if they need to call on the collateral; this implies the existence of a reliable network of certified warehouses. Banks also face problems in valuing the inventory. The possibility of sudden falls in commodity prices means that they are usually reluctant to lend more than about 60% of the value of the inventory at the time of the loan.

ROLE OF INVENTORY CONTROL

Inventory Control is the supervision of supply, storage and accessibility of items in order to ensure an adequate supply without excessive oversupply.

It can also be referred as internal control - an accounting procedure or system designed to promote efficiency or assure the implementation of a policy or safeguard assets or avoid fraud and error etc.

Inventory control may refer to:

- In economics, the inventory control problem, which aims to reduce overhead cost without hurting sales
- In the field of loss prevention, systems designed to introduce technical barriers to shoplifting.

IMPORTANCE OF STOCK MANAGEMENT

Stock management is the function of understanding the stock mix of a company and the different demands on that stock. The demands are influenced by both external and internal factors and are balanced by the creation of Purchase order requests to keep supplies at a reasonable or prescribed level.

Retail Supply Chain

Stock management in the retail supply chain follows the following sequence:

1. Request for new stock from stores to head office
2. Head office issues purchase orders to the vendor
3. Vendor ships the goods
4. Warehouse receives the goods
5. Warehouse stocks and distributes to the stores
6. Stores receive the goods
7. Goods are sold to customers at the stores

The management of the inventory in the supply chain involves managing the physical quantities as well as the costing of the goods as it flows through the supply chain.

In managing the cost prices of the goods throughout the supply chain, several costing methods are employed:

1. Retail method
2. Weighted Average Price method
3. FIFO (First In First Out) method
4. LIFO (Last In First Out) method
5. LPP (Last Purchase Price) method
6. BNM (Bottle neck method)

Weighted Average Price Method

The calculation can be done for different periods. If the calculation is done on a monthly basis, then it is referred to the periodic method. In this method, the available stock is calculated by:

ADD Stock at beginning of period

ADD Stock purchased during the period

AVERAGE total cost by total qty to arrive at the Average Cost of Goods for the period.

This Average Cost Price is applied to all movements and adjustments in that period.

Ending stock in qty is arrived at by Applying all the changes in qty to the Available balance.

Multiplying the stock balance in qty by the Average cost gives the Stock cost at the end of the period.

Using the perpetual method, the calculation is done upon every purchase transaction.

Thus, the calculation is the same based on the periodic calculation whether by period (periodic) or by transaction (perpetual).

The only difference is the 'periodicity' or scope of the calculation. - Periodic is done monthly - Perpetual is done for the duration of the purchase until the next purchase

In practice, the daily averaging has been used to closely approximate the perpetual method. 6. Bottle neck method (depends on proper planning support)

Software Applications

The implementation of inventory management applications has become a valuable tool for organizations looking to more efficiently manage stock. While the capabilities of applications vary, most inventory management applications give organizations a structured method of accounting for all incoming and outgoing inventory within their facilities. Organizations save a significant amount in costs associated with manual inventory counts, administrative errors and reductions in inventory stock-outs.

Business Models

Just-in-time Inventory (JIT), Vendor Managed Inventory (VMI) and Customer Managed Inventory (CMI) are a few of the popular models being employed by organizations looking to have greater stock management control.

JIT is a model which attempts to replenish inventory for organizations when the inventory is required. The model attempts to avoid excess inventory and its associated costs. As a result, companies receive inventory only when the need for more stock is approaching.

VMI and CMI are two business models that adhere to the JIT inventory principles. VMI gives the vendor in a vendor/customer relationship the ability to monitor, plan and control inventory for their customers. Customers relinquish the order making responsibilities in exchange for timely inventory replenishment that increases organizational efficiency.

CMI allows the customer to order and control their inventory from their vendors/suppliers. Both VMI and CMI benefit the vendor as well as the customer. Vendors see a significant increase in sales due to increased inventory turns and cost savings realized by their customers, while customers realize similar benefits.

ROLE OF STOCK CONTROL

Stock control is defined as: "The activity of checking a shop's stock".

Many shops now use stock control systems. The term "stock control system" can be used to include various aspects of controlling the amount of stock on the shelves and in the stockroom and how reordering happens. Typical features include:

- Ensuring that products are on the shelf in shops in just the right quantity.
- Recognising when a customer has bought a product.
- Automatically signalling when more products need to be put on the shelf from the stockroom.
- Automatically reordering stock at the appropriate time from the main warehouse.
- Automatically producing management information reports that could be used both by local managers and at Head office.

These might detail what has sold, how quickly and at what price, for example. Reports could be used to predict when to stock up on extra products, for example, at Christmas or to make decisions about special offers, discontinuing products and so on. Sending reordering information not only to the warehouse but also directly to the factory producing the products to enable them to optimise production.

Advantages and Disadvantages

Stock control systems ensure that just the right amount of stock are on the shelves. If there is too much stock, it ties up a company's money, money that might be better spent on reducing their overdraft, on advertising the business or on paying for better facilities for customers, for example. Too much stock means that some perishable products might not sell and would have to be thrown away and this would reduce a company's profit. If there were not enough products on the shelf, they might run out. If this happens, they would lose business and again, profits would not be as good as they ought to be.

Stock control systems save a lot of staff time. Savings may be possible by reducing the number of staff needed in the business thereby improving profits. A stock control system will not remove the necessity for checking what is on the shelves regularly - things get stolen and these won't be recorded.

Stock control systems also mean that a business may have to close down while the system is changed from a manual one. They may also involve a considerable investment in equipment and support. Stock control systems require training and some staff might find them difficult to use. They can also break down so a procedure needs to be in place so the business can continue to trade. This could involve further costs as well, perhaps requiring the purchase of backup equipment or a support agreement. Usually, the benefits of a stock control system outweigh the disadvantages.

Imagine a shop that is part of a chain of shops. It has no computer systems. At the moment, the owner of the shop orders goods. This takes up her valuable time. She knows what to order by using her experience of how quickly things sell and by looking on the shelves and seeing what is there! She also has to produce regular reports about how the business is going for Head office. This again is very time-consuming. Headquarters decide to introduce a stock control system. One simple solution would involve getting:

- A method of scanning in products at the checkout.
- A computer with a modem.
- A phone line if they haven't already got one.
- Some connections between the checkout and the computer and between the computer and the phone.
- Software.
- An ISP.
- Computer systems set up at the warehouse, the factory and Head office.
- Some training on how to use the system.
- Some support for when things don't work.
- Back-up systems in case the computer breaks down.

Theis is system in which company control his assets.

IMPORTANCE OF WAREHOUSE

Basically, A warehouse is a commercial building for storage of goods. Warehouses are used by manufacturers, importers, exporters, wholesalers, transport businesses, customs, etc. They are usually large plain buildings in industrial areas of cities and towns and villages. They usually have loading docks to load and unload goods from trucks. Sometimes warehouses are designed for the loading and unloading of goods directly from railways, airports, or seaports.

They often have cranes and forklifts for moving goods, which are usually placed on ISO standard pallets loaded into pallet racks. Stored goods can include any raw materials, packing materials, spare parts, components, or finished goods associated with agriculture, manufacturing, or commerce.

Storage and Shipping Systems

Some of the most common warehouse storage systems are:

- Pallet racking including selective, drive-in, drive-thru, double-deep, pushback, and gravity flow
- Mezzanine including structural, roll formed, racks
- Vertical Lift Modules
- Horizontal Carousels
- Vertical Carousels

A piece pick, also known as broken case pick, split-case pick, each pick, over-pack or pick/pack, is a type of order selection process where product is picked and handled in individual units and placed in an outer carton, tote or other container before shipping. Catalog companies and internet retailers are examples of predominantly piece-pick operations. Their customers rarely order in pallet or case quantities; instead, they typically order just one or two pieces of one or two items.

According to “PICK THIS!,” several elements make up the piece-pick system. They include the order, the picker, the pick module, the pick area, handling equipment, the container, the pick method used and the information technology used. Material direction and tracking in a warehouse can be coordinated by a Warehouse Management System (WMS), a database driven computer programme. Logistics personnel use the WMS to improve warehouse efficiency by directing pathways and to maintain accurate inventory by recording warehouse transactions.

Automation and Optimization

Some warehouses are completely automated, and require only operators to work and handle all the task. Pallets and product move on a system of automated conveyors, cranes and automated storage and retrieval systems coordinated by programmable logic controllers and computers running logistics automation software. These systems are often installed in refrigerated warehouses where temperatures are kept very cold to keep product from spoiling, especially in electronics warehouse where they require specific temperature to avoid damaging the parts, and also where land is expensive, as automated storage systems can use vertical space efficiently. These high-bay storage areas are often more than 10 meters (33 feet) high, with some over 20 meters (65 feet) high. Automated storage systems can be built up to 40m high.

For a warehouse to function efficiently, the facility must be properly *slotted.* Slotting addresses which storage medium a product is picked from (pallet rack or carton flow), and how they are picked (pick-to-light, pick-to-voice, or pick-to-paper). With a proper slotting plan, a warehouse can improve its inventory rotation requirements—such as first in, first out (FIFO) and last in, first out (LIFO)—control labor costs and increase productivity.

Modern Trends

Traditional warehousing has declined since the last decades of the 20th century, with the gradual introduction of Just In Time (JIT) techniques. The JIT system promotes product delivery directly from suppliers to consumer without the use of warehouses. However, with the gradual implementation of offshore outsourcing and offshoring in about the same time period, the distance between the manufacturer and the retailer (or the parts manufacturer and the industrial plant) grew considerably in many domains, necessitating at least one warehouse per country or per region in any typical supply chain for a given range of products.

Recent retailing trends have led to the development of warehouse-style retail stores. These high-ceiling buildings display retail goods on tall, heavy duty industrial racks rather than conventional retail shelving. Typically, items ready for sale are on the bottom of the racks, and crated or palletized inventory is in the upper rack. Essentially, the same building serves as both warehouse and retail store.

Another trend relates to Vendor Managed Inventory (VMI). This gives the vendor the control to maintain the level of stock in the store. This method has its own issue that the vendor gains access to the warehouse.

Large exporters/manufacturers use warehouses as distribution points for developing retail outlets in a particular region or country. This concept reduces end cost to the consumer and enhances the production sale ratio.

Cross docking is a specialized type of distribution center (DC) in that little or no inventory is stored and product is received, processed (if needed) and shipped within a short timeframe. As in warehousing, there are different types of cross docks.

Reverse logistics is another type of warehousing that has gained attention in our "green-conscious" world. The term refers to items that are going from the end user back to the distributor or manufacturer.

Cool Warehouses and Cold Storage

Cold storage preserves agricultural products. Refrigerated storage helps in eliminating sprouting, rotting and insect damage. Edible products are generally not stored for more than one year. Several perishable products require a storage temperature as low as -25°C.

Cold storage helps stabilize market prices and evenly distribute goods both on demand basis and time basis. The farmers get opportunity of producing cash crops to get remunerative prices. The consumers get the supply of perishable commodities with lower fluctuation of prices.

Ammonia and Freon compressors are commonly used in cold storage warehouses to maintain the temperature. Ammonia refrigerant is cheaper, easily available and has a high latent heat of evaporation but it is also highly toxic and can form an explosive mixture when mixed with oil containing high percentage of carbon. Insulation is also important, to reduce loss of cold and to keep different sections of the warehouse at different temperatures.

There are two main types of refrigeration system used in cold storage warehouses, a Vapour absorption system (VAS) and Vapour compression system (VCS). VAS, although comparatively costlier, is quite economical in operation and adequately compensates the higher initial investment.

The temperature necessary for preservation depends on the storage time required and the type of product. In general, there are three groups of products, foods that are alive (e.g. fruits and vegetables), foods that are no longer alive and have been processed in some form (e.g. meat and fish products), and commodities that benefit from storage at controlled temperature (e.g. beer, tobacco). Location is a very critical aspect for the success of cold storage. It should be in close proximity of growing area as well as market, be easily accessible for heavy vehicles, and have uninterrupted power supply.

Cold Storage and the Law

There are state and local laws which regulate the cold store industry, requiring safe working conditions for employees, and operational procedures must be in accordance with these laws. Those companies which do their homework and prepare in advance for inspections and other routine enforcement protocols will be able to continue operating at full capacity, ensuring greater customer service and more product flow seven days a week.

Internet Impact

Internet-based stores do not require physical retail space, but still require warehouses to store goods. This kind of warehouse fills many small orders directly from end customers rather than fewer orders of many items from stores.

Having a large and complex supply chain containing many warehouse can be costly. It may be beneficial for a company to have one large warehouse per continent, typically located centrally to transportation. At these continental hubs, goods may be customized for different countries. For example, goods get a price ticket in the language of the destination country. Small, in-warehouse adjustments to goods are called value added services.

IMPORTANCE OF WAREHOUSE MANAGEMENT SYSTEM

It is significant to note that a warehouse management system, or WMS, is a key part of the supply chain and primarily aims to control the movement and storage of materials within a warehouse and process the associated transactions, including shipping, receiving, putaway and picking. The systems also direct and optimize stock putaway based on real-time information about the status of bin utilization.

Warehouse management systems often utilize .....Auto ID Data Capture (AIDC) technology, such as barcode scanners, mobile computers, wireless LANs and potentially Radio-frequency identification (RFID) to efficiently monitor the flow of products. Once data has been collected, there is either a batch synchronization with, or a real-time wireless transmission to a central database. The database can then provide useful reports about the status of goods in the warehouse. The objective of a warehouse management system is to provide a set of computerized procedures to handle the receipt of stock and returns into a warehouse facility, model and manage the logical representation of the physical storage facilities (e.g. racking etc.), manage the stock within the facility and enable a seamless link to order processing and logistics management in order to pick, pack and ship product out of the facility. Warehouse management systems can be stand alone systems, or modules of an ERP system or supply chain execution suite. The primary purpose of a WMS is to control the movement and storage of materials within a warehouse – you might even describe it as the legs at the end-of-the line which automates the store, traffic and shipping management. In its simplest form, the WMS can data track products during the production process and act as an interpreter and message buffer between existing ERP and WMS systems. Warehouse Management is not just managing within the boundaries of a warehouse today, it is much wider and goes beyond the physical boundaries. Inventory management,inventory planning, cost management, IT applications & communication technology to be used are all related to warehouse management. The container storage, loading and unloading are also covered by warehouse management today.Warehouse management today is part of SCM and demand management. Even production management is to a great extent dependent on warehouse management. Efficient warehouse management gives a cutting edge to a retail chain distribution company.

Warehouse management does not just start with receipt of material but it actually starts with actual initial planning when container design is made for a product. Warehouse design and process design within the warehouse (e.g. Wave Picking) is also part of warehouse management. Warehouse management is part of Logistics and SCM.

Warehouse Management monitors the progress of products through the warehouse. It involves the physical warehouse infrastructure, tracking systems, and communication between product stations.

Warehouse management deals with receipt, storage and movement of goods, normally finished goods, to intermediate storage locations or to final customer. In the multi-echelon model for distribution, there are levels of warehouses, starting with the Central Warehouse(s), regional warehouses serviced by the central warehouses and retail warehouses serviced by the regional warehouses and so on. The objective of warehouse management is to help in optimal cost of timely order fulfillment by managing the resources economically. Warehouse management = “Management of storage of products and services rendered on the products within the four walls of a warehouse”.

ROLE OF COST ACCOUNTING

Cost accounting information is designed for managers. Since managers are taking decisions only for their own organization, there is no need for the information to be comparable to similar information from other organizations. Instead, the important criterion is that the information must be relevant for decisions that managers operating in a particular environment of business including strategy make. Cost accounting information is commonly used in financial accounting information, but first we are concentrating in its use by managers to take decisions. The accountants who handle the cost accounting information generate add value by providing good information to managers who are taking decisions.

Among the better decisions, the better performance of one's organization, regardless if it is a manufacturing company, a bank, a non-profit organization, a government agency, a school club or even a business school. The cost-accounting system is the result of decisions made by managers of an organization and the environment in which they make them. The organizations and managers are most of the times interested in and worried for the costs. The control of the costs of the past, present and future is part of the job of all the managers in a company. In the companies that try to have profits, the control of costs affects directly to them. Knowing the costs of the products is essential for decision-making regarding price and mix assignation of products and services.

The cost accounting systems can be important sources of information for the managers of a company. For this reason, the managers understand the forces and weaknesses of the cost accounting systems, and participate in the evaluation and evolution of the cost measurement and administration systems. Unlike the accounting systems that help in the preparation of financial reports periodically, the cost accounting systems and reports are not subject to rules and standards like the Generally Accepted Accounting Principles. As a result, there is a wide variety in the cost accounting systems of the different companies and sometimes even in different parts of the same company or organization.

The following are different cost accounting approaches:

- standardized or standard cost accounting
- lean accounting
- activity-based costing
- resource consumption accounting
- throughput accounting
- marginal costing/cost-volume-profit analysis

Classical cost elements are:

1. Raw materials
2. Labor
3. Indirect expenses/overhead

Cost accounting has long been used to help managers understand the costs of running a business. Modern cost accounting originated during the industrial revolution, when the complexities of running a large scale business led to the development of systems for recording and tracking costs to help business owners and managers make decisions.

In the early industrial age, most of the costs incurred by a business were what modern accountants call "variable costs" because they varied directly with the amount of production. Money was spent on labor, raw materials, power to run a factory, etc. in direct proportion to production. Managers could simply total the variable costs for a product and use this as a rough guide for decision-making processes.

Some costs tend to remain the same even during busy periods, unlike variable costs, which rise and fall with volume of work. Over time, the importance of these "fixed costs" has become more important to managers. Examples of fixed costs include the depreciation of plant and equipment, and the cost of departments such as maintenance, tooling, production control, purchasing, quality control, storage and handling, plant supervision and engineering. In the early twentieth century, these costs were of little importance to most businesses. However, in the twenty-first century, these costs are often more important than the variable cost of a product, and allocating them to a broad range of products can lead to bad decision making. Managers must understand fixed costs in order to make decisions about products and pricing.

For example: A company produced railway coaches and had only one product. To make each coach, the company needed to purchase $60 of raw materials and components, and pay 6 laborers $40 each. Therefore, total variable cost for each coach was $300. Knowing that making a coach required spending $300, managers knew they couldn't sell below that price without losing money on each coach. Any price above $300 became a contribution to the fixed costs of the company. If the fixed costs were, say, $1000 per month for rent, insurance and owner's salary, the company could therefore sell 5 coaches per month for a total of $3000 (priced at $600 each), or 10 coaches for a total of $4500 (priced at $450 each), and make a profit of $500 in both cases.

Elements of Cost

- Material (Material is a very important part of business)
  - o Direct material
- Labor
  - o Direct labor
- Overhead (Variable/Fixed)

- o Indirect material
- o Indirect labor
- o Maintenance & Repair
- o Supplies
- o Utilities
- o Other Variable Expenses
- o Salaries
- o Occupancy (Rent)
- o Depreciation
- o Other Fixed Expenses

(In some companies, machine cost is segregated from overhead and reported as a separate element)

They are grouped further based on their functions as,

- Production or works overheads
- Administration overheads
- Selling overheads
- Distribution overheads
- Financial Expenses

Classification of Costs

Classification of cost means, the grouping of costs according to their common characteristics. The important ways of classification of costs are:

- By nature or element: materials, labor, expenses
- By functions: production, selling, distribution, administration, R&D, development,
- By traceability: direct and indirect
- By variability: fixed, variable, semi-variable
- By controllability: controllable, uncontrollable
- By normality: normal, abnormal

Standard Cost Accounting

In modern cost accounting, the concept of recording historical costs was taken further, by allocating the company's fixed costs over a given period of time to the items produced during that period, and recording the result as the total cost of production. This allowed the *full cost* of products that were not sold in the period they were produced to be recorded in inventory using a variety of complex accounting methods, which was consistent with the principles of GAAP (Generally Accepted Accounting Principles). It also essentially enabled managers to ignore the fixed costs, and look at the results of each period in relation to the "standard cost" for any given product.

For example: if the railway coach company normally produced 40 coaches per month, and the fixed costs were still $1000/month, then each coach could be said to incur an overhead of $25 ($1000 / 40). Adding this to the variable costs of $300 per coach produced a full cost of $325 per coach.

This method tended to slightly distort the resulting unit cost, but in mass-production industries that made one product line, and where the fixed costs were relatively low, the distortion was very minor.

For example: if the railway coach company made 100 coaches one month, then the unit cost would become $310 per coach ($300 + ($1000 / 100)). If the next month the company made 50 coaches, then the unit cost = $320 per coach ($300 + ($1000 / 50)), a relatively minor difference.

An important part of standard cost accounting is a variance analysis, which breaks down the variation between actual cost and standard costs into various components (volume variation, material cost variation, labor cost variation, etc.) so managers can understand *why costs were different from what was planned* and take appropriate action to correct the situation.

The Development of Throughput Accounting

As business became more complex and began producing a greater variety of products, the use of cost accounting to make decisions to maximize profitability came under question. Management circles became increasingly aware of the Theory of Constraints in the 1980s, and began to understand that "every production process has a limiting factor" somewhere in the chain of production. As business management learned to identify the constraints, they increasingly adopted throughput accounting to manage them and "maximize the *throughput dollars*" (or other currency) from each unit of constrained resource.

For example: The railway coach company was offered a contract to make 15 open-topped streetcars each month, using a design that included ornate brass foundry work, but very little of the metalwork needed to produce a covered rail coach. The buyer offered to pay $280 per streetcar. The company had a firm order for 40 rail coaches each month for $350 per unit.

The cost accountant determined that the cost of operating the foundry vs. the metalwork shop each month was as follows:

Overhead Cost by Department	*Total Cost*	*Hours Available per month*	*Cost per hour*
Foundry	$ 7,300.00	160	$45.63
Metal shop	$ 3,300.00	160	$20.63
Total	$10,600.00	320	$33.13

The company was at full capacity making 40 rail coaches each month. And since the foundry was expensive to operate, and purchasing brass as a raw material for the streetcars was expensive, the accountant determined that the company would lose money on any streetcars it built. He showed an analysis of the estimated product costs based on standard cost accounting and recommended that the company decline to build any streetcars.

Standard Cost Accounting Analysis	*Streetcars*	*Rail coach*
Monthly Demand	15	40
Price	$280	$350
Foundry Time (hrs)	3.0	2.0
Metalwork Time (hrs)	1.5	4.0
Total Time	4.5	6.0
Foundry Cost	$136.88	$ 91.25
Metalwork Cost	$ 30.94	$ 82.50
Raw Material Cost	$120.00	$ 60.00
Total Cost	$287.81	$233.75
Profit per Unit	$ (7.81)	$116.25

However, the company's operations manager knew that recent investment in automated foundry equipment had created idle time for workers in that department. The constraint on production of the railcoaches was the metalwork shop. She made an analysis of profit and loss if the company took the contract using throughput accounting to determine the profitability of products by calculating "throughput" (revenue less variable cost) in the metal shop.

Throughput Cost Analysis	*Decline Contract*	*Take Contract*	*Accounting*
Coaches Produced	40	34	
Streetcars Produced	0	15	
Foundry Hours	80	113	
Metal shop Hours	160	159	
Coach Revenue	$14,000	$11,900	

Streetcar Revenue	$ 0	$ 4,200
Coach Raw Material Cost	$(2,400)	$(2,040)
Streetcar Raw Material Cost	$ 0	$(1,800)
Throughput Value	$11,600	$12,260
Overhead Expense	$(10,600)	$(10,600)
Profit	$1,000	$1,660

After the presentations from the company accountant and the operations manager, the president understood that the metal shop capacity was limiting the company's profitability. The company could make only 40 rail coaches per month. But by taking the contract for the streetcars, the company could make nearly all the railway coaches ordered, and also meet all the demand for streetcars. The result would increase throughput in the metal shop from $6.25 to $10.38 per hour of available time, and increase profitability by 66 percent.

Activity-Based Costing

Activity-based costing (ABC) is a system for assigning costs to products based on the activities they require. In this case, activities are those regular actions performed inside a company. "Talking with customer regarding invoice questions" is an example of an activity inside most companies.

Accountants assign 100% of each employee's time to the different activities performed inside a company (many will use surveys to have the workers themselves assign their time to the different activities). The accountant then can determine the total cost spent on each activity by summing up the percentage of each worker's salary spent on that activity.

A company can use the resulting activity cost data to determine where to focus their operational improvements. For example, a job-based manufacturer may find that a high percentage of its workers are spending their time trying to figure out a hastily written customer order. Via ABC, the accountants now have a currency amount pegged to the activity of "Researching Customer Work Order Specifications". Senior management can now decide how much focus or money to budget for resolving this process deficiency. Activity-based management includes (but is not restricted to) the use of activity-based costing to manage a business. While ABC may be able to pinpoint the cost of each activity and resources into the ultimate product, the process could be tedious, costly and subject to errors. As it is a tool for a more accurate way of allocating fixed costs into product, these fixed costs do not vary according to each month's production volume. For example, an elimination of one product would not eliminate the overhead or even direct labor cost assigned to it. ABC better identifies product costing in the long run, but may not be too helpful in day-to-day decision-making.

Lean Accounting

Lean accounting has developed in recent years to provide the accounting, control, and measurement methods supporting lean manufacturing and other applications of lean thinking such as healthcare, construction, insurance, banking, education, government, and other industries.

There are two main thrusts for Lean Accounting. The first is the application of lean methods to the company's accounting, control, and measurement processes. This is not different from applying lean methods to any other processes. The objective is to eliminate waste, free up capacity, speed up the process, eliminate errors & defects, and make the process clear and understandable. The second (and more important) thrust of Lean Accounting is to fundamentally change the accounting, control, and measurement processes so they motivate lean change & improvement, provide information that is suitable for control and decision-making, provide an understanding of customer value, correctly assess the financial impact of lean improvement, and are themselves simple, visual, and low-waste. Lean Accounting does not require the traditional management accounting methods like standard costing, activity-based costing, variance reporting, cost-plus pricing, complex transactional control systems, and untimely & confusing financial reports. These are replaced by:

- lean-focused performance measurements
- simple summary direct costing of the value streams
- decision-making and reporting using a *box score*
- financial reports that are timely and presented in "plain English" that everyone can understand
- radical simplification and elimination of transactional control systems by eliminating the need for them
- driving lean changes from a deep understanding of the value created for the customers
- eliminating traditional budgeting through monthly sales, operations, and financial planning processes (SOFP)
- value-based pricing
- correct understanding of the financial impact of lean change

As an organization becomes more mature with lean thinking and methods, they recognize that the combined methods of lean accounting in fact creates a lean management system (LMS) designed to provide the planning, the operational and financial reporting, and the motivation for change required to prosper the company's on-going lean transformation.

Marginal Costing

The cost-volume-profit analysis is the systematic examination of the relationship between selling prices, sales, production volumes, costs, expenses and profits. This analysis provides very useful information for decision-making in the management of a company. For example, the analysis can be used in establishing sales prices, in the product mix selection to sell, in the decision to choose marketing strategies, and in the analysis of the impact on profits by changes in costs. In the current environment of business, a business administration must act and take decisions in a fast and accurate manner. As a result, the importance of cost-volume-profit is still increasing as time passes.

A relationship between the cost, volume and profit is the contribution margin. The contribution margin is the revenue excess from sales over variable costs. The concept of contribution margin is particularly useful in the planning of business because it gives an insight into the potential profits that can generate a business. The following chart shows the income statement of a company X, which has been prepared to show its contribution margin:

Sales	$1,000,000
(-) Variable Costs	$600,000
Contribution Margin	$400,000
(-) Fixed Costs	$300,000
Inconme from Operations	$100,000

Contribution Margin Ratio

The margin contribution can also be expressed as a percentage. The contribution margin ratio, which is sometimes called the profit-volume ratio, indicates the percentage of each sales dollar available to cover fixed costs and to provide operating revenue. The contribution margin ratio measures the effect on operating income of an increase or a decrease in sales volume.

REFERENCES

Armony, Mor. "The Impact of Duplicate Orders on Demand Estimation and Capacity Investment".

Cecere, L., Hofman, D., Martin, R., Preslan L., The Handbook for Becoming Demand Driven, AMR Research, Juli 2005; 4

Chen, Y. F., Z. Drezner, J. K. Ryan and D. Simchi-Levi (2000), Quantifying the Bullwhip Effect in a Simple Supply Chain: The Impact of Forecasting, Lead Times and Information. Management Science, 46 pp. 436—443.

Cieslak, David, and Bob Gaby. "Programmes Provide Extensive Tools For Adaptability And Customization." *CPA Technology Advisor* 16, no. 8 (December 2006): 38.

Desbarats, Gus. 1995. "Usability: form that says function." *Industrial Management & Data Systems* 95, no. 5:3-6.

Gartner (2004) The Future of Marketing Automation Arrives With MRM, 9 April 2004

Goldberg, Harold. "10 ways to avoid CRM pitfalls." *B to B* 86, no. 17 (September 17, 2001): 11.

Hart-Davidson, William, Grace Bernhardt, Michael McLeod, Martine Rife, and Jeffrey T. Grabill. 2008. "Coming to Content Management: Inventing Infrastructure for Organizational Knowledge Work." Technical Communication Quarterly 17, no. 1: 10-34

Horngren, Datar and Foster, Cost Accounting - A Managerial Emphasis, 11th edition (Prentice Hall 2003).

Horngren, Sundem and Stratton (1996) Strategic Management Accounting, Prentice Hall, 10th Ed. pp343-345

Joachim, David. "CRM tools improve access, usability." (cover story). *B to B* 87, no. 3 (March 11, 2002): 1

Jonathan Coulter and Andrew W. Shepherd, Inventory Credit – An approach to developing agricultural markets, FAO, Rome, 1995

Ka-Ping, Yee. "User Interaction Design for Secure Systems." *Information and Communication Security* 2513, no. (2002): 278-290.

Kostelnick, Charles. "Conflicting Standards for Designing Data Displays: Following, Flouting, and Reconciling Them." Technical Communication 45, no. 4 (November 1998): 473

Lee, H, 2004. The Triple –A Supply Chain. Harvard Business Review 82; 10 102-112

Lior Arussy (2005). "Understanding the Fatal Mistakes". *Passionate and Profitable.* John Wiley & Sons, Inc..

Maher, Lanen and Rahan, Fundamentals of Cost Accounting, 1st Edition (McGraw-Hill 2005).

Martin R, 2006, GMA and AMR Research, The Demand Driven Supply Network DDSN, Your Business Operating Strategy; 15

Maskell & Baggaley (December 19, 2003). "Practical Lean Accounting". *Productivity Press, New York, NY.*

McTaggart, J.M., Kontes, P.W. and Mankins, M.C. (1994) The Value Imperative: managing for superior shareholder returns, Free Press

Mei Lin Fung, "You can learn from Dell Hell, Dell did" customerthink.com

Oliver, R.K., Webber, M.D., 1982, "Supply-chain management: logistics catches up with strategy", Outlook, Booz, Allen and Hamilton Inc. Reprinted 1992, in Logistics: The Strategic Issues, ed. M Christopher, Chapman Hall, London, pp. 63-75

Paul Hansen and Kelvin Gibson. *Effectively Slotting a Warehouse or Distribution Center*. Cygnus Supply and Demand Chain Executive. Accessed 2010-08-06.

Pennington, Lori L. 2007. "Surviving the Design and Implementation of a Content-Management System." *Journal of Business & Technical Communication* 21, no. 1:62-73.

R.S. Saxena (1 December 2009). *Inventory Management: Controlling in a Fluctuating Demand Environment*. Global India Publications. pp. 24–.

Sapp, Richard, David Crawford and Steven Rebishcke "Article title?" Journal of Bank Cost and Management Accounting (Volume 3, Number 2), 1990.

8

Focus on Select Construction Production Directives

> The whole difference between construction and creation is exactly this: that a thing constructed can only be loved after it is constructed; but a thing created is loved before it exists.
>
> —*Charles Dickens*

CONSTRUCTION PRODUCTS DIRECTIVE

Construction Products Directive (Council Directive 89/106/EEC) (CPD) is a now repealed European Union Directive with the aim to remove technical barriers to trade in construction products between Member States in the European Union. The directive is now replaced by Regulation (EU) No 305/2011. The directive was replaced in order to simplify and clarify the existing framework, and improve the transparency and the effectiveness of the existing measures. It sought to "ensure the free movement of all construction products within the European Union by harmonizing national laws with respect to the essential requirements applicable to these products in terms of health and safety." An additional objective of the directive was to "standardize the manufacturing of construction products and guarantee the unlimited use of these products within the EU."

The CPD provided the following four main elements:

- a system of harmonized technical specifications
- an agreed system of attestation of conformity for each product family
- a framework of notified bodies
- the CE marking of products

The Directive did not aim to harmonize regulations. Member States and public and private sector procurers were free to set their own requirements on the performance of works and therefore products. What the CPD sought to harmonize was the methods of test, the methods of declaration of product performance values, and the method of conformity assessment. Choice of value for intended use, was left to the regulators in each Member State. The CPD has been amended by the Council Directive 93/68/EEC of 22 July 1993 and Regulation (EC) No 1882/2003 of the European Parliament and of the Council of 29 September 2003. The directive was repealed and replaced by Regulation (EU) No 305/2011 on 9 March 2011.

Background

The construction sector has one of the most significant economic activities of the EU. Prior to the CPDs inception, there were differing standards and technical approvals among EU member states. The importance of the CPD was to remove the technical barriers to trade, market barriers and market entry strategy for the EU construction industry. Five hundred product standards and 200 testing standards are planned in the context of the CPD. The objective of the CPD (and the CPR alike) is not to define the safety of construction products, but to ensure that reliable information is presented in relation to their performance. This is achieved by providing, mainly in standards, a common technical language, to be used not only by manufacturers, but also by public authorities when defining their requirements on construction works, directly or indirectly influencing the demands placed on the products to be used in them.

Construction Products

A 'construction product' means "any product which is produced for incorporation in a permanent manner in construction works, including both buildings and civil engineering works," such as buildings, bridges, highways and other civil engineering projects.

Harmonized Technical Specifications

The Construction Products Directive recognizes the following types of Harmonized Technical Specifications:

- Harmonized European Standards
- European Technical Approvals
- European Technical Approvals without Guideline

So far 552 standards have been harmonized.

CE Marking of Construction Products

CE Marking of construction products was introduced in the CPD in 1989. CE Marking is a declaration by the manufacturer that the product meets certain public safety requirements. The public safety requirements are a set of essential characteristics that each product must satisfy and these characteristics are given in the product's harmonized standard.

There are six essential requirements which need to be addressed (by committee) and satisfied, when relevant, by the product prior to being put on the market:

- Mechanical resistance and stability
- Safety in the case of fire
- Hygiene, health and the environment
- Safety in use
- Protection against noise
- Energy economy and heat retention

CE marking is obligatory for every product placed on the EEA (European Economical area or the European Union + Norway, Iceland and Liechtenstein) market as soon as all conditions are fulfilled to enable this.

CONSTRUCTION (DESIGN AND MANAGEMENT)

The Construction (Design and Management) Regulations 2007, also known as CDM Regulations or CDM 2007, define legal duties for the safe operation of UK construction sites. The regulations place specific duties on clients, designers and contractors, to plan their approach to health and safety. They apply throughout the life of a construction project, from its inception to its subsequent final demolition and removal.

It was introduced by the Health and Safety Executive's Construction Division to help:

- Improve planning and management of projects from the very start of the project;
- Assign the right people for the right job at the right time to manage the risks on site;
- Target effort where it can do most good in terms of health and safety;
- Discourage unnecessary bureaucracy.

These regulations were a result of an EU Directive 92/57/EEC (OJ

L245, 26.8.92), the so-called 'Construction Sites Directive'. They came into force on April 6, 2007 and replaced the Construction (Design and Management) Regulations 1994, Construction (Design and Management) (Amendment) Regulations 2000 and the Construction (Health, Safety and Welfare) Regulations 1996.

The regulations are divided into 5 parts:

- Part 1 deals with matters of interpretation and application of the regulations.
- Part 2 covers general management duties of the duty holders that apply to all construction projects including those that are non-notifiable.
- Part 3 sets out additional management duties of the duty holders that apply to notifiable projects.
- Part 4 of the regulations apply to all construction work carried out on construction sites, and covers physical safeguards that must be provided to prevent danger. This was covered previously by the Construction (Health, Safety and Welfare) Regulations 1996, which are revoked by CDM2007.
- Part 5 covers issues of civil liability, transitional provisions that apply during the period when the regulations come into force, and amendments and revocations of other legislation.

CDM 2007 applies to all construction work and covers a very broad range of construction activities such as building, civil engineering, engineering construction work, demolition, site preparation and site clearance, except for Part 3, which only applies if the project is notifiable. On a notifiable project, the client must additionally appoint a competent CDM co-ordinator and a competent Principal Contractor, a Construction Phase Plan ("Construction Phase" – incorporating Mobilisation (let the building contract, appoint contractor, issue production information, arrange site hand-over, and review contractor's proposals), Construction to Practical Completion (administer the building contract and provide contractor with further information as necessary), After Practical Completion (administer the building contract after practical completion, resolve defects and make final inspections). The importance of this phase is in the inspection of expected performance standards to ensure compliance).and a Health & Safety File must be produced. Additional duties are also placed on the Client, Designers and Contractors for notifiable projects. The CDM Co-ordinator is the new title for the Planning Supervisor under CDM 1994, with increased duties and responsibilities.

- Approved Code of Practice 2007 (ACoP)

The HSE's Approved Code of Practice (ACoP): Managing Health and Safety in Construction, gives practical advice on how comply with the law. It states that if you follow the advice given you comply with the law as far as CDM regulations are concerned. If you are prosecuted for breach of health and safety law, and it is proved that you did not follow relevant provisions of the Approved Code, you must show that you have complied with the law in some other way, or a Court may find you at fault.

The ACoP came into force in April 2007. This edition is a complete re-write from the original and revised ACoP's that were written for the CDM regulations 1994.

Notifiable and Non-Notifiable Projects

Projects are classified as 'notifiable' if they take longer than 30 days or longer than 500 person days (e.g., 50 people working 10 days on the construction project). Under the CDM regulation, the client appoints a competent Principal Contractor and CDM co-ordinator, who notifies the Health and Safety Executive (HSE) by using Form 10 (F10). Failure to do so means the client must take the duties of Principal Contractor and CDM co-ordinator assigned to the parties under CDM 2007.

Non-notifiable projects are those that are likely to take less than 30 days of construction time. Although there is no legal requirement for a formal appointment of a Principle Contractor or CDM co-ordinator or a construction phase plan for non-notifiable projects, regulation does require co-operation and co-ordination between all members of the project team.

Duty Holders

Persons with specific duties under the regulations are the client, designer, principal contractor, other contractors, and a new duty holder introduced by the regulations: 'CDM co-ordinator'. Each of these duty holders, apart from the client, must be "competent" to act in the project. Details of the duties of each principal and issues about competence follow.

Client

The client is the person for whom the project is carried out. On a project, the client is the most influential person, having control over the duration, budget and appointment of various parties to carry out the work. As such they have a key role to play in the promotion of a systematic approach to the management of health and safety in construction. They set the tone of the project and make decisions crucial to its development. The legal duties of a client under CDM 2007 are:

- Verify the competence and resources of all organisations and internal teams the client engages or allocates to the project (e.g., principal contractor, CDM co-ordinator, designers, contractors)
- Ensure that suitable management arrangements are made for the project (although client doesn't have to carry out the management themselves)
- Ensure sufficient time and resources are allowed for all stages of the project including site set up
- Provide pre-construction information to the designers and contractors, or co-operate with CDM co-ordinator to collect and compile relevant pre-construction information
- Ensure co-operation and co-ordination between the client's employees and client contractors with the project contractors where the client's work activities overlap the construction work

On notifiable projects the client's additional duties are to:

- Select and appoint a competent and resourced CDM co-ordinator and principal contractor
- Cerify the sufficiency of the construction phase plan prior to construction commencement
- Cerify that suitable welfare facilities are in place prior to construction commencement and co-operate with the principal contractor to provide suitable welfare facility
- Compile and retain health and safety file from the CDM co-ordinator, keep information up to date and provide access to any person who needs to see it for health and safety purposes

Often, clients have little knowledge of managing a construction project. The regulation recognises this and doesn't require the client to manage the project themselves. Clients without construction expertise must rely on the CDM co-ordinator's advice on how best to meet their duties, and subsequently the CDM co-ordinator needs the clients support and input to work effectively. The client remains responsible for ensuring client duties are met. Note that domestic clients having work done on a property they intend to live in have no duties under CDM 2007 and are exempt from the regulations.

CDM Co-Ordinator

A CDM co-ordinator is only required on notifiable projects. Their primary roles and duties are to provide the client with a key project advisor in respect of construction health and safety risk management matters and to ensure compliance of the design and the designers with CDM 2007. Through early involvement with clients and designers, a CDM co-ordinator can make a significant contribution to reducing risks to workers during construction, and to contractors and end users who work in, or on, the structure after construction. As such, the client must appoint a CDM co-ordinator as soon as it is practicably possible. The legal duties of a CDM co-ordinator under CDM 2007 are as follow:

- Notify the project to the Health & Safety Executive when the project is notifiable
- Advise and assist the client with their duties for engaging or appointing competent and adequately resourced organisations (e.g., CDM co-ordinator and Principal Contractor)
- Assist the client with suitable management arrangements for the project (This may include design audits and construction site audits and inspections)
- Identify and collect pre-construction information and provide it in a convenient form to designers, the principal contractor, and other contractors who need it to carry out their duties
- Advise the client on the sufficiency of the time allocated for all phases of the project
- ensure that the design complies with the requirements of the regulations, paying particular attention to any late design changes
- Ensure that the designers and principal contractor co-operate and co-ordinate with each other and with those involved in the project
- Help the client verify the sufficiency of the construction phase plan to commence construction and adequacy of welfare provisions
- Prepare the health and safety file, or review and update an existing health and safety file, and give it to the client at end of construction for maintenance work

Designers

In CDM 2007, 'designer' has a broad meaning and covers person or organisations who prepare drawings, design details and those who specifies a particular method of construction or material. Therefore, by default anyone involved in the project is a potential designer, including the clients, architects, civil and structural engineers, building surveyors, building service designers, project managers, landscape architects, contractors, interior designers and shop fitters, temporary work engineers, and anyone purchasing materials where the choice has been left open.

Designers are in a unique position to reduce construction risks, and play a key role in CDM 2007. Designs develop from initial concepts through to a detailed specification, often involving different teams and people at various stages. At each stage, designers from all disciplines can contribute significantly by identifying and eliminating hazards, and reducing risks from hazards where elimination is not possible. Designers' earliest decisions fundamentally affect the health and safety of construction work. These decisions influence later design choices, and considerable work may be required if it is necessary to unravel earlier decisions. It is vital to address health and safety from the very start.

Designers' responsibilities extend beyond the construction phase of a project. The regulation places legal duties for them to consider the health and safety of those who maintain, repair, clean, refurbish, and eventually remove or demolish all or part of the structure, as well as the health and safety of users of workplaces. For most designers, buildability considerations, and ensuring the structure can be easily maintained and repaired is part of their normal work. Considering the health and safety of those who do this work should not be an onerous duty. Failure to address these issues adequately at the design stage usually increase running costs, because clients are then faced with more costly solutions when repairs and maintenance become necessary. Where significant risks remain despite available remedies, designers must provide information with the design that ensures that the CDM co-ordinator, other designers and contractors are aware of these risks.

Designers also have duties under other legislation, including those parts of the Management of Health and Safety at Work Regulations 1999 that require risk assessment.

The legal duties of a designer under CDM 2007 are:

- Ensure that the client is aware of the client's duties prior to commencing any design work
- Ensure that personnel allocated to their design team from internal resources are competent and adequately resourced
- Ensure that any designers or contractors that are engaged on the project are competent and adequately resourced
- Ensure that the design and the designers' duties are complied with by any designers engaged by them, including any designers who are based outside UK
- Eliminate or reduce health and safety risks to constructors,

users, maintainers, repairers, commissioners, testers, cleaners, demolishers etc. when preparing the design
- Co-operate and communicate with other designers, including temporary works designers, to ensure adequate co-ordination of the design
- Provide information about risks that cannot be satisfactorily addressed by their designs to the client, other designers and contractors

On notifiable projects the designers' additional duties are to:

- verify that the project has been notified and that the CDM co-ordinator has been appointed as soon as possible after commencement of initial or preliminary design;
- co-operate with the CDM co-ordinator for the verification of design and designer compliance and the co-ordination of the design;
- provide any information requested by the CDM co-ordinator for the health and safety file.

Principal Contractor

The principal contractor has a central role in managing health and safety during the construction phase. It is achieved mainly by developing a health and safety plan from the pre-construction information identified and collated by the CDM co-ordinator and provided by the client and designers, and by ensuring that the plan is followed. The principal contractor must be a contractor. A contractor is someone who performs or manages construction work and has been formally appointed as principal contractor by the client. The principal contractor is then also a contractor and must also comply with the contractor's duties. The principal contractor has the major responsibility for safety and health during the construction phase on notifiable projects only, and has the duties to:

- Demonstrate their organisation's competence and adequacy of resources to perform the principal contractor's duties on the particular project
- Verify competence and resources allocation of any sub-contracted designers or contractors
- Prepare, develop, communicate, implement and amend the construction phase plan
- Plan and manage the construction processes and ensure other contractors manage their work, including inspections and audits
- Ensure the provision of adequate welfare facilities, prevent

unauthorised access to the site, prepare and enforce the site rules and manage effective co-operation and co-ordination between contractors

- Make available to the other contractors key documents, e.g., health and safety file information, site surveys, designers' information, risk assessments, and the construction phase plan
- Inform other contractors of their mobilisation time, which should be sufficient
- Ensure the workforce is consulted on health and safety matters and provided with suitable inductions, information, and training
- Liaise with the CDM co-ordinator for any design undertaken during the construction phase and provide information for the health and safety file
- Display the project notification on the site

Contractors

Contractors and those actually doing the construction work are most at risk of injury and ill health. They have a key role to play, in co-operation with the principal contractor, in planning and managing the work to ensure that risks are properly controlled On all projects contractors must:

- Plan, manage and monitor their own work to make sure that workers under their control are safe from the start of their work on site
- Ensure that any contractor who they appoint or engage to work on the project is with the permission of the Estates project manager/supervisor and are informed of the minimum amount of time for them to plan and prepare before they start work on the site
- Provide workers under their control (whether employed or self-employed) with any necessary information, including about relevant aspects of other contractors' work, and site induction (where not provided by a principal contractor or Estates safety officer) which they need to work safely, to report problems or to respond appropriately in an emergency
- Co-operate with others and co-ordinate their work with others working on the project
- Ensure that there are adequate welfare facilities for their workers

In addition, where projects are notifiable under the Regulations, contractors must:

- Check that the client is aware of their duties, check that a CDM co-ordinator has been appointed and ensure that HSE has been notified before the work starts
- Co-operate with the principal contractor in planning and managing work, including reasonable directions and site rules
- Provide details to the principal contractor of any contractor engaged in connection with carrying out work
- Provide any information needed for the health and safety file
- Inform the principal contractor of any problems with the plan
- Inform the principal contractor of reportable accidents, diseases and dangerous occurrences

Workers

The CDM2007 places legal duties on workers to ensure they carry out the work as safely as possible and that they do not endanger the visitors/ members of the public. They must:

- Ensure they only carry out construction work they are competent to do
- Report obvious risks and hazards to the contractor
- Co-operate with others and co-ordinate work so as to ensure their own health and safety and others who may be affected by the work
- Follow site health and safety rules and procedures
- The Statutory Documents

This section covers mandatory documents for a CDM project, including project notification, pre-construction information, construction phase plan, and health and safety plan. Whilst pre-construction information should be produced for all projects, some form of the other documents must be produced for both notifiable and non-notifiable projects. Project notification is only needed for notifiable project. The Construction Phase Plan is also only required on notifiable projects, but something similar would still be required on non-notifiable projects to provide for effective health and safety management during construction. The Health and Safety File must be produced on notifiable projects, and is prepared by the CDM Co-ordinator. However, if a Health and Safety File exists for a structure the project modifies, the existing Health and Safety File must be amended to reflect changes. The client must establish who updates any existing Health and Safety Files. Even if a Health and Safety File is not required on a non-notifiable project, as-built and operational and maintenance information are still required.

Project Notification (Form 10)

The regulations require the CDM co-ordinator to notify the local HSE office of all construction work expected to last more than 30 working days and also all work which may not last this long but is expected to involve more than 500 person days or shifts of construction work. The initial notification should be made as soon as possible after appointment of the CDM co-ordinator. Further notifications would be required by changes in the information required on the notification. An additional notification would be required subsequent to the appointment of the principal contractor, if this appointment had not been made at the time of the initial notification, a change in the client or CDM co-ordinator, or a significant change in workscope and/or duration. Additional notifications are not required where designers and contractors change. This notification may be performed using the HSE Form 10(rev) or by other means, including electronic, providing it contains the information specified by Schedule 1 of CDM2007, which consists of:

1. Date of Forwarding and exact address of the construction site
2. A brief description of the project and the construction work it includes
3. Contact details of the client, CDM co-ordinator and principal contractor (name, address, telephone number and e-mail address)
4. Date planned for start of the construction phase
5. The time allowed by the client to the principal contractor referred to in regulation 15(b) for planning and preparation for construction work
6. Planned duration of the construction phase
7. Estimated maximum number of people at work on the construction site
8. Planned number of contractors on the construction site
9. Name and address of any designer and contractor already appointed
10. A declaration signed by or on behalf of the client that he is aware of his duties under these regulations

Pre-Construction Information

The pre-construction information (PCI) provides information for those designing, bidding for, or planning work and for the development of the construction phase plan. The client has a duty to obtain this information for all projects. On non-notifiable projects the client must provide all relevant information to the designers and contractors. On notifiable projects, the CDM co-ordinator assists the client with identifying what is required and collection of that information. The CDM co-ordinator also ensures the pre-construction information is in a convenient format and provide the relevant parts to designers, the principal contractor and other contractors.

The 'pre-construction information' is information regarding the project, site and other relevant issues required by the designers and contractors working on the project. This information is useful for the designers in their attempts to eliminate or reduce risks in design decisions, for bidding contractors to properly evaluate the work and associated risks, and for the contractors performing the work in their management of health and safety on the site. The client must provide all information that pertains to the site, and any other information that could be reasonably obtained. They must provide this information as soon as possible in the project so the designers can consider the information in design and planning decisions. Some of this information is also supplied to bidding contractors so they can make informed tenders for the work, or allow the construction team, in a situation where tenders are not required, to effectively plan the construction work. The pre-construction information may be discrete pieces of information in the form of drawings, reports, surveys, etc., either in electronic or hard copy format, with an index provided to all of the project team so information available to all. Alternatively, though not preferred, the 'pre-construction information' may be a single document.

Construction Phase Plan

On notifiable projects, the client must ensure the construction phase plan is sufficiently developed by the principal contractor before construction begins. A sufficient construction phase plan must contain the health and safety management systems and arrangements for the specific project and site, and the risk assessments and method statements for initial work activities. The CDM co-ordinator assists the client in assessing the construction phase plan prior to construction commencement. On non-notifiable projects involving demolition or sites or activities involving high levels of risk it is recommended that a written plan, approximating the construction phase plan should be produced and reviewed. The client must establish the need for this, probably with assistance from the designers. The CDM ACoP, Appendix 3 contains a listing of items that should be included, as required, in a construction phase plan.

Welfare Facilities

On notifiable projects the client must ensure the principal contractor has made suitable arrangements for site welfare facilities, taking into account the numbers of workers expected to work on the site, the site conditions and the project tasks, prior to allowing construction to commence. The CDM co-ordinator helps the client with this. The principal contractor has an absolute duty to prepare the construction phase plan prior to construction commencement, and develop, communicate, implement and amend the plan as necessary to maintain its sufficiency to effectively plan, manage and monitor the construction work. This should ensure that the work is performed, so far as reasonably practicable, without risks to health and safety.

Health and Safety File

A health and safety file is only required on notifiable projects however, if a health and safety file exists for a structure involved in a non-notifiable project, this file still must be updated. The health and safety file should contain the information needed to allow future construction work safely, including cleaning, maintenance, alterations refurbishment, and demolition. The file scope, structure, and format must be agreed between the client and the CDM Co-ordinator at the start of the project. Under CDM 2007 the CDM co-ordinator must prepare the health and safety file, or review and update an existing health and safety file, and pass it the client at the end of construction. This is an expansion on the requirement previously on the planning supervisor under CDM 1994, as that only required the planning supervisor to ensure that the file was prepared. On notifiable projects, contractors must promptly provide information regarding their own work that has been identified as necessary include in the health and safety file to the principal contractor for his submissions to the CDM co-ordinator. What is required, in what format and when should have been provided within the pre-construction information.

File Content

1. Description of Works: Give a brief description of the structural / building work carried out in the project to which this health & safety file relates.
2. Residual Hazards: Describe or list the residual hazards and how they have been dealt with (for example surveys or other information concerning asbestos, contaminated land, water bearing strata, buried services etc.).
3. Structural Design Principles: Description of the key structural principles incorporated in the design of the structure (e.g., bracing, sources of substantial stored energy, including pre or post-tensioned members) and safe working loads for floors and roofs, particularly where these may preclude placing scaffolding or heavy machinery there.

4. Hazardous Materials: List any hazards associated with the materials used (for example hazardous substances, lead paint, special coatings which should not be burnt off).
5. Installed Plant: Give information regarding the removal or dismantling of installed plant and equipment (for example lifting arrangements).
6. Cleaning & Maintenance: Give health & safety information about any equipment provided for cleaning or maintaining the structure.
7. Services: Give the nature, location, and markings of significant services, including fire-fighting services.
8. Access Drawings: Give information and as-built drawings of the structures, its plant and equipment (e.g., means of safe access to and from service voids, fire doors, and compartmentation).

Previous Legislation

The 2007 CDM regulations revise and bring together the CDM Regulations 1994 and the Construction (Health Safety and Welfare) Regulations 1996 into a single regulatory package.

(ANNEX)

CONFORMITY ASSESSMENT OF CONSTRUCTION PRODUCTS

Bureau Veritas provides assessment and control of construction products. A construction product means any product which is produced for incorporation in a permanent manner in construction works, including buildings, infrastructures, industries and civil engineering works.

Conformity Assessment Services – Regulatory Services

In several countries exists different regulation related to the commercialization of construction products. These laws and the standards related to its, previewed rules and task for manufacturers of the construction products and for an authorized body. Bureau Veritas is an authorized body at local and international level for the conformity assessment of constructions products.

The Construction Product Directive – CE mark

In the European Union, common standards exist for most construction products. These come under the Construction Product Directive (European Community Directive 89/106 EC) or CPD.

The CPD states that construction products commercialized in the EU must bear a CE mark. Standards for each product are published in the Official Journal of the European Union (OJEU). Bureau Veritas is an international Notified Body (NB) recognized worldwide as a Certification Body for the CPD. The CPD is regularly updated and new standards are published every 6 months. Each standard contains an annex ZA, detailing several tasks for the manufacturer and for the NB (Bureau Veritas) in order to carry out CE marking. Bureau Veritas is a Notified Body for a wide range of standards/products covered by the Construction Product Directive including: Cement , Aggregates, Road Construction Products, Precast concrete products, Masonry products, Products related to concrete, mortar and grout, Geotextiles and Geosynthetic barriers, Chimneys and conducts, Membranes, Thermal insulating products, Structural metallic products, Fire detection products, Suspended ceilings, Circulation fixtures, Structural timber products, Wood based panels.

CE Marking

The general basis of CE mark is:

- A Declaration of Conformity prepared by the manufacturer of the construction product
- A Certificate of Conformity issued by the NB (Bureau Veritas).

Once these documents have been produced, a manufacturer is able to put the CE marking on their product.

The CE mark demonstrates product or manufacturer process conformity to European Standards. It also helps to optimize manufacturing processes due to continuous monitoring. CE marking is not only an obligation, it is an opportunity to add value to a product.

What do we offer?

Bureau Veritas is a partner to help manufacturers with all tasks under the CPD. We inform clients of their obligations: standards their products must conform to if their products are subject to CE marking and the dates for when the CE mark becomes voluntary and when it becomes obligatory.

Conformity Assessment Services – Local Legislation

Bureau Veritas carries out assessments and certification to specific reference recognized at international or national level. For example, rules for ready mix concrete do not come under CE marking but are subject to national laws. Certain countries in Europe have their own rules for certain construction products where there are no harmonized standards. This is the case in Italy, Spain and other European Countries with rules governing structural products not already subject to European Legislation. Bureau Veritas is recognized and authorized body in several countries to delivery the assessment and certification previewed by the national legislation.

Conformity Assessment Services – Not mandatory scheme

The strong competitiveness, the research of excellence, the need to demonstrate it, and the specific provisions of the contract are some of the levers that triggered the process of Certification of Products for the construction industry. In order to permits and demonstrate all of it, the manufacturer needs to comply whit particular technical specification. These Technical specifications are in general standards edited by the national or international standard bodies (CEN, ISO). These standards previewed a list of tasks for the manufacturer beside to the tasks for an Accredited Body as to assure the reliability and credibility of manufacturer process and/or values and characteristics declared and assessed. For example the Fluid Piping Industry (Plastic, Cast Iron) are face to face on this affair and BV was creating the answer on this necessity. Bureau Veritas is an international Body recognized and accredited worldwide (IAF) as a Certification and Inspection Body for construction product. Bureau Veritas performs sample testing and audits at manufacturing plants, as an independent third party. Satisfactory results enable the manufacturer to obtain a Bureau Veritas Certificate showing the technical data verified and certified..

Energy and Environmental impact of Construction Products

Construction product manufacturers are increasingly concerned about the environmental impact of their processes. Hence many are now introducing green schemes such as monitoring energy consumption during production, or using a certain percentage of recycled materials in their production methods. We can attest that the manufacturers' environmental claims are true. Our certification of construction products services evolve in parallel with changing legislation and client demand. Bureau Veritas also conducts assessments according to manufacturers' own technical requirements, for example, when they want to attest to energy consumption levels during production or require a certificate attesting to the use of recycled materials at a plant.

Glossary

ADDENDUM: An addition or supplement to a document; e.g., items or information added to a procurement document.

ADVERTISE: To make a public announcement of the intention to purchase goods, services or construction with the intention of increasing the response and enlarging the competition. The announcement must conform to the legal requirements imposed by established laws, rules, policies and procedures to inform the public.

AGREEMENT: A duly executed and legally binding contract; the act of agreeing.

ALP Authority for Local Purchase: Granted by the commissioner of Administration to an individual who has successfully completed all requirements established by the Materials Management Division.

ALTERNATE RESPONSE: A substitute response; an intentional substantive variation to a basic provision or clause of a solicitation by a vendor.

AMENDMENT/CHANGE ORDER: A written modification to a contract or purchase order or other agreements.

APPROPRIATION: Sum of money from public funds set aside for a specific purpose.

BILL OF LADING: A written receipt or contract, given by a carrier, showing a list of goods delivered to it for transportation. The straight bill of lading is a contract which provides for direct shipment to a consignee. The order bill of lading is negotiable; it enables a shipper to collect for a shipment before it reaches its destination (this is done by sending the original bill of lading with a draft drawn on the consignee through a bank). When the consignee receives the lading indicating that payment has been made, the lading will be surrendered to the carrier's agent, and the carrier will then ship the goods to the consignee, and the bill of lading will be surrendered to the carrier. Note: Shippers frequently consign shipments to themselves on order bills of lading so that delivery is made only upon the shipper's order; the person or firm to be notified upon arrival of the shipment at destination must be designated.

BLANKET ORDER: A contract under which a vendor agrees to provide goods or services on a purchase-on-demand basis. The contract generally establishes prices, terms, conditions and the period covered (no quantities are specified); shipments are to be made as required by the purchaser.

BROKER: A business that carries no inventory and that has no written ongoing agreement with any manufacturer or manufacturer's authorized distributor to sell the products of the manufacturer.

BUSINESS: A contractor, subcontractor, supplier, consultant, or provider of technical, administrative, or physical services organized as a sole proprietorship, partnership, association, corporation, or other entity formed for the purpose of doing business for profit.

COMMODITY: A transportable article of trade or commerce that can be bartered or sold.

COMMODITY/SERVICE CONTRACT: Previously referred to as "M-contracts." Since the inception of MAPS, the contract number is a six-digit number assigned by the computer system. An "M" number is no longer assigned for these types of contracts.

COMPREHENSIVE PROCUREMENT GUIDELINES (CPG): Designates items that must contain recycled content when purchased by federal, state, and local agencies, or by contractors using appropriated federal funds, when these agencies spend more than $10,000 a year on any of the designated items. For example, if a state agency spends more than $10,000 a year on copy paper, and part of that money is from appropriated federal funds, then that state agency must follow the EPS guidelines and buy 30 percent post-consumer recycled paper. (Section 6002 of the Resource Conservation and Recovery Act [RCRA] and Presidential Executive Order 13101.)

CONSIDERATION: Something of value given or done as recompense that is exchanged by two parties; that which binds a contract.

CONTRACT: Any written instrument or electronic document containing the elements of offer, acceptance, and consideration to which an agency is a party.

CONTRACT ADMINISTRATION: The management of all actions after the award of a contract that must be taken to assure compliance with the contract; e.g., timely delivery, acceptance, payment, closing contract, etc.

CONTRACTOR: A person who agrees to furnish goods or services for a certain price; may be a prime contractor or subcontractor.

COOPERATIVE PURCHASING: The combining of requirements of two or more governmental units to obtain the benefits of volume purchases and/or reduction in administrative expenses.

COOPERATIVE PURCHASING VENTURE (CPV): A joint purchasing program designed by the State of Minnesota where governmental units obtain the benefits of volume purchasing and/or reduction in administrative expenses by participating in the program and purchasing from existing State of Minnesota commodity contracts.

DEALER, JOBBER OR DISTRIBUTOR: A business that maintains a store, warehouse, or other establishment in which a line or lines of products are kept in inventory and are sold to the public on a wholesale or retail basis.

DEBARMENT: The disqualification of a person to receive invitations for bids or requests for proposals, or the award of a contract by a government body, for a specified time commensurate with the seriousness of the offense, the failure, or the inadequacy of performance.

DEFAULT: Failure by a party to a contract to comply with contractual requirements.

DELIVERY: The formal handing over of property; the transfer of possession, such as by carrier to purchaser.

DEMURRAGE: The detention of a ship, railroad, car or truck beyond a specified time for loading/unloading; the payment required and made for the delay.

DESIGN SPECIFICATION: A specification setting forth the required characteristics to be considered for award of contract, including sufficient detail to show how the product is to be manufactured.

DOCUMENT TYPE: MAPS Procurement uses document type to differentiate among different functions for a requisition, solicitation, contract, or order. The document type is a field to be entered on those screens that are for requisition solicitation, contract, or order.

DROP SHIPMENT: Merchandise which is shipped by a manufacturer directly to a customer in response to the seller who collects orders but does not maintain an inventory.

EMERGENCY ACQUISITION: A threat to public health, welfare, or safety that threatens the functioning of government, the protection of property or the health or safety of people.

ENERGY STAR: A federal standard applied to office equipment for the purpose of rating the energy efficiency of the equipment. Energy Star computers, monitors, and printers save energy by powering down and going to "sleep" when not in use, resulting in a reduction in electrical bills and pollution levels.

FISCAL YEAR: The 12 months between one annual settlement of financial accounts and the next; a term used for budgeting, etc. The fiscal year for the U.S. Government is October 1 to September 30; the fiscal year for the State of Minnesota is July 1 to June 30.

HAZARDOUS WASTE: Any waste (solid, liquid, or gas) which because of its quantity, concentration, or chemical, physical, or infectious characteristics pose a substantial present or potential hazard to human health or the environment when improperly treated, stored, transported, or disposed of.

JOINT VENTURE: The temporary association of two or more businesses to secure and fulfill a procurement bid award.

LABOR SURPLUS AREA: A civil jurisdiction designated by the U.S. Department of Labor, usually updated annually in the late fall. Used as one of the criteria for designating economically disadvantaged (ED) vendors.

LEAD TIME: The time that it would take a supplier to delivery goods after receipt of order.

LEASE: A contract conveying from one entity to another the use of real or personal property for a designated period of time in return for payment or other consideration.

LESS-THAN-TRUCKLOAD (LTL): A quantity of freight less than the amount necessary to constitute a truckload.

LIFE CYCLE COSTING: A procurement evaluation technique which determines the total cost of acquisition, operation, maintaining and disposal of the items acquired; the lowest ownership cost during the time the item is in use.

LINE ITEM: An item of supply or service specified in a solicitation for which the vendor must specify a separate price.

LIQUIDATED DAMAGES: A specific sum of money, agreed to as part of a contract to be paid by one party to the other in the event of a breach of contract in lieu of actual damages, unless otherwise provided by law.

LIST PRICE: The price of an article published in a catalog, advertisement or printed list from which discounts, if any, may be subtracted.

LOWEST RESPONSIBLE VENDOR: The vendor with the lowest price whose past performance, reputation and financial capability is deemed acceptable.

MANDATORY: Required by the order stipulated, e.g., a specification or a specific description that may not be waived.

MAPS: The Minnesota Accounting and Procurement System. Quite often MAPS or AGPS is referred to when speaking of the Procurement side of the system and GFS is referred to when speaking of the accounting side.

MANUFACTURER: A business that makes or processes raw materials into a finished product.

MARKET: The aggregate forces (including economics) at work in trade and commerce in a specific service or commodity. To sell, analyze, advertise, package, etc.

MATERIAL VARIANCE/MATERIAL DEVIATION: A variance or deviation in a response from specifications of conditions that allows a responder a substantial advantage or benefit not enjoyed by all other responders or that gives the state something significantly different from what the state requested in the solicitation document.

MATERIALS MANAGEMENT: Embraces all functions of acquisition, standards, quality control and surplus property management.

OPEN MARKET REQUISITION (OMR): The requisition document type used in MAPS Procurement to request the purchase of a non-contract item when the requested item's estimated cost exceeds the authority for purchase level of the buyer. An OMR conveys the request for purchase to the person with the authority to purchase. The resulting order type is most often the Purchase Order Requisition (POR).

OPTION TO EXTEND/RENEW: A provision (or exercise of a provision) which allows a continuance of the contract for an additional time according to permissible contractual conditions.

PARTIAL PAYMENT: The payment authorized in a contract upon delivery of one or more units called for under the contract or upon completion of one or more distinct items of service called for thereunder.

PERFORMANCE BOND: A contract of guarantee, executed subsequent to award by a successful vendor to protect the buyer from loss due to the vendor's inability to complete the contract as agreed.

PRE-CONSUMER MATERIAL: Material or by-products generated after the manufacture of a product but before the product reaches the consumer, such as damaged or obsolete products. Pre-consumer material does not include mill and manufacturing trim, scrap, or broken material which is generated at a manufacturing site and commonly reused on-site in the same or another manufacturing process.

PREFERENCE: An advantage in consideration for award for a contract granted to a vendor by reason of the vendor's residence, business location, or business classifications (e.g., minority, small business).

PREPAID: A term denoting that transportation charges have been or are to be paid at the point of shipment.

PREQUALIFICATION OF VENDORS: The screening of potential vendors in which such factors as financial capability, reputation and management are considered when developing a list of qualified vendors. See Vendors List, Qualified Vendor/Responsible Vendor.

PRICE AGREEMENT: A contractual agreement in which a purchaser contracts with a vendor to provide the purchaser's requirements at a predetermined price. Usually involves a minimum number of units, orders placed directly with the vendor by the purchase, and limited duration of the contract. See Blanket Order and Requirements Contract.

PROCUREMENT: The combined functions of purchasing, inventory control, traffic and transportation, receiving, inspection, store keeping, and salvage and disposal operations.

PUBLIC PURCHASING: The process of obtaining goods and services for public purpose following procedures implemented to protect public funds from being expended extravagantly or capriciously.

PURCHASE MANUAL: A document that stipulates rules and prescribes procedures for purchasing with suppliers and other departments.

QUALITY: The composite of material attributes, including performance features and characteristic, of a product or service to satisfy a given need.

RESPONSIBLE BIDDER: A bidder whose reputation, past performance, and business and financial capabilities are such that the bidder would be judged by an appropriate authority as capable of satisfying an organization's needs for a specific contract.

RESPONSIVE BIDDER: A bidder whose bid does not vary from the specifications and terms set out in the invitation for bids.

REUSED PRODUCT: Any product designed to be used many times for the same or other purpose without additional processing other than specific requirements, such as cleaning, painting or minor repairs.

RFP OR RFB CONFERENCE: A meeting arranged by a procurement office to help potential bidders understand the requirements of an RFB or an RFP.

SEALED: A method determined by the commissioner to prevent the contents being revealed or known before the deadline for submission of responses.

SERVICES: Unless otherwise indicated, both professional or technical services and service performed under a service contract.

UNSUCCESSFUL VENDOR: A vendor whose response is not accepted for reasons such as price, quantity, failure to comply with specifications, etc.

Bibliography

Armony, Mor. "The Impact of Duplicate Orders on Demand Estimation and Capacity Investment".

Ashby, Michael; Hugh Shercliff and David Cebon (2007). *Materials: engineering, science, processing and design* (1st ed.). Butterworth-Heinemann.

Askeland, Donald R.; Pradeep P. Phulé (2005). *The Science & Engineering of Materials* (5th ed.). Thomson-Engineering.

Brunner, P.H.; Rechberger, H. (2004). *Practical Handbook of Material Flow Analysis*. Lewis Publishers, New York.

Chris Hendrickson (September 2008). "What Is Construction Project Management?". PM Hut. http://www.pmhut.com/what-is-construction-project-management. Retrieved 2010-07-04.

David Blanchard (2010). Supply Chain Management Best Practices, 2nd. Edition, John Wiley & Sons.

Desbarats, Gus (1995). "Usability: form that says function." *Industrial Management & Data Systems* 95, no. 5: 3-6.

Gartner (2004). The Future of Marketing Automation Arrives With MRM, 9 April 2004

Horngren, Sundem and Stratton (1996). Strategic Management Accounting, Prentice Hall, 10th Ed. pp343-345

Lee, H. (2004). *The Triple –A Supply Chain*, Harvard Business Review 82; 10 102-112

Lior Arussy (2005). "Understanding the Fatal Mistakes". *Passionate and Profitable*. John Wiley & Sons, Inc..

Martin R. (2006). GMA and AMR Research, *The Demand Driven Supply Network DDSN*, Your Business Operating Strategy; 15

Mentzer, J.T. et. al. (2001). Defining Supply Chain Management, in: *Journal of Business Logistics*, Vol. 22, No. 2, 2001, pp. 1–25.

Nakamura, S.; Kondo, Y. (2009). *Waste Input-Output Analysis. Concepts and Application to Industrial Ecology*. Springer.

Oliver, R.K., Webber, M.D. (1982). "Supply-chain management: logistics catches up with strategy", Outlook, Booz, Allen and Hamilton Inc.

Reprinted 1992, in Logistics: The Strategic Issues, ed. M Christopher, Chapman Hall, London, pp. 63-75

Pennington, Lori L. (2007). "Surviving the Design and Implementation of a Content-Management System." *Journal of Business & Technical Communication* 21, no. 1: 62-73.

Shaw, R. and Kotler, P. (2010). Marketing Efficiency: leaner, faster and better marketing; Market Leader Quarter 1 2010

Taylor, Frederick Winslow (1911). *The Principles of Scientific Management.* New York, NY, US and London, UK: Harper & Brothers. LCCN 11010339. OCLC 233134.

Thomas, Rhané (June 15, 2009). "IT Managers and Project Management". PM Hut. Retrieved December 13, 2009.

Veen, Annelies van der; Jan van Bon (2007). *Foundations of ITIL V3.* Van Haren Publishing.

Weele, Arjan J. van (2010). *Purchasing and Supply Chain Management: Analysis, Strategy, Planning and Practice* (5th ed. ed.). Andover: Cengage Learning.

Index

K

L

M

N

O

P

Q

R

S

T

V

Q

■■■